A Bilingual Library of Contemporary Chinese Master Writers

当代中国名家双语阅读文库

丛书主编 | 许诗焱　杨昊成
丛书副主编 | 李钟涛

ZHAO
BEN
FU

赵本夫

| 卷 |

南京师范大学出版社
NANJING NORMAL UNIVERSITY PRESS

图书在版编目（CIP）数据

当代中国名家双语阅读文库.赵本夫卷：汉英对照／赵本夫著；许诗焱,杨昊成主编. — 南京：南京师范大学出版社，2020.10
ISBN 978-7-5651-4720-3

Ⅰ.①当… Ⅱ.①赵… ②许… ③杨… Ⅲ.①中国文学－当代文学－作品综合集－汉、英 Ⅳ.①I217.1

中国版本图书馆CIP数据核字（2020）第176698号

丛 书 名	当代中国名家双语阅读文库
丛书主编	许诗焱 杨昊成
书　　名	当代中国名家双语阅读文库·赵本夫卷
著　 者	赵本夫
译　 者	Shelly Bryant，Jeremy Tiang，Florence Woo，Mark McConaghy，Jesse Field
封面题字	徐　燕
策划编辑	郑海燕　王雅琼
责任编辑	张泽芳
出版发行	南京师范大学出版社
地　 址	江苏省南京市玄武区后宰门西村9号（邮编：210016）
电　 话	（025）83598919（总编办）　83598412（营销部）83373872（邮购部）
网　 址	http://press.njnu.edu.cn
电子信箱	nspzbb@njnu.edu.cn
照　 排	南京开卷文化传媒有限公司
印　 刷	江苏凤凰通达印刷有限公司
开　 本	880毫米×1230毫米　1/32
印　 张	11.375
字　 数	279千
版　 次	2020年10月第1版　2020年10月第1次印刷
书　 号	ISBN 978-7-5651-4720-3
定　 价	38.00元
出 版 人	张志刚

南京师大版图书若有印装问题请与销售商调换
版权所有　侵犯必究

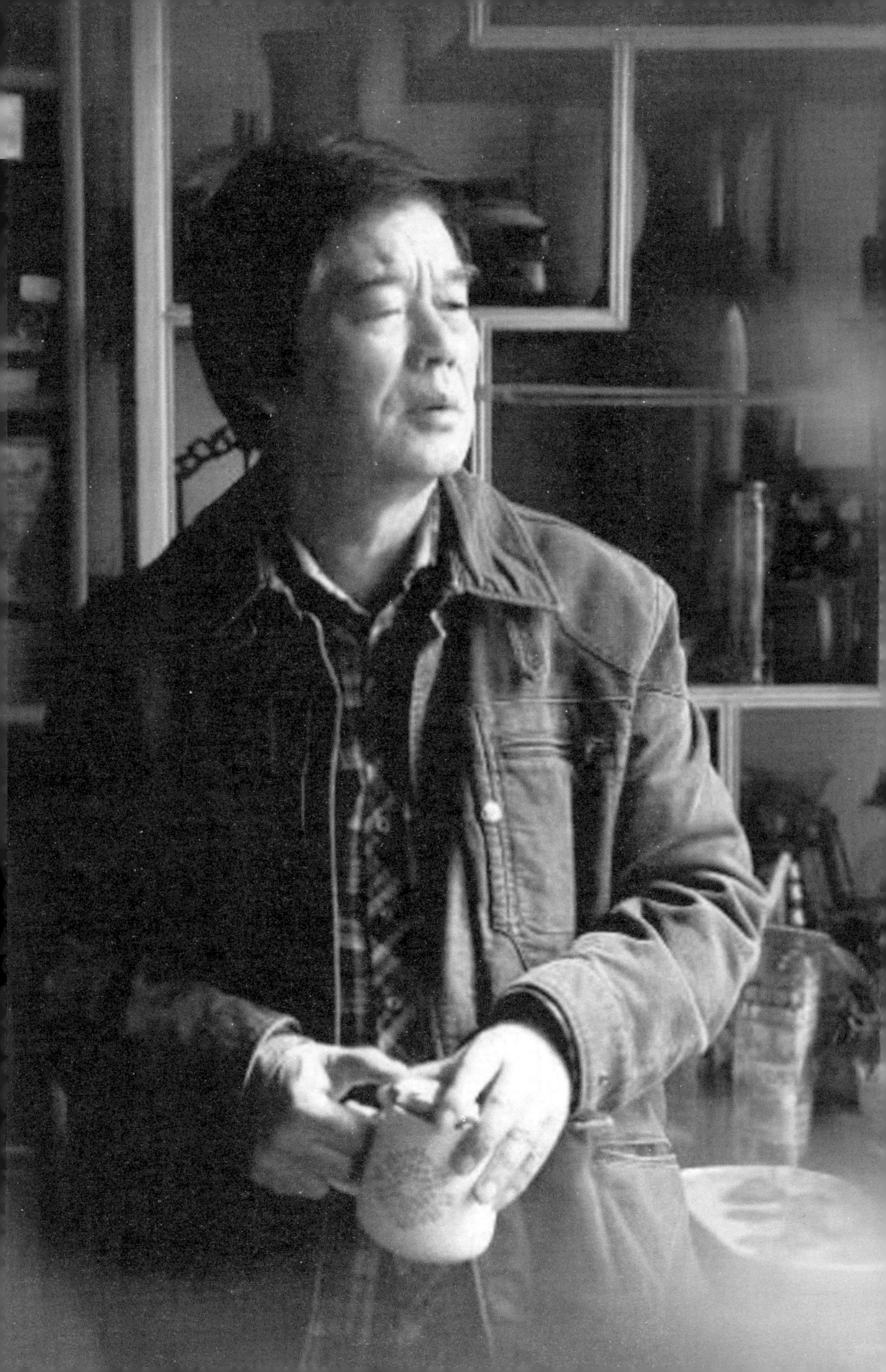

赵本夫

中国作家协会第七、第八届主席团委员，原江苏省作家协会专职副主席，大型文学双月刊《钟山》杂志主编，江苏省中华文化促进会副主席。先后就读于北京大学、南京大学。1981年发表处女作《卖驴》，获当年全国优秀短篇小说奖。至今已发表小说、散文500多万字，出版作品40多部。代表作有小说《卖驴》《绝唱》《鞋匠与市长》《走出蓝水河》《天下无贼》《地母》三部曲等。先后获得全国优秀短篇小说奖、《雨花》文学奖、《上海文学》奖、《天津文学》奖、《钟山》文学奖、紫金文学奖、《小说月报》百花奖、《小说选刊》全国文学奖、《中国作家》文学奖、《文艺报》年度人物奖、人民文学出版社优秀作品奖、国家新闻出版署优秀作品奖、江苏省委省政府"首届紫金文化奖章"等20多种文学奖项。部分作品被译为英、法、德、俄、挪威、日、韩文等语种，在国外发行。

Zhao Benfu

He, ex-vice-president of the Writers' Association of Jiangsu Province, also served as a committee member in the seventh and eighth session of the Presiding Board of the Chinese Writers' Association. He is the editor-in-chief of *Zhongshan*, an influential literary bimonthly in China, as well as vice-president of the Chinese Culture Promotions Society of Jiangsu Province. He once studied in Beijing University and Nanjing University. In 1981, his debut story "Selling Donkeys" was awarded the National Prize for Outstanding Short Stories of the Year. And since then, he has published a vast multitude of works—approximately 5 million words in more than 40 works. His representative works include "Selling Donkeys," "Last Song," "The Cobbler and the Mayor," *Leaving the Blue Water River*, "A World without Thieves" and the *Mother Earth* trilogy. He has won more than a score of literary prizes and accolades, including the National Prize for Outstanding Short Stories, *Yuhua* Literary Prize, *Shanghai Literature* Prize, *Tianjin Literature* Prize, *Zhongshan* Literary Prize, Zijin Literary Prize, The Hundred Flowers Award from *The Fiction Monthly*, The National Literary Prize from *The Selected Fictional Works*, *Chinese Writers* Prize, The Writers of the Year Award from *The Literature and Art Weekly*, the Excellent Works Award from the former State Administration of Press and Publication and The Zijin Cultural Medallion of Jiangsu Province. His works have been translated into English, French, German, Russian, Norwegian, Japanese and Korean and published abroad.

总　序

近年来，中国文学外译以前所未有的蓬勃势头展开。在江苏省委宣传部的直接领导下，南京师范大学外国语学院与江苏省作家协会、凤凰出版传媒集团合作，于2014年4月在伦敦书展上推出全英文期刊《中华人文》，之后又与南京师范大学出版社合作，于2018年推出《当代中国名家双语阅读文库》（第一辑）。这无疑

Preface

In recent years, translation of Chinese literature has gained unprecedented momentum. With the support of the Publicity Department of Jiangsu Provincial Party Committee, in cooperation with Writers' Association of Jiangsu Province and Phoenix Publishing & Media Group, the School of Foreign Languages and Cultures at Nanjing Normal University launched *Chinese Arts & Letters*, a journal introducing Chinese literature in translation to English-language readers in April, 2014. In 2018, the School of Foreign Languages and Cultures at Nanjing Normal University collaborated with Nanjing Normal University Press to launch the first volume of

是中国文学"走出去"的一次主动尝试。

杨昊成教授之前一直担任《中华人文》和《当代中国名家双语阅读文库》（以下简称《文库》）的主编，然而，2018年10月他不幸因病去世。杨昊成教授生前一直饱受病痛之扰，但他始终追求卓越，不仅逐字逐句审读这两份出版物中的每一篇文章，对于封面设计、文字配图等细节也都亲力亲为。《文库》的总序原来由杨昊成教授撰写，作为继任者，我理应对总序稍加修改，并表达对杨昊成教授的感谢和怀念。

对于这个文库，至少有两点可以一说。首先，它是在中国文化"走出去"这个时代背景下诞生的，这对于《文库》的出版意义重大。一个国家在世界经济中获得坚强地位后——正如中国强有力地向外部世界所展示的那样，就希望在诸如文化等其他各个方面全面出击，这是很正常的事。从历史上看，法语联盟、英国文化协会、歌德学院等都是这样，它们都是各自国家从事文化交流的重镇。虽说它们多半是民族自信和自豪的产物，但它们的存在似乎完全没有错。关键问题还是在于一个国家的文化如何走出

A Bilingual Library of Contemporary Chinese Master Writers. This work is a vibrant initiative of Chinese literature Going Global.

Professor Yang Haocheng was the editor-in-chief of *Chinese Arts & Letters* and *A Bilingual Library of Contemporary Chinese Master Writers* until he passed away in October, 2018. He had suffered from serious illnesses all his life, yet always continued to pursue excellence. Not only did he read every word of all the pieces printed in both publications, but he also devoted himself to the details of cover design and selection of illustrations. This Preface was originally written by Professor Yang. As his successor, I am revising it, and I would like to express my gratitude to him. I dearly cherish his memory.

There are two things that must be said. First, the present *Library* was born amidst the favorable climate of Chinese culture Going Global which was a significant factor in its publication. It is natural that when a country has earned a stronghold in the world economy, as China has now done so robustly, it will desire to go all out in other respects, including culture. Historically, it has been true of such institutions as the Alliance Française, the British Council, and the Goethe-Institut, all important channels for their respective countries' cultural flow and interaction. It is probably a matter of national self-confidence and pride, but there is nothing wrong with that. The question that remains is how a country's culture should go global. Two forces are at work: various

去。有两股力量在做着这方面的工作：一是各级官员，二是诸如学者、作家、翻译家、编辑等专业人士。这两股力量有着同一个目标，但在将自己的文化成就介绍到外部世界去的时候，他们所采取的策略和手段却不尽相同。前者中不乏不通外语及外国文化者，想把自己认为的宝贝强行兜售给潜在的买家，殊不知文化交流很大程度上犹如贸易，是建立在平等交换及买家自愿选择的基础之上的，任何一厢情愿的强卖是注定要失败的。后者比前者要更懂行，却在政治方向和经济资助上有赖于前者，因此常常陷入这样一种困境：他们想按自己认为的正确的道路前进，却不时遭遇不受欢迎的指示或干扰。《中国文学》这份挣扎了整整五十年的官方杂志就是一个很好的教训。虽然《中国文学》在它的后半段有杨宪益这样多产又具有人格魅力的翻译家担任主编，但杨宪益一人显然无力抵御他那个时代的政治影响。《中国文学》有着明显的时代印记，这也解释了为什么这么多年它在海外一直不怎么为人所接受。

非常幸运的是，《文库》得以坚持自己既定的标准，《文

bureaucrats, and professionals such as researchers, writers, translators, editors, and publishers. The two forces have the same aim, but each espouses different strategies and approaches for introducing their cultural achievements to the outside world. Some ignorant of the foreign languages and their cultures, bureaucrats want very much to sell what they deem to be precious material to a potential buyer, not knowing that cultural exchange is, to a great extent, like trade and is built on the basis of equal give-and-take and willingness on the side of the buyer, while any one-sided forced selling is doomed to fail. Though much more informed, the professionals are reliant on the bureaucrats for political direction and financial support, and are thus left in a dilemma. They want to proceed with what they regard as the right path, but are frequently met with undesirable obstacles, including unwelcomed directions or interferences from the bureaucrats. The case of *Chinese Literature*, an officially sponsored magazine that has struggled for a full fifty years, is instructive. Though *Chinese Literature* has had as its chief editor the prolific, charismatic translator Yang Xianyi for the second half of its fifty-year life, Yang alone certainly would not have had sufficient strength to stay clear of the political influences of his day. *Chinese Literature* bears the clear hallmark of its time, which explains its low readership overseas over the years.

Fortunately, the present *Library* is able to adhere to its set standard, and what is collected here are either representative works

库》内收集的都是当今中国最负盛名的作家的代表作或得到人们高度认可的作品。数十年的意识形态斗争过去了，我们终于可以回归到文学创作的本体研究。所有收录在本文库的翻译作品，虽然它们对待文学的手法和角度有着天壤之别，却都道出了人性和人生的共性，那就是人类的喜、怒、哀、乐。这些短篇，以其洗练的笔法、精巧的结构、典型的人物事件，成为当代中国文学宝库中极为重要的组成部分。为了更好更立体地呈现作家及其作品，除了少数例外，我们还为每个作家收录了一篇评论和一篇访谈。

其次，从事翻译的人都清楚，当目标语为母语时，译者们做得就要好一些。译者的母语是英语，从事汉译英就会得心应手得多，这是不争的事实。杨昊成老师曾就《水浒传》的翻译给沙博理先生（Sidney Shapiro）打电话，电话中沙博理先生非常坦诚地表示："对我来说，翻译像《水浒传》这样的作品比将英文材料译成中文要容易得多。虽然早在1963年我就入了中国籍，但中文毕竟不是我的母语。"

本文库以拥有一支高超的职业翻译家队伍为豪，他们的母语

or highly recognized pieces of some of the most famous writers from contemporary China. After the lapse of dozens of years of ideological struggles, we are able to return at last to the ontological study of literary creation, and all the works translated here speak of the commonality of human nature and human life—humankind's happiness, anger, sorrow, and joy—despite their vastly different approaches and perspectives toward literature. With their succinct style, exquisite structure, and typical characters and events, these stories constitute an extremely important, integral part of the treasure house of contemporary Chinese literature. For a better, more three-dimensional presentation of the authors and their works, we have also included a critique and an interview for each author, with only a few exceptions.

In addition, it is common knowledge among translators that they do better when translating into their mother tongue. It's an undeniable fact that translators whose mother tongue is English will be much more at home when it comes to Chinese-English translation. Professor Yang Haocheng used to call Sidney Shapiro about his translation of *Outlaws of the Marsh*. Mr. Shapiro once said to him on the phone, "Translating things like *Outlaws of the Marsh* is much easier for me than translating English materials into Chinese. After all, Chinese is not my mother tongue, though I became a Chinese citizen all the way back in 1963."

The present *Library* boasts a terrific pool of professional

是英语,又全都是双语或多种语言的使用者。他们同时也都是《中华人文》的译者。这就完全不一样了。事实上,无论是《中国文学》还是几乎所有其他由中国人办的期刊杂志,都有着相同的问题:它们的译者大都是非母语使用者,其英语是作为第二语言习得的,无法跟母语是英语的职业翻译家相比。更为难得的是,这些译者对中文的掌握都是一流的,其中不少人是世界公认的汉学家或老牌的中国通。Denis Mair(梅丹理)、Nicky Harman(韩斌)、Natascha Bruce、Luisetta Mudie、Shelly Bryant(白雪莉)、Josh Stenberg(石峻山)、Helen Wang、Jeremy Tiang、Eric Abrahamsen、Michael Day、Simon Patton、Florence Woo等,是我们最为尽职而宝贵的翻译家中的一部分。出自他们之手的译作,乍看之下可能并无特殊之处,实际却很是地道,常令我们击节叹赏。

因此,《文库》的目标读者首先是对翻译感兴趣的读者,尤其是学习翻译的本科生和研究生。杨昊成老师在审阅译稿时,时常忍不住把译者的精彩译文抄录下来,并加以点评:"她有着凹凸有致的身材"译为"She has a figure of voluptuous curves"。还

translators whose mother tongue is English, and all of them are bilingual or multilingual. They are the same translators who are working for *Chinese Arts & Letters*. This makes all the difference. In fact, both *Chinese Literature* and almost all other journals and magazines run by Chinese publishers have the same problem. Many of their translators are non-native speakers or writers of the target language, and their English was learned as a second language. They cannot be compared with professional translators whose mother tongue is English and, better still, whose command of the Chinese language is superb. Many of them are internationally recognized sinologists or old China hands to boot. Denis Mair, Nicky Harman, Natascha Bruce, Luisetta Mudie, Shelly Bryant, Josh Stenberg, Helen Wang, Jeremy Tiang, Eric Abrahamsen, Michael Day, Simon Patton, and Florence Woo are among our most conscientious and treasured translators. What comes out of their hands may seem at first glance to be nothing special, yet their work is so idiomatic that we cannot help but admire.

The target audience of the present *Library*, then, should first of all be readers interested in translation, especially undergraduates and graduate students studying translation. When Professor Yang Haocheng was reading the manuscripts prepared by these translators, he often could not keep himself from copying their wonderful translations with careful analysis, such as the rendering of,"她有着凹凸有致的身材"(meaning "She has a figure of

有一个高度口语化的专门词语可以用来描述这样的女孩，即zaftig，所以我们经常可以听到人们说：她是那种身材火辣、招蜂引蝶的女孩儿（She is a sort of zaftig, coquettish girl）。"包二奶"如今已是很常见的一个说法了，我们的译者将它译成"to keep a bit on the side"，"当小三"也就顺理成章地译作"to be sb's bit on the side"；bit意为"水性杨花的女子"，on the side意思是"悄悄地""私下里"，不过还带点幽默。如今许多年轻人喜欢用的"吃货"一词，在英文里也有相对应的说法，即"greedy guts"［注意是guts而非gut，如He is a greedy guts（他是个吃货）］，虽然在已故陆谷孙教授主编的《中华汉英大词典》中有诸如foodie、glutton、gourmand、gastronaut、food aficionado等其他译法。"恶搞"（to kuso）事实上来自日语，但已进入英语词汇，令to parody、to lampoon、to snark等稍显过时。phubber是phubbing一词的逆构，据说是由澳大利亚的几个语言学家、词典编纂家和作家从phone和snub两个词合并创立的一个新词。这个新词用来描述那种不顾周围人事、一心看手机的人，和目前流行的中国词语"低头族"完全一致。这个词只有几年的历史，尽管

voluptuous curves"). There is a special word, albeit highly colloquial, to describe that kind of girl, "zaftig." So we constantly hear people say, "She is a sort of zaftig, coquettish girl." Similarly, "包二奶" is a very common term today, and our translator renders it "to keep a bit on the side." Accordingly, "当小三" is "to be sb's bit on the side," "bit" meaning a loose woman, and "on the side," in secret or on the sly, but with a bit of humor. Likewise, "吃货," a term enjoyed by many young people today, has also its English equivalent, "greedy guts." (Mind you, it's *guts* and not *gut*. For instance: *He is a greedy guts.*) This is aside from other possible renderings, such as foodie, glutton, gourmand, gastronaut, or food aficionado, as listed by the *Chinese-English Dictionary* chief-edited by the late Professor Lu Gusun. And "恶搞" actually has a Japanese term "to kuso," which has already entered the English language, making "to parody," "to lampoon," and "to snark" seem somewhat outdated. "Phubber," the reverse formation of "phubbing," which is said to be a new coinage by some Australian linguists, lexicographers, and authors from "phone" and "snub," a neologism to describe the habit of snubbing people around you in favor of a mobile phone, is an exact equivalent of the the popular Chinese term "低头族." It only has a history of several years, and though already included in the *Australian National Dictionary*, most other dictionaries or thesauruses have not yet included it. And such simple oral sayings as "过了这村儿没这店儿" and "金窝银窝, 不如自家狗

已被收入《澳大利亚国家词典》，其他绝大多数词典或工具书却尚未收入。简单而口语化的说法如"过了这村儿没这店儿"和"金窝银窝，不如自家狗窝"，被高超地译成了简洁有力的"It's now or never"，和至今为止最贴近原文的"Gold dish, silver dish, they cannot compare to your own dog's dish"，它们分别是从平淡无奇的"last chance"和同样令人难忘却丢失了原意象的"East or west, home is best"中生出的天才的产物。仅此一点就足以使本文库成为对翻译感兴趣的读者的一个很好的阅读材料。事实上，这些材料对我们编辑自己而言，也是一个了解两种语言以及全面提升自己的极好机会。目前已有不少高校使用本套《文库》作为笔译课程的教材，并将其列为翻译硕士考试的参考书目。

《文库》的目标读者还包括比较文学和中西文化比较研究的学者。在系统的规划、组织和支持下，中国文学作品外译输出的数量和质量都有了很大的提高，但中国文学的海外影响力仍然有限，尚未成为世界文学中的"活跃存在"。我们认为，解决这个问题的关键在于，不仅仅要关注中国文学的海外翻译，同时更要窝" are masterfully translated into the pithy phrase, "It's now or never," and the most faithful to date, "Gold dish, silver dish, they cannot compare to your own dog's dish," respectively, both genius outgrowths from the prosaic "last chance," and the equally memorable—though losing the image—clause, "East or west, home is best." This alone is a good reason why the *Library* is a good read for all who are interested in translation. In fact, editing these works has turned out to be a great opportunity for us editors to learn about the two languages, and it has generally uplifted us. Many universities have chosen the *Library* as the textbook for their translation courses and have included it in the list of reference books for the entrance examination for their Masters in Translation and Interpretation programs.

The target audience of the present *Library* also includes scholars of comparative literature and comparative study of the cultures of East and West. With systematic planning, organization, and support, the quantity and quality of translations of Chinese literature have greatly improved. However, their influence overseas is still limited, and Chinese literature in translation is still not an "active presence" in World Literature. We believe that the key to addressing this problem is to emphasize not only international translation of Chinese literature, but also international literary criticism. At the Symposium on Chinese Literature Going Global

注重中国文学的海外评论。在"从莫言获奖看中国文学如何走出去"学术会议上，宋炳辉教授指出："中国文学要真正走出去，其实在很大程度上还要依靠文学研究者对文学作品本身的阐释，对文学作品内涵的有效和多元阐释是实现本土文学国际化的一个重要因素。"在当代中国文学外译中，这一维度目前未受到应有的重视，而我们正努力在这方面有所突破。杨昊成教授去世之后，南京师范大学外国语学院邀请盛宁教授担任《中华人文》主编，对于《文库》的译介内容选择，尤其是访谈和评论的选择，盛宁教授都全程给予指导。盛宁教授曾担任我国外国文学研究顶级期刊《外国文学评论》主编，众多中国学者通过这一高端平台对外国文学进行多角度的解读与评论，极大地促进了外国文学在中国的"活跃存在"。我们希望通过《文库》，鼓励学者评论翻译成英语的、作为世界文学组成部分的中国文学。换句话说，盛宁教授以前工作的重心是引导学者用汉语评论外国文学，而现在则是引导更多的学者用外语评论中国文学，当然包括海外汉学家的评论。我们要让中国文学不但有效地"走出去"，而且能够真正

since Mo Yan won the Nobel Prize, Professor Song Binghui pointed out that "for Chinese literature to really go global, it must, to a large extent, depend on literary scholars' interpretation of the literary works, and having effective multiple interpretations of the literary works is an important factor in realizing the internationalization of local literature." When contemporary Chinese literature has been introduced to the world, this dimension has not received due attention, so we are trying to achieve a breakthrough in this area. After Professor Yang Haocheng passed away, we invited Professor Sheng Ning to be the editor-in-chief of *Chinese Arts & Letters*. Selection of the content for the *Library*, especially the interviews and criticisms, followed Professor Sheng Ning's suggestions. Professor Sheng Ning was formerly the editor-in-chief of *Foreign Literature Review*, the top-level journal in the field of foreign literature studies. On this platform, many Chinese scholars interpret and criticize foreign literature from various perspectives, facilitating the "active presence" of foreign literature in China. We hope that the *Library* will encourage scholars to criticize Chinese literature translated into English and as a part of World Literature. In other words, Professor Sheng Ning formerly focused on guiding scholars to criticize foreign literature in Chinese, but now he is focusing on guiding more scholars to criticize Chinese literature in foreign languages, including literary criticism from foreign sinologists. We hope to ensure that Chinese literature is not only

地"走进去"。

《文库》还希望能够引起译学界对文学翻译过程研究的关注。如前文所述,《文库》的译者均为母语为英语的海外汉学家;与此同时,依托南京师范大学外国语学院,选择专门从事文学、翻译研究的教师作为编辑,通过译者—编辑合作模式完成译稿。合作基本程序为译者翻译第一稿,在翻译的过程中译者与编辑随时进行交流,译稿完成后编辑进行校对,并与译者共同修改,修改完成后由主编进行最后审定。我本人并非翻译专业出身,但在参与《中华人文》的编辑工作伊始,就被这一过程中所出现的各种问题深深吸引。尽管知道翻译理论研究并非自己的专业,但我在2014年还是忍不住写了一篇完全基于自己编辑实践的论文——《译者—编辑合作模式在中国文学外译中的实践——以毕飞宇三部短篇小说的英译为例》,由此开启了学术研究的新方向,并至今乐此不疲。目前《中华人文》正在着手建立翻译过程语料库,《文库》的翻译过程语料也将加入其中。语料库拟对所有研究翻译的学者开放,开展多角度的研究,丰富翻译研究的路径。翻译过程语料库

effectively Going Global, but is also truly being appreciated.

The present *Library* also aims to attract scholars' attention to the process of literary translation. As mentioned above, the translators of the *Library* are all sinologists whose mother tongue is English. At the same time, they collaborate with Chinese editors who are teachers from the School of Foreign Languages and Cultures at Nanjing Normal University, specializing in literature or translation. The basic collaboration process involves the translator finishing the first draft and communicating with the editor whenever questions arise. After the first draft is finished, the editor proofreads it, then revises it with the translator. After the revision is completed, the editor-in-chief checks and approves the final draft. I am not a translation major, but from the time I began my job as editor at *Chinese Arts & Letters*, I was drawn to the various challenges that arose during this process. Although I knew little about translation theory, I could not wait to write an article entirely based on my own editing experience, "The Translator-Editor Collaboration in Translating Chinese Literature—Three Short Stories by Bi Feiyu as Case Studies" in 2014. It has opened a new direction in my academic research, in which I have never lost interest. At present, *Chinese Arts & Letters* is setting up a Translation Process Corpus, and the materials in the translation process of the *Library* will be added to the Corpus as well. The Corpus will be open to all translation scholars to conduct studies from various perspectives and enrich the approaches to translation

体现了母语为英语的译者与母语为中文的编辑之间的充分交流：译者和编辑各自发挥自己的母语优势，在两种语言、两种文化之间互动交融，努力使译文既符合目标读者群的阅读习惯与审美趣味，又准确传达原文背后深刻的文化内涵。我们甚至可以设想，如果能将这种集中了翻译场域中人类智慧的翻译过程语料，以合适的方式对人工智能进行"投喂"，让人工智能进行深度学习，将来也许可以将语言的细微之处翻译出精妙的美感，真正突破人工智能在翻译水平方面的瓶颈。

尽管以上所提到的目标读者都相对专业，但我们仍然希望《文库》雅俗共赏，成为文学爱好者的枕边书。杨昊成教授曾对当代青年只看手机不看书的状况提出严厉的批评：他们"似乎更喜欢来自新媒体的碎片化阅读，严肃文学因此令人悲哀地受到轻视或藐视，被遗忘在图书馆的书架上，满是尘埃，仅成为少数书生的精神食粮"。他希望本文库能挽回一部分"迷途的羔羊"，让他们"回到传统的纸质阅读的正常轨道上来"。我觉得自己没有资格批评——尽管我已经不能算作是"当代青年"，但我看手机的

studies. The Translation Process Corpus showcases the communication between the translator who is a native speaker of English and the editor who is a native speaker of Chinese. They each exert their own mother tongue advantages, and interaction occurs between the two languages and cultures. They seek to make the translated text not only satisfy the target audience's reading habits and aesthetic preferences, but also convey the deepest cultural connotations of the original text. We may even imagine that if these materials crystalizing human intelligence in the translation field were "fed" in the proper way into an artificial intelligence and became deep-learning materials for AI, AI would one day translate every subtlety of the language with delicacy and beauty, breaking the bottleneck in AI translation.

Though, as mentioned earlier, the target audience of these works is relatively professional, we hope that the present *Library* will suit both refined and popular tastes and be put beside the pillows of all readers who are interested in literature. Professor Yang Haocheng once criticized young people today for being interested only in cellphones instead of books, saying, "So it is fragmented reading from the new media that college students seem to be enjoying today, and serious literature is woefully slighted or neglected, forgotten in the dust-covered shelves of the libraries, becoming the spiritual food for a minority of bookish souls." He hoped the *Library* would bring back some of "the lost lambs to the

频率已经远远超过了看纸质书的频率,应该也算是杨昊成教授所批评的"迷途的羔羊"之一。然而,我们还是希望《文库》能让大家稍稍改变一下习惯,每天花一点时间阅读纸质书,《文库》中的短篇小说也许就是最好的开始。本文库第一辑所译介的作家之一苏童曾说:"短篇小说就像针对成年人的夜间故事,最好在灯下读,最好是每天入睡前读一篇,玩味三五分钟,或者被感动,或者会心一笑,或者怅怅然的,如有骨鲠在喉,如果读出这样的味道,说明这短暂的阅读时间没有浪费,培养这样的习惯使一天的生活终止于辉煌,多么好!"《文库》中不仅有精彩的短篇小说,更有相对照的英文版,相信读者一定会有双重的乐趣与收获。

文学评论家吴义勤、学者及翻译家许钧都从他们各自不同的视角出发,对本文库的出版表示了强有力的支持。两位都是他们各自领域的重要人物,他们的意见更增加了本文库的权威性。

《当代中国名家双语阅读文库》是开放性的,它会不断地出下

normal track of conventional paper book reading." I don't think I myself have the right to criticize young people today. Although I am not young, I read my cellphone much more frequently than I read paper books, which makes me one of "the lost lambs" criticized by Professor Yang Haocheng. But it is our hope that the *Library* will change our reading habits a little. If we plan to spend some time every day reading books, the short stories in the present *Library* are an ideal starting point. As Su Tong, one of the writers introduced in Volume One of the *Library,* once said, "Short stories are like bedtime stories for adults, preferably being read beside the lamp, one piece per night. They can be tasted for three or five minutes, moving, amusing, depressing, or overwhelming the reader. If you experience these feelings, it shows that this short period of time has not been wasted. A habit like this ensures that each day will end in magnificence. How wonderful it is!" The *Library* contains wonderful short stories in both Chinese and English, which, we believe, will surely bring readers double happiness and growth.

Literary critic Wu Yiqin, and academic and translator Xu Jun, have both voiced their strong support for this *Library,* each speaking from their different perspectives. Both of them are towering figures in their own fields, and their opinions add to the authority of the *Library.*

This *Library* is meant to be open ended, though it is set to be developed on a five-author basis, which includes five short stories

去。它以五位作家为一辑，每位作家为一卷，每卷包括五个短篇并附有一篇评论和一篇访谈，其中个别卷会略有变化。为了本文库的出版，各方面的人员做出了很多努力或给予了很大支持，其中包括我们杰出的翻译家、作家、评论家、《中华人文》和南京师范大学出版社的领导、编辑等，可以说这是一次令人快乐又组织有序的大合唱。历史会铭记我们的现任总指挥盛宁教授，会永远怀念首任主编杨昊成教授！

许诗焱

2020年9月

alongside a critique and an interview for each author, with slight variations in each issue. Various people have contributed their effort and lent their support to the publication of the *Library,* including our terrific translators, authors, critics, editors from *Chinese Arts & Letters* and Nanjing Normal University Press, and the Press's leadership, so you may say it's a joyful, well-orchestrated tutti. History will remember our current conductor, Professor Sheng Ning, and will cherish our memory to Professor Yang Haocheng as our first editor-in-chief.

Xu Shiyan
September, 2020

目　录

绝　唱　　　　　　　　　　　　　　030
天下无贼　　　　　　　　　　　　080
鞋匠与市长　　　　　　　　　　　134
斩　首　　　　　　　　　　　　　168
临　界　　　　　　　　　　　　　202

附录
|评论
　　赵本夫论/吴秉杰　　　　　　　262
|访谈
　　文学如何呈现记忆？——赵本夫访谈录/沙家强　　322

Contents

Last Song	031
A World without Thieves	081
The Cobbler and the Mayor	135
Decapitation	169
On The Verge	203

Appendices
|Critique
  On Zhao Benfu/*Wu Bingjie*   263
|Interview
  How Does Literature Present Memory?
    —An Interview with Zhao Benfu/*Sha Jiaqiang*   323

绝　唱

　　一园翠竹，约八亩许。园内枝叶扶疏，绿荫映罩，地面上松松地长着一簇簇青草，开着红的、黄的、紫的、白的各种野花，招引得蜂蜂蝶蝶在竹园里飘飞穿行。

　　园主人姓尚，官称尚爷，七十多岁，圆脸，白净，没有胡须，年轻时像竹园一样风流，娶过三个女人。早年间，他做过一家地

Last Song

Translated by Shelly Bryant

In a garden of bamboo covering about eight *mu* of land, branches with luxuriant leaves spread out gracefully, forming a canopy of green shade. Clumps of green grass grew loosely on the ground, blossoming with red, yellow, purple, white, and all kinds of wild flowers, attracting butterflies and bees to flit through the bamboo garden.

The owner of the garden was Shang, and officially people called him Lord Shang. He was in his seventies, with a round, clean face. He did not have a mustache, and had been as romantic as the bamboo garden in his younger days. He had been married to three

主的账房，会背一些诗文，尤爱柳永词，高兴时还研墨挥毫写一写。

尚爷一生无所长，不善理家，嗜好听戏、养鸟，且精。后来，他因为和这家地主的贴身丫头私通，被辞去账房职务。尚爷二话没说，一年的工钱没要，买下那丫头，领回家做了二房。他家有十几亩薄地，原有一个妻子。两个女人相处很和睦，共同爱着一个男人，种地兼管生孩子。尚爷很放心，依旧是听戏、养鸟，养鸟、听戏。他喜欢女人，从来不打骂她们。尚爷会大红拳，手重。他说："女人不禁打，一打骨头就碎了。"

有一年，从河南来了个野戏班子，尚爷天天跟着听。戏班子挪一村，他跟一村，一个多月后，跟到徐州府，距家已有近二百里地了。他迷上了戏。这个戏班子是唱豫剧的，一个武生，一个闺门旦，唱得特别好。尚爷喜欢他们，更喜欢那个唱闺门旦的姑娘。那姑娘老在前排看见他，心也动了。唱野戏很苦，四海漂流，

women. In the early days, he was an accountant for a landlord. He could recite some poetry, and had a special love for Liu Yong's poems. When he was in a good mood, he would even take up a brush to write or draw.

Lord Shang had no special skills. He was not good at managing his household, loved going to the opera and rearing birds, and was quite expert at both. Later, he had an illicit affair with the landlord's personal maid, which cost him his job as their accountant. Lord Shang said nothing, but gave up one year of his salary and bought the maid. He took her home and made her his second wife. He had more than a dozen acres of poor quality land in his family and one wife. The two wives got along very well, shared their love for the same man, worked the land, and added children to the family. Lord Shang felt at ease, going about his usual business of enjoying the opera and rearing birds. He liked women and did not lay a hand or use harsh words on them. He knew the art of Hung Kuen and could dish out hard blows. He said, "Women cannot take a beating. It will shatter their bones."

One year, a roving opera troupe came from Henan, and Lord Shang followed it around. Whenever the troupe moved to a new village, Lord Shang followed. After more than a month, he had followed them all the way to Xuzhou Prefecture, nearly two hundred miles from his home. He was fascinated with opera. This opera troupe sang Henan opera, with one actor playing a martial role and another playing a maidenly female role. They sang extremely well. Lord Shang liked them, especially the girl who played the maidenly female role. The girl always saw him in the front row, and she too was moved. Being in a roving opera troupe was tough, wandering

没有定所，而且常受人欺负。姑娘早就不想唱戏了。她知道，前排那个白脸后生是奔她来的。他爱她，她也爱他，有这样一个痴心汉子，一辈子也值了，正是精诚所至，金石为开。一个在台上唱戏，一个在台下听戏，两个眉来眼去，姑娘连戏词都忘了，回到后台就挨打。尚爷跟到后台，一把扯住姑娘的胳膊："走吧，跟我走吧，我不会亏待你！"姑娘抹抹泪，当真就跟他来了。当时，尚爷手里还提着鸟笼子，很像个阔少。领班的不敢拦阻，只好眼睁睁看着他们去了。

这时候，前台的戏还正唱着。

尚爷领着那姑娘，出了徐州府，沿黄河故道一路西行。天黑得伸手不见五指，荒草野洼，连个人影儿也不见。姑娘牵着他的衣襟，吓得直打哆嗦。尚爷安慰她说："别怕，你看这个！"路旁有一棵对把粗的柳树，尚爷一手提鸟笼子，一手抓住小柳树，只一拧，"咔嚓！"树身断了。姑娘高兴了："啃！你这么大的劲儿？"尚爷说："你唱一段吧？""谁听呀？""我听。"姑娘唱起来："花木

from place to place without a permanent residence. They were also bullied by people. For a long time, she had wanted to quit the opera. She knew that the young man in the front row with the clean face came because of her. He loved her, and she reciprocated his love. To the girl, having such an infatuated male follower made her life was worth the living. The old saying, the utmost sincerity can influence even metal and stone, applied to this couple. One sang on the stage, and the other listened before the stage, making eyes at each other. Once when the distracted girl forgot her lines, she got a beating backstage.

Lord Shang went backstage and grabbed hold of the girl's arm. "Let's go. Follow me! I won't treat you poorly."

The girl wiped her tears away and followed him. Lord Shang held a bird cage in his hand, with an air of a rich young master. The leader of the troupe did not dare hold her back, but just watched helplessly as the couple left.

The opera was still going on onstage throughout the whole exchange.

Lord Shang led the girl out of Xuzhou, heading west along the old course of Yellow River. When night fell, the wilderness was deserted and pitch dark. The girl grasped the front of his jacket tightly and trembled in fear. Lord Shang consoled her, "Don't be afraid. Look at this!"

A willow tree stood beside the road. Holding the bird cage in one hand, he caught the little willow tree with the other, twisting it. Snap! The tree broke. The girl was delighted, "Wow! Aren't you strong?"

Lord Shang said, "Why don't you sing a tune?"

兰，羞答答……"

"站住！"

背后突然大喝一声。姑娘戛然声止，又尖叫着，扑到尚爷身上。尚爷以为是遇上了拦路打劫的。他回头看看，十几步开外，一个后生仔一手擎火把，一手持钢刀，正一步步向他逼来。

尚爷把姑娘拉到背后，又把鸟笼子递给她，撩起长袍掖在腰间，迎上去。两人相距有十步远，尚爷突然撸下头上的礼帽，一扬手："噗！"一团黑影飞过去，那人以为是暗器，一拧身子，同时举起钢刀相迎，却没有金石之声。就在这一眨巴眼的工夫，尚爷一个箭步跟上，飞起一脚，"哨啷！"钢刀泛着寒光抛落到一丈开外的草丛里。那人丢下火把，亮开架势打来。尚爷弓步出手，只一招，对手就倒了。尚爷正要上前按住，不料那人一个后滚翻，从地上闪开。轻捷！尚爷心里叫一声好，一个燕子抄水，凌空扑去，就势抓住那人的脖颈，脚下一绊，又把他放倒地上。尚爷脚下踩着个硬东西，伸手一摸，正是踢飞的那把刀。他一把抓起来，

"Who's going to listen?" asked the girl.

"Me," answered Lord Shang.

The girl started singing, "Hua Mulan, shyly..."

"Don't move!"

The loud command came from behind. The girl stopped singing suddenly, screaming as she flung herself onto Lord Shang. Lord Shang thought they had met with some bandits, but looking behind him, he saw a dozen steps from them a young man holding up a torch in one hand and a steel sword in the other. He was closing in on them.

Lord Shang moved the girl behind him, handing her the bird cage. He lifted his robe and tucked it in at his waist, then rushed towards the young man. When they were ten steps apart, Lord Shang suddenly rolled the hat off his head and tossed it. Whoosh! A black shadow flew towards the young man. Thinking it was a dart, the fellow twisted and raised his sword to block it. There was no sound of metal hitting against metal. In the blink of an eye, Lord Shang lunged out with a hefty kick. Plunk! The sword, glinting and cold, was kicked to a clump of grass more than a foot away. The young man threw down his torch and took a fighting stance as he rushed towards them. Lord Shang assumed the bow stance and, with one move, his opponent fell. Lord Shang was about to move in and hold his opponent down when the latter unexpectedly did a back flip and flashed to the side, raising himself from the ground. Smooth! Lord Shang applauded inwardly. With the swallow-lifting-water move, he flew in the air toward the young man and caught hold of his neck in one fluid motion. With his leg, he tripped his opponent, sending the fellow to the ground. Stepping on something

按住那人的肩胛，扭头向姑娘说："杀了吧？"

"啊……不不不！我不要你杀人！我不要……"那姑娘已瘫在地上，一叠声叫着。

尚爷转回头，松开手，又把刀丢在地上："你走吧！"他刚站起身，那人却在地上绝叫一声："不！你还是杀了我吧！"尚爷一愣，又拾起刀："好，我成全你。"正要举刀，那唱闺门旦的姑娘却发了疯似的扑过来，拦腰抱住尚爷："别别别！……你不能杀他呀！"

尚爷犹豫着又站起来。

"你是……关山?!"姑娘扑到那人身上，哽咽起来。

关山是谁？她认识？……关山躺在地上，动也不动，任凭姑娘推揉哭叫，死了一般，毫无反应。

尚爷如坠五里雾中，走开几步，捡起那人先前丢掉的火把，"噗噗"连吹几口，又冒出火苗来，亮堂堂一片。他拿回来弯腰照了照，咯噔！尚爷傻了，关山就是那个野戏班里的武生！他一下子明白过来：这武生也爱着闺门旦呢！他是卸了装追来的。怪不

hard, Lord Shang felt with his hand. It was the sword he had kicked away. He raised it and pressed it to the man's shoulder. Turning his head, he asked the girl, "Shall I kill him?"

"Ah... no no no! I don't want you to kill him!" The girl was lying on the ground, crying in fear.

Lord Shang turned back to his opponent and released him, throwing the sword on the ground, "Go!"

Just as Lord Shang stood up, the man yelled desperately, "No, please kill me!"

Taken aback, Lord Shang picked up the sword again. "All right, I'll grant you your wish."

He was about to raise the blade again when the girl pounced on him wildly, throwing her arms around his waist. "Don't don't don't... you can't kill him!"

Lord Shang hesitated again and stood up.

"Are you... Guan Shan?" The girl flew into the man's arms and started sobbing.

Who was Guan Shan? She knew him? Guan Shan lay on the ground motionless, and no matter how the girl pushed and shoved him, he did not respond, as if he were dead.

Lord Shang felt like he had fallen into a thick fog. He walked a few steps to one side and picked up the torch thrown down by his opponent. He blew on it a few times and rekindled the flame, brightening up the place. He came back, shining the torch on them. Lord Shang was shocked. Guan Shan was the actor playing the martial role in the opera troupe! He suddenly understood. This actor also loved the girl. He had taken off his make-up and pursued the girl all the way here. No wonder he was so nimble, but he could

得身子那么轻捷，只是不禁打，没真功。这么说，他是讨姑娘来了。

尚爷惭愧了，一抱拳："对不住，我不知道……"他要把姑娘送还。可是姑娘又不肯，关山只一个劲地要求："杀了我吧！杀了……"

这事有点麻烦。尚爷也坐下了。三人都坐在草地上，似乎在商量杀不杀的事。商量了半天，没结果。尚爷火了："我看你也没出息！为个女人让我杀你。我不能杀你！我经眼的角色多啦。据我看，你能唱出好戏来！唱、做、念、打，无一样不出众，十年以后，肯定会成名流。我杀你是罪过！懂吗，我不能杀你！"

关山坐在草地上，半天没吭声。闺门旦又嘤嘤地哭起来："我不是……不想嫁你……可我怕苦……学不……出来……"

关山叹了一口气，站起来，喉头哽塞着向尚爷说："请你……好生待承她！"转脸要走，尚爷心头一热，一把拉住："关山，实在对不住。你要不嫌弃，咱磕个头吧？老实说，我是个戏迷，我喜欢你的戏，也佩服你的人品！"

not actually fight, and he did not know real martial arts. So, he had come for the girl.

Lord Shang was ashamed. He wrapped one hand around his clenched fist and pulled his hands to his chest, "I'm so sorry, I didn't know..."

He wanted to return the girl to Guan Shan, but she would not agree.

Guan Shan kept begging, "Kill me!"

This situation was a little tricky. Lord Shang sat down too. The trio sat on the grass and seemed to be discussing about whether or not to kill Guan Shan. They discussed it for a long time, but no conclusion was reached. Lord Shang grew angry. "I see you're pretty useless. You want me to kill you because of a girl. I can't kill you. I've seen many kinds of people. In my opinion, you are a very good opera singer. You're outstanding in every area of this art. In another ten years, you'll surely become famous. It would be a sin for me to kill you. Do you understand? I can't kill you!"

Guan Shan sat on the ground, not saying anything for a long time. The girl started sobbing again. "It's not that... I don't want to marry you... but I'm afraid of hardship... that I can't ever... be good at..."

Guan Shan let out a sigh, stood up, and said with a lump in his throat, "Please... treat her well!"

He turned around, preparing to leave. Lord Shang suddenly felt great warmth toward this man. He held onto him and said, "Guan Shan, I'm very sorry! If you will, let's part as sworn brothers. To tell you the truth, I'm an opera enthusiast, and I like your acting. I also admire your character."

关山想了想,这事也无法怨人家,谁叫咱是个穷戏子哩?连个女人也养不起!这人倒豪爽,也是个识家,高山流水,知音难觅哩。好!

两人重新报了姓名,说出生辰年庚,聚沙为炉,插草为香,两个头磕下去,成了把兄弟。尚爷年长五岁,为兄;关山小五岁,为弟。姑娘破涕为笑了。

分手时,关山把那把刀送了尚爷:"路上做个帮手吧!"尚爷无以为赠,把鸟笼子给了他,里头养着一只百灵:"我养了十年啦。送你。这是百灵十三口,叫得正欢。望你专心学戏,也做个百灵十三口!"

关山挥泪洒别,独自去了。尚爷兀自站着未动,手捧钢刀,心里一阵酸痛,觉得很对不起他。

尚爷把姑娘领回家,续成三房。再细看那把刀,倒吸一口气:"这是一把宝刀哩!"闰门旦告诉他:"在戏班里时,我见过这把

Guan Shan thought for a moment. He felt he had no reason to resent Lord Shang. It was not others' fault that he was a poor opera actor, too poor to even keep a woman. This man was very forthright and could appreciate talent when he saw it. This was hard to come by. That was good, then.

The two men introduced themselves properly, exchanging their dates of birth. Gathering sand in place of a censer and using grass as joss sticks, they kowtowed to each other and performed a ceremony making them sworn brothers. Lord Shang was five years older than Guan Shan, so he became the older brother. The girl smiled through her tears.

When they were parting, Guan Shan gave Lord Shang his sword as a gift. "Use it to help you on the road."

Lord Shang did not have a gift, so he gave his brother the bird cage with his lark inside it. "I've kept this bird for ten years. You take it. This is a lark with 'thirteen voices,' so it can imitate thirteen calls very well. I hope you'll put your heart into learning opera and will become as accomplished as this lark."

Guan Shan bade them a teary farewell and left alone. Lord Shang stood holding the sword, not moving, and sensed a little pain in his heart, feeling very sorry for Guan Shan.

He brought the girl home to become his third wife. He examined the sword again carefully, then sucked in his breath. "This is a treasure."

The girl told him, "I've seen this sword in the troupe. Guan Shan said it has been passed down for generations in his family. He hardly let anyone touch it."

Lord Shang felt even guiltier. The girl, the treasured sword—

刀。关山说是家传，平日摸都不让人摸的。"尚爷更惭愧了。姑娘，宝刀，两大爱，都送给自己了。有心胸！

关山自别了尚爷，刻意求进，十年以后，果然风靡舞台。苏、鲁、豫、皖四省交界之地，没个不知道关十三的。关十三的名号和他养的那只百灵十三口有关。百灵十三口，是说它能学十三种禽鸟的叫声，如喜鹊噪枝、公鸡打鸣、母鸡下蛋、麻雀嬉戏、燕子哺雏、黄鹂鸣柳等。百灵叫百口，是泛说，褒言，其实叫不了那么多。一般讲，百灵十三口就是上品了。关山精心养那只百灵，也时时记着尚爷的鼓励，竭力把戏路拓宽，不管演主角还是配角，都一丝不苟。一般人看戏，眼睛老盯住主角。其实行家看戏，不仅看主角，还看配角，老爱从配角身上找毛病。逢到关山演配角时，一招一式都有讲究，都有韵味。但又绝不喧宾夺主。好的配角能把主角抬起来，差的配角能把主角砸下去，这里有功夫，也有戏德。主角好，配角也好，这台戏就演圆了。所以，演员都爱

Guan Shan's two great loves were now his. What a big heart his little brother had!

After parting from Lord Shang, Guan Shan painstakingly sought improvement. Ten years later, he swept the stage. In the region where the four provinces of Jiangsu, Shandong, Henan, and Anhui joined, everybody knew Guan Shisan (Guan Thirteen). His renowned name came from the lark with "thirteen voices" he kept. A lark with "thirteen voices" could make the calls of thirteen different birds. For example, the sounds made by magpies on a branch, cocks crowing, hens laying eggs, sparrows frolicking, swallows feeding, orioles crying on a willow tree, and so on. Saying a lark had "a hundred voices" was a general statement or commendatory remark. Actually, such a bird was incapable of making that many calls. Generally speaking, a lark with "thirteen voices" was considered top grade. Guan Shan took great care of his lark, and he always remembered Lord Shang's encouragement, so did his utmost to expand his acting career. Whether he was the lead or supporting actor, he was meticulously attentive. When ordinary people watched the show, their eyes were glued to the leading actor, but connoisseurs would not only watch the leading actors, but would also notice the supporting actors and try to point out their faults. When it was Guan Shan's turn to play a supporting role, he was fastidious about his every move, giving it a lasting appeal. He also took care not to act like a presumptuous guest usurping the host's role. A good supporting actor could lift up the leading actor, while a bad one would squash the leading actor. Real skill was involved here, and it also showed an actor's ethics. If both the supporting and leading actors were good, the play was consummate. So, all the

和关山做搭档。他抬大家，大家抬他，关十三的名字越叫越响。

关山的戏路宽，生、旦、净、末，都行。但他最拿手的戏还是《单刀会》。那是祖上的戏，关山演得很虔诚。每次开戏前，他都要净手焚香，对空叩拜。关山本是赤红脸，大高个，一上装，活似关羽再生。武功自不必说了，单是唱腔就令人叫绝了。他唱大红脸，有膛音，露天野台，三里外都能听到："大江东去浪千叠，引数十人驾着这小舟一叶。又不比九重龙凤阙，可正是千丈虎狼穴。大丈夫心别，我觑这单刀会，似赛村社……"高腔大嗓，豪气冲天。常常是关十三余音未绝，那掌声、喊好声便山呼海啸般响起来。

其间喊得最响的，又常是尚爷。关山只要到黄河故道一带演戏，尚爷是场场必到。一是为听戏，他完全为之倾倒了；二是为了照应关山，怕人欺负他。有一次，关山从前台回到后台，还没卸装，过来几个地痞，说要和"关二爷"较较武功。尚爷一步挡

actors liked to pair with Guan Shan. He lifted everybody up, and everybody lifted him up in turn. The name of Guan Shisan gained increasing fame.

Guan Shan could render a wide range of characters. The good guys, both male and female, roles with painted faces, and the ugly roles. He could do them all. His masterpiece was "Lord Guan Goes to the Feast." It was a play about his ancestor Guan Yu, and he acted piously. Before every opening, he would offer incense with clean hands and kowtow to the sky. Guan Shan had a naturally flushed face and was tall. When he put on his costume, he looked like Guan Yu reincarnated. Needless to say, his martial arts were excellent, and even just his voice alone was amazing. When he rendered the role of Guan Yu in this play, the sound was sonorous and could be heard three miles away in an open field: "A thousand billows flow eastwards; A few dozen rowers are with me in this small craft. I go to no nine-storeyed dragon-and-phoenix palace, but a lair, ten thousand feet deep, of tigers and wolves. A stout fellow is never afraid, I go to this feast as if to a country fair." His high, loud voice was bold and powerful. Usually, Guan Shisan's voice still lingered when the applause and cheers had already started crashing like a tsunami.

It was usually Lord Shang who cheered the loudest. When Guan Shan's troupe was playing in the old Yellow River course area, Lord Shang attended every show. His main reason for going was to enjoy the opera, because he admired it unreservedly. His second reason was to look out for Guan Shan, fearing that he might be bullied. Once, Guan Shan retired backstage and had not even taken off his make-up when some local ruffians appeared and wanted to

开，抱拳微笑说："哪儿不周全，各位有话好说。"一头说，一头亲热地拉住前头那人的手，一使劲："嘎嘣"一声，把他手腕上的骨头捏碎了。那家伙锐叫一声，在地上翻滚起来。其余几个大惊失色："你是关十三什么人？""把兄弟兼保镖！"几个人都喘了，架起那人就走，尚爷从怀里掏出几块钢洋扔过去："看好病再来！"

事后，这几个人一打听，才知他是尚爷，故道两岸谁不知他的名气？要面子，爱管闲事，还会武功，光师兄弟就二百多。咂咂舌头算了。至此，关十三在这一带演戏，从没有人再敢刁难。

到一九四九年后，关十三不大到这一带来了。他所在的野戏班成了河南一个大城市的市剧团，他当了业务团长。剧团每天在城市剧场演出，难得到乡下来一趟。只在合作化一片红和人民公社成立的时候，应邀来演出过两次。那两次，尚爷都去了，是关十三请去的。不知为什么，尚爷有些惆怅，看完戏也没有喊好。不是演得不好，不是。连他自己也说不上为什么。关山看尚爷不

challenge Guan Shan to a fight. Lord Shang took a step forward, one clenched fist in the other hand at the chest and smiled as he said, "If there's anything you're not satisfied with, let's talk civilly."

As he spoke, he warmly tugged one of the ruffian's hands, applying sudden force. Snap! He had broken the bones in the man's wrist. The man gave out a sharp cry and rolled on the ground. The other ruffians went pale with fear. "How are you related to Guan Shisan?"

"Sworn brother and body guard!" he replied.

The ruffians gasped, picked up their friend, and turned to leave. Lord Shang fished out a few silver dollars from the pocket at his chest and tossed them over. "Go see a doctor, then come back!"

Later, the ruffians asked around and found out that he was Lord Shang. He was famous on both sides of the old course. He cared about his reputation, liked to meddle in others' business, and was skilled in martial arts. He had over two hundred fellow apprentices. They might as well just hold their tongue and walk away. From that time on, when Guan Shisan performed around this area, nobody dared make things difficult for him.

After 1949, Guan Shisan did not frequent this area. The roving opera troupe he belonged to became the local troupe of a big city in Henan, and he became the head of the troupe. The troupe performed at the city theater every day, hardly ever traveling to the village. They were invited to the village to perform twice, first time during the peak of the Cooperative Movement and then at the establishment of the People's Commune. Lord Shang went both times, invited by Guan Shisan, but for some reason, Lord Shang seemed a little depressed. He did not even applaud after the show.

高兴，猜出一点什么，安慰他说："大哥，在家住够了，就到我那里去玩几天，我陪你。"后来，尚爷接到关山的信，果然去过两趟。不过，也就两趟。一次住了十天，一次住了七天。其实，第二趟还是为了给他送百灵才去的。头一趟去，他发现那只百灵十三口不叫了。那只百灵在尚爷手上玩了十年，在关十三手里玩了近二十年，老了。一只百灵活三十年。老辈人说，从光腚玩鸟，谁一辈子也玩不了三只百灵，这话有道理。尚爷这次送去的百灵是十四口，比那一只还好。关山爱如性命，练功时挂在练功房，唱戏时挂在后台，从来不离身子。关山当上了团长，还是照常演戏，拳不离手，曲不离口，他不能一天不看见百灵，也不能一天不唱戏。

可惜，十年动乱时，那只百灵十四口被人从笼子掏出来。摔死了。那只鸟只活了八年，正叫好口。关山疼得直吸溜嘴，泪珠子扑嗒扑嗒往下掉。之后，他被下放到环卫所当淘粪工，十年没唱戏，嗓子也倒了。后来重回剧团，一张嘴，没音！憋得脸红脖

It was not because the show wasn't good. In fact, he did not even know the reason himself. Seeing that Lord Shang was not happy, Guan Shan guessed the reason. He consoled him, "Brother, if you're bored at home, come visit me. I'll keep you company."

When Lord Shang received Guan Shan's invitation, he visited him twice, but only twice. He stayed for ten days the first time, and seven days the second. Actually, the second time he only went because he was delivering a lark to Guan Shan. During his first visit, he discovered that the lark with "thirteen voices" did not sing any more. It had lived with Lord Shang for ten years, and with Guan Shan for close to twenty. It had grown old. The life span of a lark was said to be thirty years. The old folks used to say, "If you start keeping a bird from the time you're a baby, you still won't go through three larks in your lifetime." That made sense. The new lark Lord Shang gave Guan Shan was a lark with "fourteen voices," making it a step better than the previous one. Guan Shan absolutely loved it. When he practiced martial arts, he hung it in his training room, and during his performance, he hung it backstage. It never left him. After Guan Shan became the head of the troupe, he still acted, practiced martial arts, and sang. He could not go a day without seeing the lark, or without singing opera.

Unfortunately, during the ten years of unrest, the lark with "fourteen voices" was snatched from the cage and smashed to death, having only lived for eight years. It was destroyed just as it was singing at its best. Guan Shan was so heartbroken he sobbed, teardrops streaming down his face. After that, he was sent to the Sanitation Department to be a waste collector, and he did not sing for ten years. In fact, he lost his voice. Later, he returned to the

子粗，才哑哑地有一点微响，关十三气得一跺脚，昏倒后台。

他还当团长，可是再不能登台演戏了。他老是郁郁不乐的，就给尚爷写了一封信。尚爷去了，又带去第三只百灵，是十二口。关山很喜欢。这一趟，尚爷一住就是一个月，每天陪他走走玩玩，有时也喝点酒。关山因为唱戏，一辈子烟酒不沾，现在开始喝酒了，是尚爷劝他喝的。他喝了，但也只喝一点。他还想恢复嗓子。尚爷理解他的心情，就给他说："十三，行！我看你能行。还能恢复，只是别急，悠着来。"

但这次尚爷说的不是心里话。他看关山已是五十大几的人了，丢过十年功，再恢复不易。可他又不忍心直说，就讲了假话。人总该有点希望。

尚爷有眼力，关山的嗓子到底毁了。虽有百灵做伴，心里还是苦凄。他一辈子献身舞台，成家很晚，只有一个女儿，在外地工作，老伴前些年也死了。平日，他就一个人在家。关山老得很快。

troupe, but still no sound emerged from his throat. He turned blue in the face trying to force himself to sing, but only a little sound came out. Guan Shisan stomped his feet in frustration, fainting backstage.

He was still the head of the troupe, but he was not able to act any more. Constantly depressed, he wrote to Lord Shang. Lord Shang visited him again and brought him a third lark, this one with "twelve voices." Guan Shan liked it very much. This time, Lord Shang stayed for a month. He accompanied Guan Shan everywhere, even drinking a little wine on occasion. Guan Shan had not smoked or drunk when he was still singing opera, but now, he started drinking, persuaded by Lord Shang. He drank, but just a little. He still wanted to resume singing. Understanding his feelings, Lord Shang encouraged him, saying, "Shisan, you can do it! I think you can recover. But don't rush it; be patient."

But this time, his words were not heartfelt. He saw that Guan Shan was already in his fifties, and he had not sung for ten years. It would not be easy to recover his voice. Lacking the heart to tell him the truth, he lied. He believed everyone should live with some hope.

Lord Shang's assessment was correct. Guan Shan's voice was totally destroyed. Though he had the lark by his side, he was bitter and desolate. He had given his life to the stage, marrying very late. He only had one daughter, and she worked in another part of the country. His wife had also passed away a few years earlier, so he was at home alone most of the time, causing him to age very rapidly.

By contrast, Lord Shang's days were quite satisfying during these years. His three wives bore him seventeen children altogether.

这几年，尚爷的日子倒挺惬意。三个女人共给他生了十七个孩子，其中五个女儿都出了嫁，十二个儿子也都成了亲，真叫子孙满堂了。解放初贯彻婚姻法，三个妻子离掉俩，只留一个结发原配，另两个其实是离婚不离家，还住一个院。尚爷爱上哪屋上哪屋。外人谁也不问。后来，原配和丫头都死了，只剩一个闺门旦。尚爷又和她复了婚。这样过日子毕竟方便一些。尚爷家人口多，一家伙分了百多亩地。儿孙们搞联营，种田的种田，跑生意的跑生意，两部汽车，两台大拖拉机，日子过得轰轰烈烈的。邻居都说尚爷治家有方。尚爷一背手走了："屁！我才不操那份闲心。"他让孩子们为他辟出一块地，正好八亩，栽上湘竹，搭了个茅草屋，在野地里看起竹园来了。他对儿孙们说："卖了竹子，钱是你们的。我只要这个窝。"他图清静，家里一摊子都交给闺门旦了。

关山又来了信，说已经退休。尚爷立刻回信一封，让他到这里来同住。关山真的来了。

All five daughters and twelve sons were married and had their own families. He was a man blessed with a houseful of children and grandchildren. Because of the enforcement of marriage laws at the beginning of Liberation in 1949, he had been forced to divorce two of his wives, leaving him with just the first. He was divorced from the other two wives, but they did not leave the family, still sharing the same compound. Lord Shang could go to whichever house he pleased, and outsiders had no business questioning him. Later, his first wife and the maid both died, and only the opera girl was left. Lord Shang married her again, making life more convenient for themselves. The population in Lord Shang's household was large, and more than a hundred acres of land were allocated to them altogether. Some of the children and grandchildren engaged in joint ventures, some were farmers, and some went into business. With two cars and two huge tractors, they lived their lives on a grand, spectacular scale. The neighbors praised Lord Shang for his good housekeeping. He clasped his hands at the back and walked away, saying, "Nonsense! I don't burden my mind with such things."

He asked his children to lay out a piece of land for him. It was exactly eight acres. He planted some mottled bamboo, built a thatched cottage, and attended to the bamboo garden in the wild country. He told his children and grandchildren, "When the bamboo is sold, you can have the money. This cottage is all I need."

He just wanted to seek a quiet life, and so left the opera girl to run the household.

Another letter came from Guan Shan, telling him that he had retired. Lord Shang replied immediately, inviting him to the bamboo garden. Guan Shan took up the invitation.

现在,他们就同住一个茅草屋,品茶、下棋、玩百灵,或者到竹园里走一走,真是神仙一样。但尚爷很注意,从来不说唱戏的事。

关山来时,把那只百灵十二口也带来了。这只鸟性子烈,爱学新口,可是老学不上来,就气得在笼子里乱扑腾。因为火气大,老爱烂眼、长尾疮。尚爷有办法。到附近田里捉一种本地叫"舌头栗子"的东西。这种小动物形同壁虎,一般不知道它的好处。其实,是一种极珍贵的药材,美称"鸟中参"。捉活的剥皮捣碎,能治百鸟百病,神得很。但在喂百灵以前,一定要洗手。百灵爱干净。

两个老人为捉一只"舌头栗子",常常在田埂上扑倒几次,弄得一脸一身都是土,终于捉到一只,于是哈哈大笑起来。那只百灵十二口再也不得病了,水灵灵地挂在竹园里,一天到晚地叫。看见什么鸟,学什么鸟,渐渐,能叫到十三口、十四口了。他们也就倍加喜欢。

这一天,不知从哪里飞来一只竹鸡,色灰黄,样子像笋鸡或鹧鸪。这种鸟一般生活在山区,性凶好斗,冷不丁叫起来,能吓

They stayed in the thatched cottage together, drinking tea, playing chess, enjoying their larks, and taking strolls among the bamboo. They lived like gods. Even so, Lord Shang was very careful not to talk about the opera.

When Guan Shan came, he brought his lark with "twelve voices" with him. This bird had a strong temperament and loved to acquire new "voices," but it had a hard time learning them. It would get frustrated and start scrambling in the cage. With its bad temper, its eye and long tail often developed sores, for which Lord Shang had a cure. He went to the fields nearby and caught a creature called "tongue millet." This small creature looked like a lizard, and people usually did not know what they were good for. In fact, it was a kind of precious Chinese medicine, called "bird ginseng." If you caught one alive, skinned it, and pounded it to pieces, it could cure all kinds of diseases in birds. It was truly miraculous. But, before giving it to the lark, one had to wash his hands, because larks loved cleanliness.

Hoping to catch a "tongue millet," the two old men would drop into the ridge of the field several times, covering their faces and bodies with mud. When they finally caught one, they broke into laughter. The lark with "twelve voices" never got sick again. It kept singing cheerfully from morning until night in the cage hung in the bamboo grove. Whatever bird it saw, it learned its call. Gradually, it could make thirteen, then fourteen different calls. The men loved it even more.

One day, a bamboo partridge flew in from some unknown place. It was grey-yellow and looked like a young chicken or quail. This kind of bird usually lived in mountainous areas, and it had a

人一跳。这只竹鸡不知是在山区住够了,还是和谁闹别扭,孤零零飞到这里来了。它正在空中飞行,突然发现下面一片竹林,就一抖翅扎了进来。

百灵挂在一簇竹梢上,好奇地打量着这位新来的朋友,不时吹起悦耳的口哨,表示欢迎。竹鸡飞飞跳跳,落到笼子旁边一根逸出的竹枝上,竹枝儿一颤悠,站住了。两只鸟相距有三尺远近,互相歪起头看看。竹鸡突然大叫起来:"嘎嘎嘎嘎!……"百灵惊得在笼子里翻跳了几下,才落到横架上站稳,心想,这家伙是个怪脾气!其实才不是,竹鸡也是表示友好,只是嗓门大了点。它惭愧地摇了摇尾巴,表示歉意。百灵立刻懂了,人家没什么歹意,就是这么叫。这是一种完全陌生的叫声。虽然凶猛,却别有一番山野味。百灵对它发生了浓厚的兴趣。它对竹鸡又吹了一个口哨:"嘟嘟!……"——辛苦!

这时候,尚爷和关山正在竹园边树荫下下棋,竹鸡一阵凶猛的叫声,他们同时都听到了,对视了一眼,又同时站起来。这种鸟叫没听到过!两个老人都激动了。平原地区鸟少,这对百灵学口有很大限制,能出现一种新的鸟,就意味着会有一种新的鸟叫,

ferocious, pugnacious nature. It could startle a person with its sudden cries. This partridge must have grown tired of its mountain residence, or it was fighting with another bird, leading it to fly to this area alone. Flying in the air, it suddenly discovered the patch of bamboo forest, shook its wings, and hurled itself downwards.

The lark was hanging in a cluster of bamboo shoots, sizing up its new friend curiously. It whistled pleasantly now and again to express its welcome. The partridge flew and hopped, and finally settled next to the cage on a bamboo branch that overhung the cage. The branch trembled, then steadied itself. The two birds were three feet apart, slanting their heads to look at each other.

The partridge suddenly cried out, *Gaggle, gaggle,* scaring the lark out of its wits. It jumped around in panic inside its cage for a while, then settled down on its perch. It felt the new fellow had a strange temperament. Actually, the partridge was trying to express its friendliness, but its voice was too loud. It shook its tail in embarrassment, indicating its regret. The lark understood that the partridge had no ill will, but it was a completely unfamiliar call. It was ferocious, untamed but charming. The lark was deeply interested in it. It whistled to the partridge again, *Doo doo*!...— you've worked hard.

At this moment, Lord Shang and Guan Shan were playing chess under the shade beside the bamboo garden. They both heard the ferocious cries of the partridge. They looked at each other and stood up together. They had not heard this kind of bird call before. Both men were very excited. There were very few birds in the plains, and this prevented the lark from learning new voices. The appearance of a new bird meant the lark could learn a new call. If it mastered that

百灵如能学上来，将会成为百灵十五口——十五口！不得了！那将是百灵上上品，稀世珍禽了！尚爷玩了一辈子鸟，也见过无数玩百灵的人，没有谁的百灵能叫十五口。关十三更没见过。一对老朋友都激动得脸红气喘了，虽然一句话没说，却都知道对方在想什么。他们玩鸟一辈子，没想晚年终于要达到那个奇妙的境界了！

那么，当务之急，是不要惊了那只鸟，要稳住它，让它在竹园落户。他们不敢径直走进竹园子，尚爷在前，关十三在后，弯下腰轻轻分开竹丛，猫一样毫无声息地往竹园里迂回前进。那只竹鸡又叫起来："嘎嘎嘎嘎！……"几只麻雀被它惊飞了："吱棱——"

他们的心在怦怦乱跳，手也有些哆嗦。干脆，尚爷和关山把身子匍匐下来，趴在地上一寸寸地往前爬动。若不是他们那老迈的身躯和一双布满皱纹的脸，真叫人以为那是两个顽皮的孩子，在做什么诡秘的游戏。

他们在竹丛的缝隙间缓缓爬动着，野花野草都被压在身下，手脸沾满了泥土、草叶和花瓣，谁也顾不上擦一擦，只是神态紧

call, it would become a lark with "fifteen voices." Fifteen voices! That would be incredible. It would become an ultra-high-grade lark, a rare, precious bird. Lord Shang had kept birds all his life and had known numerous people who kept larks. He had never come across someone who owned a lark with "fifteen voices." This was even more true of Guan Shan. The pair of old friends were so excited that their faces grew flushed as they panted. They did not say a word, but each knew what the other was thinking. They had kept larks their whole lives, and they had not expected to reach such a wonderful realm in their old age.

The urgent task at hand was not to startle the bird, but to secure it and allow it to make the bamboo garden its home. They did not dare walk directly into the garden. Lord Shang led the way, followed by Guan Shan. They stooped and parted the bamboo clusters gently, and as fleet-footed as cats, they advanced along a circuitous route. The bird started crying again, *Gaggle, gaggle*! A few sparrows flew away in fright.

The two men's hearts were thumping, and their hands trembled slightly. Lord Shang and Guan Shan got down on their hands and knees and crawled forward inch by inch. If it were not for their aging bodies and wrinkled faces, they would have been mistaken for two mischievous children playing some strange game.

They crawled slowly among the gaps in the bamboo grove, crushing the wild flowers and grass under their bodies. Their hands and faces were covered with mud, grass, leaves, and petals, but they did not bother to wipe them off. Their eyes were glued nervously to the front, looking upwards searching the bamboo plants. They were getting close to the cage where the lark was.

张地盯住前方，从竹丛间往上搜寻……渐渐近了，快要接近挂百灵的笼子了……看见笼子了！百灵正在里头欢跃。现在离笼子还有十几步远，不能再靠近了！尚爷小心地往后摆了摆手，关十三贴着他的脚后跟，立刻趴下不敢动了。他们开始寻找那只新来的鸟。可是，湘竹的细枝太稠密了，密匝匝地挡住了视线，什么也看不见。"嘎嘎嘎嘎！……"那只鸟又叫起来，分外清晰，分外响亮！两个老人吓得大气不敢喘。急忙又把头往下低了低，唯恐被那只鸟发现。如此沉默了几分钟，没什么动静，就是说，那只鸟还在。关十三忍不住又往前爬了几下，和尚爷并肩靠齐了。尚爷神色严肃地盯了他一眼，关十三忙讨好地笑了笑。

一阵微风掠过，整个竹林发出一阵轻轻的涛声，面前的湘竹摇动起来。一蓬枝叶闪了闪，露出那只鸟的形体，两人眼睛一亮，同时看到了。风一拂动，那只鸟兴奋起来，不停地在竹枝上腾动着身子，甚是矫健！尚爷定睛看了一阵，不认得，平原上没这种鸟。他回头看看关山。关山正眯起眼打量，似乎在回忆，突然兴奋地把嘴凑上去，压低了嗓门说："竹鸡！山里鸟。"尚爷信然，点点头。关山过去唱野戏，跑的地方多，因为养百灵的缘故，所

There it was! It was hopping happily inside the cage. They were about a dozen steps away from it. They could not go any closer. Lord Shang waved his hand behind him. Guan Shan, who was following at his heels, lay flat on his belly on the ground, not moving. They started to search for the new bird, but the fine branches of the mottled bamboo were too thick, blocking their line of sight. They could not see anything. The bird started calling again, *Gaggle, gaggle*! It was distinct and bright. The two old men were so afraid that they didn't even breathe heavily. Quickly, they lowered their heads, fearing the bird would discover them. All was quiet for several minutes and nothing stirred which suggested that the bird was still around. Unable to stand it, Guan Shan crawled a few steps forward, coming abreast with Lord Shang. The latter gave him a hard stare, and Guan Shan smiled sheepishly.

A breeze brushed past, and the gentle sound of rustling wafted through the bamboo forest. The mottled bamboo in front of them swayed. A fluffy branch bent aside, revealing the shape of the mysterious bird. The men's eyes brightened, seeing it at the same time. When the wind blew, the bird got excited, moving back and forth on the bamboo branches. It was so robust! Lord Shang scrutinized the bird. He did not recognize it, as it did not belong to the plains. He turned to look at Guan Shan. The latter was squinting as he sized up the bird, looking like he was digging into his memory. He suddenly brought his mouth close to Lord Shang, and lowered his voice to say excitedly, "A bamboo partridge. Mountain bird."

Believing him, Lord Shang nodded his head. During Guan Shan's opera days, he had been to many places, and because of his

以特别留意鸟。他还是十三年前在大别山见过的,现在猝然想起来了。

"嘎嘎嘎嘎!……"竹鸡又对着百灵叫起来,像是挑逗。百灵站在横梁上,歪起头看住它,一动不动,似乎在揣摩它是怎么叫的。"嘎嘎嘎嘎!……"竹鸡越发叫得欢了。百灵把头转正了,嗉囊鼓了几鼓,一张嘴:"呀!"却突然卡了壳,发音不对,而且没有连声。竹鸡骤然又叫起来:"嘎嘎嘎嘎!……嘎嘎!"……叫着、跳着,像是疯笑一般。它在嘲笑百灵,就像山里的野小子在嘲笑没见过大山的平原小姑娘。百灵羞窘得低下了头。竹鸡还在疯笑,没完没了地疯笑,一会儿飞起,围着百灵的笼子绕一圈,一会儿又落在那根竹枝上,它简直是得意极了。

尚爷和关山匍匐在草丛里,不安地对视了一眼。他们没想到竹鸡这么爱挑衅。这只百灵是急性子,一时学不上来,怕会气坏,那就糟啦!百灵学口,有时会出现这种情况,一张嘴学不上来,憋住一口气,从此再不叫了,连以往会叫的也不叫了,此谓"叫落"。"叫落"的时间一长,嗓子也就坏了。这很像演员唱戏,嗓子一倒,任你是什么好角色,也成了舞台弃物。百灵"叫落"一

lark, he paid special attention to birds. He had seen bamboo partridges thirteen years earlier, when he was at Dabie Mountains and all of a sudden, and he recalled that meeting now.

Gaggle, gaggle! The partridge was calling out towards the lark, as if teasing it. The lark stood on its perch and tilted its head to look at the partridge. It did not move, contemplating how its new friend made those sounds. *Gaggle, gaggle*! the partridge called ever more happily. The lark righted its head, puffed its crop up and down and opened its beak, *Ya*! It suddenly stopped. It was not the right sound, and it was not fluid. The partridge started calling abruptly again, *Gaggle, gaggle*! It jumped up and down as it called, like it was laughing wildly. It was mocking the lark, just like a wild fellow laughing at a girl from the plains who had never seen a mountain before. The lark was so embarrassed that it lowered its head. The partridge continued laughing, wildly and endlessly. It flew up and circled the lark's cage, then settled down on its branch, then repeated this cycle over and over again, extremely pleased with itself.

Lord Shang and Guan Shan exchanged an uncomfortable look as they lay on their bellies in the grass. They never thought the bamboo partridge could be so provocative. This lark had an impatient nature, and if it could not learn the new call, it might get frustrated. That would be disastrous. There were cases when a lark could not learn a call, and it would hold its breath, never singing again, not even the sounds it had already acquired. This was known as "call down." When the "call down" period was long, the bird's voice would be destroyed. This was very similar to an opera singer. When the singer lost his or her voice, he or she would fall into

久，这只百灵也就废了。两个老人真是紧张极了。午后的斜阳钻进竹林，斑斑驳驳的，并没有力度。可他们多皱的额上却沁出了汗珠子。

然而，不管他们心里怎样担心，最不愿出现的情况还是出现了。百灵在竹鸡无情的嘲笑中，由羞惭而变得愤怒了！它缓缓抬起头，定定地盯住三尺以外的竹鸡。竹鸡还在叫："嘎嘎嘎！……"百灵的嗓子一鼓一鼓的，两眼要喷出血来。它不跳，不动，不叫，就那么沉默着……

尚爷和关山也沉默着，两只肘吃力地撑着地面，连喘气也粗了。可他们仍然不敢动。时间在一分一秒地过去，天色开始暗下来。因为一直在注视着那只可怜的百灵，竹鸡什么时候飞走的都不知道。百灵还保持着原来的姿势，望着前面，望着那早已不存在的竹鸡。

尚爷悲哀地叹了一口气，转回头轻轻地向关山说："完啦，百灵完啦。"关山没有吭声。

"起来吧，天晚了，把百灵提回屋里去。"尚爷说着，艰难地爬起身。关山也随后爬了起来。在地上趴伏了半天，浑身的筋骨

oblivion, no matter what great roles he or she used to play. When a lark suffered a long period of "call down," it would become handicapped. The two old men were very anxious. The afternoon sunlight crept into the bamboo forest. It was weak and dappled, but the two men's wrinkled foreheads were covered with sweat.

No matter how much they worried, the most undesirable scenario unfolded before them. The lark's embarrassment turned to anger before the cruel mocking of the bamboo partridge. It slowly raised its head and stared at the partridge three feet away. The bamboo partridge continued calling, *Gaggle, gaggle*! The lark's crop puffed up and down, its eyes looking like they would spray out blood. It did not hop, move, or cry. It just stood silently.

Lord Shang and Guan Shan remained silent too, their elbows straining to support their bodies as they breathed heavily, but they still did not dare move. The time was ticking by, and it was starting to get dark. They were paying so much attention to their poor lark that they did not notice when the partridge flew away. The lark remained in the same position, looking straight ahead at the partridge that was no longer there.

Lord Shang sighed sorrowfully and turned his head to say softly to Guan Shan, "Gone. The lark is gone." Guan Shan did not utter a word.

"Let's get up. It's late. Let's carry the lark into the house," Lord Shang said, getting up with difficulty. Guan Shan followed. Having lain on the ground for half the day, they felt as if their muscles and bones were falling apart. They walked towards the lark, one in front of the other. Lord Shang bent the mottled bamboo and took down the cage. He was about to turn around when the lark

像散了架。他们一前一后走向百灵。尚爷把湘竹弯了弯,摘下鸟笼,正要转回身,百灵却突然在笼子里乱窜起来,翅膀和头重重地撞在笼子上,还是不停地乱窜。怪事!平常收笼从来没这样过。尚爷疑惑地看了关山一眼。关山伸手接过笼子,又重新挂在竹梢上:"它不愿意走!还放这儿吧。"果然,百灵不飞也不撞了,依然蹲在横梁上,又出起神来。尚爷不明白,怎么关山一下子就猜准了它的心事!

那么,就只好这样了。只是晚间把百灵挂在竹园里,怕遇到伤害,必须守夜才行。但若不这么办,看来百灵愣飞愣撞,今夜非气死不可。他们第一次感到,这只小动物竟是如此执拗!他们都有些感动了。关山似乎更感动一些,"这么着吧,大哥,我守上半夜,你守下半夜。""行吧。"

他们轮流着守了一夜。时值初秋,晚间的风很凉。尽管他们都披着大衣,天明还是都受了寒。

第二天一早,尚爷就对前来送饭的儿子说:"三天以内,不许任何人进入竹园!送饭来,也别喊叫,放屋里就行了。"老子的事,儿子们向来不打听。但回去一说,一家四五十口人还是大惑

suddenly flew wildly inside its cage. It crashed its wings and head hard against the bars as it continued struggling wildly. It was strange! It did not normally behave like that when they carried it into the house. Lord Shang looked at Guan Shan uncertainly. The latter took the cage and hung it on the branch again, "It doesn't want to leave. Let's leave it outside."

The lark stopped crashing itself against the cage. It stood on its perch and seemed to be in a trance once more. Lord Shang did not understand how Guan Shan could guess the bird's wishes so quickly.

They had no choice but to leave the bird outside. However, they were afraid some harm might come to it if the lark was left alone in the bamboo garden at night, so they decided keep guard. If they did not, the lark might just smash itself against the cage, and it definitely would not live through the night if that happened. They felt for the first time just how obstinate this little creature was. They were a little moved, particularly Guan Shan. He said, "Brother, let me do the first shift, and you do the second."

"That will work," Lord Shang replied.

They took turns guarding the lark that night. It was the beginning of fall, and the wind was chilly at night. Even though they were wearing jackets, they both caught colds before morning.

The next day, Lord Shang said to his son, who was bringing them food, "Don't let anyone set foot in the bamboo garden for three days. When you bring food, please don't shout. Just leave it in the house."

Lord Shang's sons usually did not ask about their father's business, but when the son went home and told the rest of the family what had happened, the forty or fifty more members of the

不解了，不知两个老人要在竹园里搞什么名堂。

尚爷有尚爷的考虑。他对百灵还抱着最后一点希望。现在，这只百灵显然是"叫落"了，要回嗓不容易。但他不甘心就这么把它废了！百灵"叫落"有时也有例外。就是在沉默了多少天以后，突然学出了新口，一下子叫出声来，于是一切都恢复正常，而这只百灵也就进入一个新的等级，从而身价倍增。百灵到了十三口以后，每再增加一口，都是极难的。而从十四口增加到十五口，就更难！老实说，这只百灵回嗓的可能性，如果按常例算，仅有万分之一。就是说，极小极小。但尚爷凭着对这只鸟秉性的熟悉和昨晚的神态，却有一种预感：它能叫出来！现在最要紧的是保持竹园的安静，企望那只竹鸡重新飞回来，在百灵面前多叫几遍。这样虽然会加剧百灵的苦恼，但却增加了它熟悉对方叫声的机会。

又是整整一天，竹鸡没有来。百灵除了偶尔喝一点水，什么也不吃，仍然站在横梁上发呆。

第三天过去了，竹鸡仍没有来。百灵干脆不吃也不喝，形体明显地憔悴了。一股风吹来，它都要在横梁上打个栽，尚爷不时悄悄靠上去，在十几步远的地方看一看，心里也像那只百灵一样

household were puzzled, wondering what the two old men were up to in the bamboo garden.

Lord Shang had his own thoughts. He still held out a last little hope for the lark. This lark was obviously in a state of "call down" now and it would not be easy for it to recover its voice. He was unwilling to lose the lark in this way. Sometimes, there were exceptions to the "call down" of a lark. He was hoping that the lark would suddenly master the new voice after a few days of silence. If it started calling and everything returned to normal, it would enter a new rank and become really valuable. After a lark had acquired thirteen voices, each addition was extremely difficult. It was even more difficult for a lark to increase from fourteen to fifteen voices. The truth was, in normal circumstances, the chance of this lark recovering its voice was one in a hundred, an extremely slim chance. But based on his familiarity with the nature of this lark and its expression the previous night, Lord Shang had a gut feeling that it could recover its voice. The important thing now was to maintain the quietness of the bamboo garden, in hopes that the bamboo partridge would return and cry a few more times in the presence of the lark. Even though that might increase the lark's distress, it would also increase the chances of the bird familiarizing itself with the partridge's cries.

Another whole day passed without the partridge appearing. The lark would not eat, but just drank a little water as it stood on its perch in a daze.

The third day passed with no sight of the partridge. The lark gave up eating and drinking, growing extremely wan and sallow. Even a slight gust of wind caused it to stagger on its perch. Lord

憋闷得慌。他可怜这小小的生命。心想，何必这么认真？叫不出来就叫不出来，算啦。你也是出过力的鸟，你已经是出类拔萃的百灵了。就是从此哑了，尚爷还会养着你，还会爱惜你，放心！尚爷一辈子说话算话，还不行吗？可是百灵还是固执地站在横梁上，身子都打颤了。

关十三似乎从来就没有离开过竹园。他也像那只百灵一样，不吃也不喝，只是匍匐在十几步开外的草丛里，眼巴巴地看着百灵，似乎在等待着什么。可有时候，他布满血丝的双眼又十分空茫，看似看着百灵，其实又什么也没看。谁知他在想什么呢？尚爷见了，不时摇头叹息，这倒好！百灵呆了，人也呆了！

第四天早上，百灵几乎在横梁上站不住了。可正在这时，那只失踪了三天的竹鸡，不知到哪里转了一圈，又突然回来了。而一回来，就飞到那根逸出的竹枝上，"嘎嘎"地叫起来，好像在嘲弄百灵，怎么，你到底没学上来吧？

谁也没有料到，奇迹也正在这时候出现了！百灵突然一抖精神，对着竹鸡大叫起来："嘎嘎嘎嘎！……"竹鸡反倒被吓了一跳，愣住了。尚爷和关十三更是愣住了！百灵不仅学得极像，而且更洪亮、更圆润！在十几步远的竹丛间，尚爷激动得抓耳挠腮，

Shang sometimes went near the cage stealthily, watching the bird from about a dozen steps away, his heart as dejected as the lark. He pitied this tiny life. He thought to himself, Why so serious? Just give up if you can't learn the new voice! You've worked hard. You're already an outstanding lark. Even if you lose your voice, I will still keep and treasure you. Don't worry! I always keep my word. Why don't you give up? But the lark still stood on the perch, trembling.

Guan Shisan did not leave the bamboo garden at all. Like the lark, he would not eat or drink, but lay in the grass about a dozen steps away, watching the lark, as if waiting for something. Sometimes, his blood-shot eyes looked empty, like he was watching the lark, but also like he was staring into space. Nobody knew what was going through his mind. When Lord Shang saw this, he shook his head and sighed. Not only had the bird gone crazy; Guan Shan had gone crazy too.

The fourth morning, the lark seemed too weak to stand on its perch. But just then, the bamboo partridge, which had disappeared three days earlier came back, having made its round some other place. It went straight back to its perch on the protruding bamboo branch. Wasting no time, it cried out, *Gaggle, gaggle*! It seemed to be mocking the lark. What? You haven't learned this voice yet?

Unexpectedly, a miracle unfolded before them. The lark suddenly came alive, crying at the partridge, *Gaggle, gaggle*! The partridge, startled in its turn, was dumbstruck. Lord Shang and Guan Shisan were even more astonished. The lark had not only learned the voice well, but also did it louder, mellower, and fuller than the partridge. Lord Shang, who was standing a dozen steps

而关十三的泪水却刷刷地流出来。叫出来了，叫出来啦！百灵十五口，稀世珍禽，谁见过这样有志气的鸟吗？没有！他觉得心里特别畅快，憋了三天——不！憋了十几年的闷气，似乎都被百灵吐出来了！

两个老人几乎同时起步，像发了疯一样，蹒跚着扑上去。竹鸡吓得怪叫一声，"嗖"一下飞跑了。而那只百灵却站在高高的横梁上，向着竹鸡飞去的方向，继续昂首大叫："嘎嘎嘎嘎！……嘎嘎嘎嘎！……嘎嘎嘎！……"它几乎一刻不停地叫着。它如痴如醉了！它疯了！它傻了！"嘎嘎嘎嘎！……嘎嘎！……"关十三还在围着鸟笼子抚掌大笑，尚爷的脸色却陡然变了！一个尘封的记忆在脑子里闪了一下：这叫"绝口"，又叫"绝唱"，就是说，它会一直叫下去，一直到叫死！年轻时，尚爷只听老辈人讲过，却从来没有见过。据传说，只有世上最优秀最有志气的百灵才会这样。莫非，我真要经验一回了！

果然，百灵越叫声音越小。关十三也感到了事情的不妙，直直地看着尚爷。他急得伸手要摘笼子，尚爷一把按住："别动，晚了！"的确，是晚了。百灵几天不吃不喝，已经心力交瘁，它在用生命的全部力量，歌唱着它的志气，宣告着它登上一个百灵世界

away among the bamboo clusters, was so excited he started scratching his ears and cheeks. Guan Shisan's tears gushed and flowed. The lark had done it! It had become a lark with "fifteen voices." It was a rare, wondrous bird. Who had ever seen such an ambitious bird? Guan Shisan felt especially carefree. Three days of suppression—no, the rancor he had endured for over ten years—seemed to have been released by the lark.

The two old men started at the same time, rushing toward the birds like they had lost their minds. The bamboo partridge cried out in fright and flew away. The lark stood on its high perch and, looking in the direction the partridge flew, continued calling proudly, *Gaggle, gaggle...* It could not stop. It was intoxicated. It had gone crazy. It had lost its mind. *Gaggle, gaggle...* Guan Shisan circled the cage, clapping his hands and laughing. Lord Shang's expression suddenly changed. A remote memory flashed through his mind: This is called the "last voice," or the "last song," which meant the lark would continue calling until it died! When he was young, Lord Shang had heard the old people say that, but he had not witnessed it himself. According to legends, only the best and most ambitious larks would do that. Was he going to witness it now?

Sure enough, the lark's call became softer and softer. Feeling something was wrong, Guan Shisan stared at Lord Shang. Panicked, he wanted to take the cage down. Lord Shang stopped him, "Don't move. It's too late!"

It was really too late. The lark had not been eating or drinking for days, and it was mentally and physically exhausted. It was using all its life energy to sing of its ambition, proclaiming that it had

最辉煌的阶梯!

终于,它拼尽全力,叫出最后一串声音:"嘎嘎嘎嘎!……"一头从横梁栽下来,翻个滚,死了。它死得这么突然,这么痛快,这么悲壮!……

尚爷和关十三为百灵做了一只很精致的木匣,然后将它安葬在竹园中心。这是一座小小的禽冢,周围是湘竹、青草和鲜花。百灵没有了。可是百灵那最后的叫声,却一直在竹园里游荡。

一个多月以后,关十三突然也去世了。他病得很急,死得也很快。临死前,他握住尚爷的手,老泪止不住地流淌:"我……还不如……那只……百灵……"

尚爷居然一滴泪也没有掉。他理解他,却没法安慰他,只是神色庄重地摇了摇头:"十三,别难过。我不会叫你孤独的。"

安葬那天,来了许多祭奠的人。根据关十三的遗嘱,没有通知他所待过的那个剧团和唯一的女儿,倒是当地的艺人来了不少。他们都尊敬这位艺术前辈。有的还自动带来了笙、箫、唢呐之类吹打乐器。

尚爷把一切葬事所必需的事情安排就绪,让儿孙们在外面照应着,一个人进了屋。过了片刻工夫,有人突然发现,尚爷在屋

ascended to the most glorious pedestal of the lark world.

Finally, it expended all its strength and let out a series of sounds, *Gaggle, gaggle!* ... Then it stumbled from its perch, flipped over, and died. It happened so abruptly, so simply, so movingly, and so tragically!

Lord Shang and Guan Shisan made an exquisite wooden box for the lark and buried it in the middle of the bamboo garden. This was a tiny bird tomb, surrounded by mottled bamboo, green grass, and fresh flowers. The lark was gone, but its last song continued to wander around the bamboo garden.

More than a month later, Guan Shisan suddenly departed from this world. His sickness came upon him quickly, and he died quickly too. Before he died, he held Lord Shang's hand, and said with tears falling down his aging face, "I... cannot... even... measure up to... that... lark..."

Lord Shang did not shed a single tear. He understood Guan Shisan, but did not console him. He only shook his head and said with a serious expression, "Shisan, don't be sad. I won't let you be lonely."

On the day of the burial, many visitors came. According to Guan Shisan's wishes, they did not inform the opera troupe he acted with or his only daughter of his death. Many local actors came to the funeral. They all respected this master of art. Some even brought musical instruments of their own to play on the funeral service. Lord Shang made all the necessary arrangements for the burial and let his children and grandchildren take care of the rest. He entered the house alone. After a while, somebody discovered that he had killed himself there, slitting his own throat. Blood still gurgling from the

里自杀了！他脖子上割开一个豁口，血还在汩汩地流。身子旁边，卧着一把钢刀。那还是当年关十三送他的。他在桌子上留下一个纸条："我陪十三去了。"

一切都这么意外，一切都毫不意外。闺门旦和儿孙们痛哭一场，闻讯而来的人们唏嘘着，帮着把尚爷和关十三埋葬了。他们的坟都在竹园里，相距只有三步，中间是那座小小的禽冢。

一园翠竹，约八亩许……

1985 年

wound. Beside his body rested a steel sword. It was the one Guan Shisan gave him. He left a note on the table: I'm going to accompany Shisan.

Everything was so unexpected, and yet so expected. The opera girl and Lord Shang's children and grandchildren wept inconsolably. Everyone who heard about this sighed and mourned, and they came to help to bury Lord Shang and Guan Shisan. Their tombs were situated in the bamboo garden, three steps apart. In the middle was the tiny bird tomb.

It was a garden of bamboo, covering about eight *mu* in total.

1985

天下无贼

傻根要回家了。

傻根已经五年没回家了。

傻根出来做工时才十六岁,现在已是二十一岁的大小伙子。

村上同来的几十个人,每年冬天都要回去过年,大约两个月的假期,把当年挣来的钱带回去,看看老婆孩子,看看老人。但

A World without Thieves

Translated by Jeremy Tiang

Silly Boy was going home.

Silly Boy hadn't been home for five years.

Silly Boy had gone off to work aged sixteen, and was now a strapping lad of twenty-one.

A few dozen people from his village had come with him. The others went home for the Spring Festival at the end of each winter with the money they'd accumulated that year, a two-month vacation to visit their wives and kids, and pay their respects to their elders.

傻根从没回去过。傻根是个孤儿,来回几千里路,回去做什么?再说大伙都走了,也没人看工地。那些砖瓦、木料、钢筋堆了一个很大的场子。傻根就一个人住在料场,一天转悠几遍,然后睡觉。夜里起来解手,摸黑再转悠一遍,左手捏个手电棒子,右手提个木棍。傻根提个木棍主要是防狼,不是防贼的。这里是大沙漠,几百里路没人烟,就附近有个油田,新发现的。他们就是为新油田盖房子的。

傻根夜间时常碰到狼,三五一群,跑到料场里躲风寒。看到傻根走来,就站住了,几点绿光闪烁,傻根握住木棍冲上去,大喊一声:"快跑啊!"

狼就跑走了。

它们主要怕他手里的电棒子。

有几天夜间看不到狼,傻根会感到寂寞。就提上木棍跳到料场外的沙丘上,拿手电棒子往远处的夜空照几下,大喊几声:"都来啊!"不大会就汇集一群狼来,有几十匹之多,高高低低站在对面的沙丘上,一丛绿光闪烁。它们和傻根已经很熟了。傻根先用手电棒子照照狼群,然后响亮地咳一声,说:"现在开会!"狼们就专注地看着他。

Silly Boy had never returned. He was an orphan and didn't see the point traveling all that distance. Besides, if everyone were to go, who would watch the work site? All those bricks, tiles, timber and steel girders, piled across the large area. Silly Boy lived alone in the materials yard, patrolling it several times a day before going to bed. If he got up for a piss, he'd make one more round in the dark, flashlight in his left hand, wooden truncheon in his right. The truncheon was to be used against wolves, not bandits. In the middle of the desert, there wasn't a soul for hundreds of miles—only a newly-discovered oil field nearby. This construction project would provide housing for the oil field workers.

In the middle of the night, he often encountered small packs of wolves scurrying into the yard to escape the bitter wind. When they saw Silly Boy approach, they'd freeze, their eyes dots of green glistening in the dark. Silly Boy would run at them brandishing his truncheon, screaming, "Scram!"

And they'd run away.

They were mostly afraid of his flashlight.

If several nights passed without any wolves, Silly Boy began to feel lonely. He'd grab his truncheon, leave the yard and clamber to the top of a sand dune, shining his flashlight into the night sky, screaming, "Show yourselves!" Before long, there'd be a gathering of wolves, twenty or thirty or more, scattered about the dunes opposite, a forest of green flickers. They and Silly Boy knew each other well by now. He'd turn his light on the beasts, then clear his throat resonantly and proclaim, "I declare this meeting open!" They'd continue to stare steadily at him.

"嗯，开会!"

"嗯，张三李四，嗯，王二麻子!"

"嗯!……"

开完会，傻根照例放电影，就是把手电棒子捏亮了往天上照，一时画个圆一时画个弧一时交叉乱画。整个大漠奇静。只见天空白光闪闪，神出鬼没。狼们就肃然无声，只把头昂起追踪电光，却怎么也追不上。正看得眼花缭乱，突然一道白光从天空落下，如一根长大的棍子打在左边的沙丘上，那棍子打个滚，倏然消失。傻根就很得意，挥挥棍子大喊一声："快跑啊!"就转身跑走了。狼们都没跑，仍然站在沙丘上，有些疑疑惑惑的样子。

但现在傻根要回家了。

傻根要回家，带工的副村长觉得很突然。他一直干得很安心。别人每年冬天回家，他理也不理的，到底没什么牵挂。可是去年腊月村上人回家时，傻根似乎有点心动，当时他扯扯副村长的袖口，说大叔我多大啦？有些吞吞吐吐的。副村长没听明白，说什么多大啦？傻根就松了手抱住膀子笑，笑得有点狡黠，说我问你我今年几岁。副村长有点不耐烦，当时正收拾东西，说你问这干

"Yes, start the meeting!"

"Yes, Mr Zhang, Mr Li. Yes, Mr Wang, Pock-face."

"Yes!"

After the meeting, Silly Boy usually screened a movie. This consisted of him aiming the flashlight beam at the sky, drawing circles and arcs, or sometimes just random lines. The whole desert was preternaturally quiet, no movement except the weird white flashes in the sky. The animals were silent, raising their heads trying to follow the light, which they could never quite keep up with. Just as they were growing cross-eyed, the white beam would come straight down and land like a giant baton on a sand dune to the left, circle it quickly, then disappear into thin air. Silly Boy, feeling pleased with himself, would wave his truncheon and shout "Get lost!" before dashing off himself. The wolves stayed put on the sand dunes, looking confused.

But now, Silly Boy was going home.

The leader of their work team, who was also the Deputy Headman of their village, was startled by Silly Boy's sudden urge to depart. Every winter when the others left, he never seemed to mind staying—after all he had no attachments back home. Last time round, though, Silly Boy seemed to have something on his mind. He'd tugged at the Deputy Headman's sleeve and asked, hesitantly, *Uncle, how old am I?* The Deputy Headman didn't quite understand. *How old what?* Silly Boy stood with his arms crossed, smiling craftily, repeating, *I asked you how old I am.* The Deputy Headman, busy packing, didn't have the patience for this. He said, *What are you asking this for, haven't the cadres written it down*

什么，干部给你记着呢。傻根却站着不走，很固执的样子。副村长只好直起腰，说好吧好吧我给你算算，就扳起指头算，说你来那年是十六岁，在沙漠待了五年，应当是二十一岁了。傻根说噢，二十一岁，噢，就有些怪怪的。

那时副村长并没有意识到他想回家。傻根自小由村里人拉扯大，睡过所有人家的被窝，吃过所有女人的奶子，一切都不用操心，连年龄也由村干部给记着。傻根也就养成无心无肺的性情。那次忽然打探年龄，副村长以为不过是随便问问，就没往别处想。

副村长没有想到，傻根有心思了。

去年秋末的一天，傻根去了一趟油田小镇，其实就是一条街，其实一条街也算不上，就是有几家小商店，这是方圆几百里最热闹的去处了。那天他在街上闲荡，迎面看到几个穿着鲜艳的女子从身边擦过，然后看到一个少妇坐在商店门前的台阶上奶孩子，少妇半敞开怀，胸脯白花花一片。傻根像被电击了一下，脑袋里嗡嗡响，他慌乱地张望了几眼，便赶紧回来了。就是从那天开始，傻根有了心思。

这一个冬天，他过得有些焦躁。

for you? But Silly Boy stubbornly stood his ground, until the Deputy Headman had no choice but to straighten up, saying *All right, all right, let me work it out*—and here he began counting on his fingers—*you were sixteen when you came to work with us, and you've been in the desert five years, so you should be twenty-one now*. Silly Boy said, *Oh, twenty-one, oh*. in a strange tone of voice.

Even then, the Deputy Headman didn't realize Silly Boy was thinking of going home. From a child, Silly Boy was brought up by the village as a whole. He'd slept under every roof, sucked from every woman's teat, free of worry. Even his age was recorded by the village cadres. Silly Boy was simply contented. Now, when he suddenly asked how old he was, the Deputy Headman assumed it was idle curiosity, and didn't think any more of it.

The Deputy Headman didn't notice, but Silly Boy was beginning to have Certain Thoughts.

The year before, on a day towards the end of autumn, Silly Boy had gone to the small town by the oil field—which was actually just a road, or not even that, a few shops clustered together. Still, this was the most exciting place for hundreds of miles. Strolling down the street, he saw a few girls walking towards him in brightly-colored dresses, then a young mother on a shop's steps, feeding her child with her blouse half-open, exposing a dazzling white expanse of breast. Silly Boy felt an electric jolt. His brain buzzed. In a state of confusion, he stared as long as he dared and then hurried away. After that day, he began having Certain Thoughts.

He suffered through that winter in a state of some anxiety.

Not long after the Spring Festival, when the migrant workers

春节过后不久，村上的民工都回来了。傻根对副村长说，我要回家。副村长说回家做什么，好好的。傻根说回家盖房子娶媳妇！说这话的时候，口气很硬，完全没有商量的余地。副村长先是愣了一阵，接着哈哈大笑，往傻根肩上捶了一拳头，说中中！这么大的个子，还不该娶媳妇吗？啥时动身？傻根也笑了，说赶明儿就走。

头一天，傻根已把五年的工钱从油田小镇取了回来。他的钱一直由油田储蓄所代管的，一共有六万多块，这是一笔很大的钱了。傻根提在手里很高兴，沉甸甸的像几块小砖头。当傻根提着钱走出储蓄所时，小镇上许多人都吃惊地看着他，直到他晃晃荡荡走出小街。

这天晚上，同村来的民工都来看他，说傻根你不能这么把钱带在身上。傻根说咋的？同村人说路上很乱，几千里路，碰上劫贼，弄不好把命都丢了。傻根不信，说怎么会，我从小就没碰到过贼。副村长说还是从邮局汇吧，这样保险。傻根说要多少汇费？副村长很随便地说要六七百块吧。副村长其实也没汇过钱，每年回家也都是随身带走工钱。但因为是大家结伴回家，并不担心安

from the village returned, Silly Boy told the Deputy Headman, *I want to go home*. The Deputy Headman said, *You're doing fine here, what do you want to go back for?* Silly Boy said, *I want to go back and build a house and find a wife*. His tone of voice was firm, no room for negotiation. The Deputy Headman was stunned for an instant, then burst out laughing, thumping Silly Boy on the back. *Well said! A lad your age, still not married? When do you want to go?* Silly Boy laughed too, and said, *I'll set off tomorrow.*

The previous day, Silly Boy had already retrieved his five years of wages from the little town, where they'd been deposited with Oil Field Savings. There was more than sixty thousand *yuan*—an enormous sum. Silly Boy felt happy just holding it, heavy as little bricks. As he walked out with all those banknotes, the townsfolk stared at him in astonishment till he'd swaggered out of sight.

This evening, many of his fellow villagers came to bid him farewell, saying, *Silly Boy, you shouldn't carry so much cash on you*. Silly Boy said, *What are you talking about?* They told him, *The journey will be chaotic, and in so many thousands of miles, you're bound to encounter some thieves, if you're unlucky you may even lose your life*. Silly Boy didn't believe them, protesting, *How could that be, I've never met a thief in all my life*. The Deputy Headman said, *Why not let the Post Office remit it, safer that way*. Silly Boy asked, *How much are the fees?* The Deputy Headman casually said six or seven hundred, though he'd never actually remitted money himself, just carried it on him—but that was with everyone traveling together, so they weren't concerned about safety. Silly Boy laughed, *Then I'd rather bring it myself*.

全问题。傻根笑起来，说我还是带身上。大家都有些着急，说傻根不是吓唬你，路上不太平，汽车上火车上常有抢东西的，这么走非出事不可，傻根还是不信。傻根的确从小没见过劫贼。老家的村子在河南一个偏远的山区，一辈辈封在大山里，民风淳朴，道不拾遗。有人在山道上看到一摊牛粪，可是没带粪筐，就捡片薄石围牛粪画个圈，然后走了。过几天想起去捡，牛粪肯定还在。因为别人看到那个圈，就知道这牛粪有主了。这样的地方怎么会有劫贼？傻根在大沙漠待了五年，同样没碰到过贼。村里人说路上有贼，傻根怎么也不信，说你们走吧，我要睡觉了。

大伙只好摇摇头走了，说傻根还是傻，这家伙只一根筋。

第二天，傻根跟一辆大货车离开大沙漠。副村长派个民工陪着，说要把他送到三百里外的小火车站。傻根就很生气，也不理他。心想六万块钱还不如一块砖头沉，怕我拿不回去？就扭转头看车外的沙丘。正有七八头狼追着货车跑，一直追了十几里路，傻根站起身冲它们挥挥手。狼群终于站住，在一座大沙丘上抬起头嚎了一阵子。渐渐消失了。傻根朝其他搭车的人看看，很骄傲

Everyone grew flustered and said, *Silly Boy, we're not trying to scare you, but it really isn't safe out there, people are always getting mugged on the bus or train, and if you insist on doing this, something really terrible will happen to you.* Silly Boy continued to brush them off. He truly had never seen a thief. His home village was in a remote district of Henan where generations of villagers, tucked away behind those mountains, lived simple, honest lives. If someone saw a pile of cow dung on a hill path but didn't have his dung basket with him, he'd scratch a circle around the dung with a flake of stone, and then go on his way. When he came back several days later, the dung would still be there, because anyone else seeing that circle would know there was a prior claim. How could there be any form of robbery in such a place? There hadn't been any thieves in his five years in the desert either. So when the villagers told him the journey home was full of bandits, he simply refused to believe them, saying, *You should all go now, I want to sleep.*

They could only leave, shaking their heads, lamenting that Silly Boy was still so silly, not to mention so damn stubborn.

The next day, Silly Boy got a lift out of the desert on a truck. The Deputy Headman sent one of the migrant workers to accompany him the three hundred miles to the train station. Silly Boy, enraged by this, decided to ignore him. Sixty thousand *yuan* wasn't even as heavy as a brick, did they think he wouldn't be able to carry it? Instead, he turned his head and stared at the sand dunes passing by. Seven or eight wolves loped alongside the truck for more than ten miles. Finally Silly Boy stood up and waved at them, at which they stopped at the crest of a large dune and howled, receding into the

的样子。

※　※　※

傻根装钱的帆布包挂在脖子上,包里还装了几件单衣裳和一个搪瓷缸子,塞得鼓鼓囊囊的。货车上六七个搭车的,都看他。同村的民工就有些紧张,附在傻根耳朵上小声说当心。傻根装作没听见,便冲那些人笑笑,一副无可奈何的样子。他们也笑笑,但没人吱声。只有一个瘦瘦的年轻人在打盹,汽车颠得他脑袋一晃晃的。同村的民工早就注意到他了,他觉得这家伙最可疑。傻根头一天取款时,油田小镇很多人都知道,尾随来完全可能,就用肘碰碰傻根,朝那人抬抬嘴巴。傻根朝那人看看,心想这有什么看头,人家在睡觉。不觉打个哈欠,自己也打起盹来。

护送的民工不敢打盹,用手搓搓脸硬撑着。不大会儿,搭车的六七个人都打起盹来。先前打盹的瘦瘦的年轻人却醒了,坐在角落里抽烟,专注地望着车外一望无际的大沙漠。汽车颠得厉害,一座座沙丘往后去了。从一大早动身,到太阳转西还没跑出大沙漠。这期间,护送的民工一直在研究那个瘦子。他发现他瘦瘦的脸上起码有三处刀疤。便在心里冷笑,他相信这个刀疤脸不是什

distance. Silly Boy glanced at the other passengers, proud of himself.

*   *   *

Silly Boy kept the money in a canvas bag around his neck, which also contained several thin shirts and an enamel mug, packed tight as a drum. The six or seven other passengers stared at him, agitating the accompanying villager, who leaned close and whispered, *Be careful*. Silly Boy pretended not to hear, but smiled at everyone else, a picture of helplessness, and they smiled back, but no one made a sound apart from a skinny young man dozing off, the vehicle's motion shaking his head from side to side. The villager had already marked him down as a suspicious figure. Many people in the small town knew about Silly Boy withdrawing all his money the day before, and it was entirely possible that someone had followed him. He nudged Silly Boy with his elbow and indicated the dozing man with his chin. Silly Boy looked over but felt there was nothing to see, just someone having a nap. He started yawning himself, and was soon snoozing too.

The fellow villager didn't dare to shut his eyes, but pinched his face to stay awake. Before long, he was the only one not napping. Then the skinny young man who'd fallen asleep first woke and sat in a corner to smoke, looking out over the borderless desert. The truck shook violently, passing one sand dune after another. They'd set off at the crack of dawn, and even now that the sun was low in the west, they hadn't left the vast desert. All day long, the villager had been studying the skinny man, and had noticed at least three knife scars on his bony face. He smiled grimly to himself, certain this

么好东西。

傍晚时，大货车终于吼叫着冲出沙漠。进入戈壁公路，车速明显加快，又跑了个把小时，终于到达小火车站。小火车站十分简陋，只有一个卖票的窗口，没有候车室，等车都在站台上。同来的六七个人都买了票，包括刀疤脸也在等车。傻根买好票，对跟来的民工说，你该走了吧，待会车就来了，不会有事的。民工还想做最后的努力，说傻根这会还不晚，你把钱交给我，天明从这里寄走，你人到家，钱也差不多到家了。傻根真是有点火了，说你傻不傻？汇费要几百块，能买一头牛，我干吗要花这冤枉钱？就紧紧抱住帆布包。傻根的声音像吵架，所有的人都转头。民工就有些窘，赶忙说你小点声，当心露了马脚。傻根气得笑起来，声音更大说什么露了马脚！我就不喜欢你们这些小男人，嘀嘀咕咕。我这钱不是偷的捡的，是我在大沙漠干了五年的工钱，露了马脚又怎的？哈！怕人抢？喂喂——傻根把脸转向站台上几十个等车的人，放开嗓门喊，说你们谁是劫贼？站出来让他瞧瞧？几十个人面面相觑，没人搭理。有人笑笑，把脸转向一旁去。傻根得意地回头说，咋样？你看没有劫贼吧？人家笑话你呢，快回去

Scarface couldn't be good news.

It was evening by the time the truck finally roared out of the desert. Once on the Gobi road its speed increased significantly. After a couple more hours, they reached the train station, a rundown place with just one ticket window and no waiting room—you did your waiting on the platform. The six or seven other passengers all bought their tickets, including Scarface. Silly Boy got his ticket and said to his fellow villager, *I guess you should be going now, the train will come soon, nothing will happen to me*. The villager made one final effort and said, *Silly Boy, it's not too late, give me the money and I'll post it tomorrow, it'll arrive home around the same time as you do*. Silly Boy, now a little angry, said, *Are you stupid, the fees are several hundred yuan, I could buy a cow with that, why should I just throw that money away?* He clutched the canvas bag tight. His quarrelsome tone of voice made everyone turn to look at him. The accompanying villager, embarrassed, said, *Careful, don't give yourself away*. Silly Boy laughed with irritation, and shouted even louder, *Give what away? I don't like small men like you, fussing around. I didn't steal my money, I didn't pick it up in the street, it's mine, my wages from five years, working in the desert, what's there to give away? Ha! You think I'm afraid of robbers? Hey, hey!*—and here he turned to the people waiting on the platform, raising his voice—*Any of you robbers? Step forward, let him see*. The few dozen people looked awkwardly at each other, but no one spoke. Some chuckled, turning their faces aside. Silly Boy turned back with a satisfied smile and said, *So, I guess there aren't any thieves? Look, everyone's laughing at you, you should*

吧。这时傻根有些怜悯那个民工了。要说呢，他也是一番好意，又是副村长派来的。可是村里人啥时学得这么小心眼？咱们村上人向来不这样的，谁也不提防谁，全村几十户人家就没有买锁的。这好，出来几年都变了，到处防贼，自己吓唬自己。

终于，那个民工很无奈地走了。走的时候很难过，他想傻根完了。这家伙没法让他开窍。

这是一趟过路车，傻根随大伙拥上去时，心情格外好。车厢里很空，几十个人随便坐。他到处看看，便捡一处靠窗的位置坐下了。一同来的那个刀疤脸随后坐他对面，也靠窗。傻根冲他笑笑，那人没理，掏出一本杂志看，封面是个半裸的女人。傻根不识字，就伸过头去，也想看看那个封面。对方赶紧翻过去，很严厉地瞪了他一眼，仿佛那是他老婆。傻根忙讨好地笑笑。女人，他想。

这时一对男女走过来。男人三十岁上下，高大魁梧，一脸大胡子，女子二十六七岁，有一张好看的圆圆脸。看光景像一对夫妻。女子友好地笑笑挨傻根坐下了。男子则坐对面，和刀疤脸挨着。刀疤脸打量他们一眼，便合上杂志，扭转头望窗外。傻根闻

leave. By now, Silly Boy was feeling rather sorry for his fellow villager, who after all was only trying to help, and had been sent by the Deputy Headman. But when had people in the village learned to be so narrow-minded? The village never used to be like that, no one needed to fear anyone else, not a single house in the whole place had a lock on it. And yet, after just a few years away, they saw thieves at every turn, frightening themselves.

Finally, the accompanying villager had no choice but to go. He was filled with sorrow, certain that Silly Boy was done for. There was just no persuading the lad.

This is a passing train. As Silly Boy surged towards it with the rest of the crowd, he was in exceptionally high spirits. The carriages were mostly empty, and everyone could sit where they liked. He looked around and chose a seat by the window. The scar-faced man from the truck sat opposite him, also against the window. Silly Boy smiled directly at him, but the man didn't respond, instead he pulled out a magazine with a half-naked woman on its cover. Silly Boy was illiterate, but when he stretched his neck out, trying to get a better view of the image, the man hastily flipped it round and glared at him sternly, as if it were his wife. Silly Boy quickly smiled ingratiatingly. Women, he thought.

Just then a couple walked by. The man was thirty or so, tall and imposing, with a huge beard. The woman was twenty-six or seven, with a round, pretty face. They looked like husband and wife. The woman smiled as she sat next to Silly Boy, while her man sat opposite, next to Scarface. After eyeing them a second, Scarface

到一股好闻的香气，顿时不安起来。列车已缓缓启动，傻根的脑袋里也咣咣响，慌乱中又有些高兴。一路上有个年轻女人坐身旁，无论如何是一件愉快的事。

不时有人往这边窥探。

先前大家忙着放行李找座位，这时都安顿下来。火车已经正常运行，心情都有些悠然。这个车厢里所有的人都知道那个傻乎乎的小子身上带了许多钱，不免为他担心。这趟车向来不安全，时有偷窃和抢劫发生，不少人吃过亏。当然也有人暗自高兴，傻小子钱在明处，遇上抢劫者，肯定会瞄上他，自己可以安全了。

当那一对大胡子男女靠傻根坐下时，一些人兴奋起来。车厢里空位不少，干吗要挤在一起呢？看来要有什么事发生了。大家开始窃窃私语，说你看那男人有些匪气呢，那女子挨傻小子那么近，一对大奶子要耷他脸上了。有人装着上厕所，经过旁边看一眼，回来报告点消息。一车厢目光如探照灯，围住傻根晃来晃去。所有的人都在等待一场好戏开演。

* * *

大家的猜测没错，这一对男女确实是贼。

closed his magazine, turning to look out of the window instead. Silly Boy sniffed a delightful scent and felt a moment of unease. The train had slowly started moving and there was a pounding in his head too, yet also some joy within his confusion. A young woman sitting beside him on this journey was, in any case, a reason to be happy.

From time to time, people peeped in their direction.

The chaos of stowing luggage and finding seats died down, and there was a moment of calm. The train was on schedule, and the atmosphere was relaxed. Everyone on board knew this foolish young man was carrying a great deal of money, and couldn't help being worried for him. This route had never been safe; many had fallen victim to thefts and robberies. Of course there were also those who secretly rejoiced, thinking: *this idiot is an obvious target, so the rest of us should be safe while the thieves go for him.*

There was a stir when the bearded man and his lady sat beside Silly Boy. The carriage was full of empty seats, why squeeze together like this? It seemed something was about to happen. The passengers began whispering, *You see that man, doesn't he look like a bandit, and the way that girl is sitting right against that silly fellow, her huge breasts practically hitting him in the face.* Some people pretended they needed the toilet, glancing in Silly Boy's direction as they passed, coming back to report what they'd gleaned. A carriageful of eyes were like search lights, surrounding Silly Boy and darting about. Everyone was awaiting a good show.

* * *

The crowd hadn't guessed wrongly. This couple were, indeed, thieves.

男子叫王薄，大学毕业，学美术的。女子叫王丽，大专毕业，学建筑设计的。他们并不是夫妻，只是一对搭档。两人有个共同的爱好，就是旅游。他们就是旅游途中认识的。两人原都有工作，后来都辞了，现在就是四处漂流。

两人并不时常作案，一年也就二三次，够花了就住手。要动手就瞄住大钱，比如老板、港商、厅级干部，后来也偷处级干部。因为有一次在一座省城听人闲聊，说现在全中国最掌实权的就是处级干部，厅、局级干部其实只是原则领导，不管那么细。下头市、县到省里办事，比如上个项目要点指标什么的，光厅、局长点头没用，还得去实际负责操作的处长那里，这层关节打不通，厅长批了也没用，拖住不办，让你干着急。县处级干部就更有实权，掌管上百万人一个县，一路诸侯，大到干预办案，小到提拔干部，想腐败是很容易的。后来两人看报纸，专门研究反腐报道，果然发现揪出来不少处级干部。揪出来的厅、局级干部就很少，

The man was called Wang Bo, a university graduate with a degree in fine arts. The woman was Wang Li. She had a college degree in architectural design. They weren't married, just partners. Their shared hobby was sightseeing, and in fact they'd met in the course of their travels. Both had left their jobs, and now spent their days wandering around the country.

They didn't commit many crimes, maybe two or three a year. As long as they had enough money for their immediate needs, they'd hold back. They picked big marks—company owners, Hong Kong businessmen, department-level cadres. Later they also hit division-level ones—because once at a provincial capital, they'd overheard some gossip that in the whole of China, the officials with the most actual power are division-level cadres. The bureau- and department-level cadres only provide general guidance, without caring much about the practical details. When city- or county-level officials need to get something done at the provincial level, such as getting government grants for a project or some quota, it's no use if the bureau director-general nods his head; actually making it happen requires the co-operation of the division director. The approval of the bureau chief means nothing— your case may drag along without actually being resolved, causing nothing but anxiety. The county division cadre has even more practical power—controlling the fate of an entire county, more than a million people. They are the local autocrats—the sole arbiter of everything from influencing a case to promoting a cadre, an easy position from which to fall into corruption. Then the two of them read the newspaper, focusing on anti-corruption reports, that sure enough quite a few division-level

科级以下也少。据说是往上难查，往下不够档次，处级干部既够分量又好查处。王薄王丽就很感慨，说看起来九十年代就该处级干部倒霉。有回在宾馆碰到一个处长，贼溜溜乱瞅女人，王丽就恶心，然后去钓他，果然一钓一个准。睡到半夜，王丽悄悄打开门放王薄进来，王薄把处长拍醒，说处长咱们谈谈，处长惊得张口结舌。王薄摸摸大胡子，说你别怕我没带刀子，你睡了我女朋友，得赔点钱。王丽把他的保险箱提过来，说你自己打开吧。处长说我这钱是有大用途的，王薄说咱们这事也很重要。处长一脸汗水，抖抖地打开保险箱，有五万块，说你们要多少？王薄说要两万吧，给你留三万。两人就拿两万元走了。出了门王丽说你这人没出息，手太轻。王薄说算了，他也不容易，回去说不定把官撤了。

这两人做贼并不以敛钱为目的，有了钱就花。有时还寄些钱给希望工程。某省希望工程办公室收到一万元捐款，署名"星

cadres had been seized. Comparatively few department-level ones had been uncovered, and at the staff level or below, hardly any. They said it was too difficult to investigate anyone higher up than that, and the lower-downs weren't worth bothering about. Only at the division level did one find the substance and ease of access. Wang Bo and Wang Li sighed at this, saying how unlucky the nineties were for division-level cadres. They had once encountered the director of a division in a hotel. Wang Li was repulsed by the sleazy way he leered at every woman who walked past, and went after him. Soon, he was hooked. In the middle of the night, Wang Li quietly let Wang Bo into the hotel room, and he smacked the cadre awake saying, *Sir, we need to talk*. The director's mouth hung open, tongue-tied. Wang Bo stroked his luxuriant beard and said, *Don't worry, I haven't brought a knife, but you've slept with my girlfriend, you'll need to compensate me*. Wang Li hefted over his security case and said, *Go on, open it*. The director said, *This money is earmarked for important things*. Wang Bo said, *Our business is important too*. The cadre's face was streaming with sweat. Hands shaking, he opened the case, which contained fifty thousand *yuan*. He said, *How much do you want?* Wang Bo said, *Twenty thousand will do, we'll leave thirty for you*. And the two of them departed with twenty thousand. As they walked out, Wang Li said, *You're useless, you went far too easy on him*. Wang Bo said, *Forget it, this won't go well for him, he might even lose his position*.

    The point of their heists wasn't to accumulate wealth; they spent whatever they got. Sometimes they even sent cash to the

月",登报寻找叫"星月"的好心人。他俩看到了大笑,说咱们也成好心人了。两人最喜欢的事是旅游,数年内走遍了全国的名山大川。他们是贼,可他们爱山水。

当初王薄就是因为没钱旅游才做贼的。旅游是为了寻找灵感,可是跑了几年也没找到,越跑越没有感觉。王丽就取笑他,说艺术是圣女,你太脏,找不到的。王薄咂咂嘴,不吱声。

这次他们来大沙漠实在是因为没什么地方好去了,没想到来到大沙漠一待就是几个月。他们以车站小镇为基地,不断往沙漠深处走,有两次遇上沙暴差点送命,还有几次碰上狼群差点被狼吃了。王丽吓坏了,老是闹着要走。王薄说要走你走,我还要住些日子。王丽只好陪着。王薄被大沙漠镇住了,这是他自己都没有想到的。

大沙漠并没有任何风景,大沙漠里只有沙丘,光溜溜的沙丘,百里千里都是沙丘。站在大沙丘上极目远眺,沙丘一个接一个,重重叠叠,无边无际,在阳光下光波粼粼,一如浩瀚的大海。而在阴霾的天气里,大漠则雾气缭绕,隐现的沙丘如几百里连营,

Hope Project, which built schools in poverty-stricken rural areas. When one of the Project's provincial offices received a gift of ten thousand *yuan* from "Moon and Stars", they published an ad in the papers searching for this great benefactor. The couple laughed when they saw this, saying *Hey look, now we're philanthropists.* But above all, the two of them loved to travel, and over the years had visited all the famous scenic spots in China. They may have been thieves, but they also had an appreciation of fine landscapes.

Initially, Wang Bo took to thievery because he didn't have money to travel—he needed to travel to search for inspiration, even though inspiration didn't come after several years on the road, and in fact it faded the more he chased. Wang Li laughed at him, *Art is a sacred virgin and you're too profane, you'll never find her.* Wang Bo clicked his tongue, not disputing this.

They came to the desert because they had nowhere better to go. They didn't anticipate that they would spend several months there. They used the small town with the train station as their base, wandering again and again into the deepest reaches of the dunes. Twice, they encountered sandstorms and almost died, and a few times almost got eaten by wolves. Wang Li was terrified and kept clamoring to leave, but Wang Bo said, *Go if you want to, I'm staying here a bit longer.* She had no choice but to stay. Wang Bo was enraptured by the desert, which even he had not expected.

The desert had no particular scenery to speak of, only thousands of miles of smooth, shiny sand dunes. Standing atop a tall crest and staring into the distance, you saw only more dunes, one after another, rows and rows of them, borderless, heartbreakingly

你甚至能听到隐隐的号角和厮杀，让人森然惊心。相比之下，他所见到的那些百媚千娇的山水，就显得轻浮和机巧了。

王薄在大沙漠里流连，翻过一座沙丘又一座沙丘，喘吁吁不得要领。他真是弄不明白，这单调得不能再单调的大沙漠何以如此震撼人的心魄？但后来他突然明白了，大沙漠的全部魅力就是固执，固执地构筑沙丘，固执地重复自己，无论狂风、沙暴还是岁月，都无法改变它。

回到小镇休息几日，两人谁也没再提起沙漠。过去每游一处山水，回来总爱戏谑一番，现在沙漠却成了禁忌，王薄变得沉默寡言。几天后他终于开口，说："我要回去画画了。"王丽幽幽地看着他，很久没搭话，半夜里突然说："咱们该分手了。"

他们终于决定告别大沙漠。

在车站看到傻根完全是个意外，两个人全愣住了。

这个从沙漠走出来的傻小子，居然固执地认为世界上没有贼！就像大沙漠一样固执。

那一瞬间，王丽突然有点感动。

她扯扯王薄的衣袖小声说："这小子……特像我弟弟，傻里傻

clear against the sunlight, like the wide ocean. In hazy weather the desert was shrouded in mists, dunes poking through like a few hundred miles of army tents, so you almost believed you heard the shouted commands and killings, making you shiver in the dead silence. After this, the more obvious charms of mountains and rivers seemed frivolous and dainty by comparison.

Wang Bo lingered in the desert, climbing one sand dune after another, panting and wondering what the point was. How could this most monotonous place have so completely shaken his soul? Later, he understood that the magic of the desert lies in its obstinacy. It stubbornly keeps constructing sand dunes, repeating itself, regardless of strong winds, sandstorms or time passing, refusing ever to change.

Returning to the small town for a few days' rest, the two of them didn't mention the desert. Normally, after each excursion they liked to banter about what they'd seen, but the desert seemed a forbidden subject. Wang Bo became silent and withdrawn. Days later, he finally spoke: "I want to go back to painting." Wang Li looked at him gloomily and didn't reply for a long time. In the middle of the night, she suddenly said, "It's time we split up."

And so they decided to say goodbye to the desert.

At the train station, encountering Silly Boy was an accident. They were both shocked.

For such a foolish young man to emerge from the desert—stubbornly insisting there are no thieves in the world! As obstinate as the great desert itself.

In an instant, Wang Li's heart was stirred.

气的。"王丽时常给弟弟寄钱,可弟弟不知她是贼。

王薄转头看着她,目光怪怪的,没吱声。

上车后,王丽说:"坐哪儿?"

王薄说:"随你。"

* * *

这是一趟慢车,差不多个把小时就停一次,每停一次就上来许多人。座位上早就坐满,过道上挤了不少人,大包小包竹筐扁担,横七竖八。幽暗的灯光下弥漫着热烘烘的气味,不时有人大声争吵。一个看上去有点瘸腿的老人在过道上挤来挤去,老是找不到一个可以立足的地方,急得骂骂咧咧。傻根看到了,站起身正要招呼让座,被身旁的王丽一把拉回座位上,低声说:"少管闲事!"傻根又乖乖地坐下了。他有些不太明白这女子什么意思,仿佛他是她的什么人。但他似乎乐意服从她,就重新坐好,仍是东张西望。这时他看到王丽挤到过道上,靠近那个瘸腿老人说了一句什么,老人一愣,慌慌地往另一车厢去了。等她回来坐好,傻根本想问她说了什么,却憋住了没问。就有些纳闷。

傻根一直处在兴奋中,每次停车,他都要打开窗户往外看,

She tugged Wang Bo's sleeve and whispered, "That little one—he's like my brother. So silly." Wang Li sent money to her brother from time to time, though he didn't know she was a thief.

Wang Bo turned to look at her, his expression odd. He said nothing.

After boarding, Wang Li said, "Where should we sit?"

"Up to you," he replied.

* * *

This was a slow train, stopping almost every hour, hordes of passengers flooding onto the carriage at each station. The seats were soon all taken, the passageway crowded with people, bags and bamboo baskets jostling for room, stacked all over the place. Steamy air swirled under dim lighting. From time to time, a loud argument broke out. An old man with a bit of a limp squeezed back and forth along the corridor, unable to find a place to stand, shrieking with anxiety. Silly Boy was about to stand and offer his seat when Wang Li dragged him back down and murmured, "Not your problem." Obediently, he sat down again. He didn't quite understand what the lady meant, talking as if they knew each other, but he was quite happy to do as she said. He resumed his position, still glancing around. Then (he saw) Wang Li squeezed onto the walkway and said a few words to the old man. The old man looked shocked, then hurriedly moved to the next carriage. When Wang Li came back, Silly Boy was dying to ask what she'd said to him, but swallowed the question. It was puzzling.

Silly Boy was in a state of constant excitement. Each time the train stopped, he insisted on opening the window to look outside.

黑黢黢的村庄小镇越来越多，就有一种重返人间的亲切感。小站稀疏昏暗的灯光，举着菜篮在窗口叫卖的女人，都让他感到新奇无比。几年待在大沙漠里，恍若隔世，他想对每一个人都笑笑，对每一个人说我挣了六万块钱，要回家盖房子娶媳妇啦！傻根的心窝窝里像注着蜜，想让所有的人和他分享。

这时王丽好像受不住车厢里混浊的气味，熏得想呕吐，猛起身扑向窗口，半个身子压在傻根身上。傻根立刻感到她软乎乎的身子，窘得手足无措。可是王丽突然尖叫一声："哎哟！"又反弹回来，原来是对面的瘦子站起伸懒腰踩了她的脚。王丽气恼地瞪他一眼："干什么你！"瘦子阴阴地往下瞅瞅，慢吞吞说："对不起，一不当心。"王薄冲王丽挤挤眼，呵呵笑起来。王丽生气地说："你还笑！"

王薄觉得有趣极了。先前王丽制止傻子让座，并把那个瘸腿老人赶走，是王丽看出瘸子是个扒手。他骂骂咧咧是装样子的。这种小伎俩骗得了傻根，却骗不了王丽。王丽把他赶走，是不想让他在这个车厢里作案，准确地说是不想让傻根发现真有贼，她宁愿让那个傻小子相信天下无贼。他知道王丽有时候很聪明，有

Villages and small towns became more frequent, grimy and sour-looking, but still he had the tender feeling of returning to humanity. In the diffuse, dim light of each little station, even the women with baskets of vegetables calling out their wares seemed refreshing. So many years in the great desert was like being cut off from the world. He wanted to smile at everyone he met, and tell them, *I've earned sixty thousand yuan and I'm going home to build a house and marry a girl!* Silly Boy felt as if honey had trickled into his heart. He wanted to share this sweetness with the rest of the world.

By this point, Wang Li seemed to have had enough of the bad air in the carriage, which was suffocating her. Nauseous, she lurched towards the window, half her body pressed against Silly Boy's, who felt embarrassed as her soft form draped over his, uncertain what to do. But suddenly, she shrieked and fell back into her seat. The skinny man opposite was stretching, and had stepped on her foot. She glared at him, "What do you think you're doing?" And he glanced down at drawling coolly, "Sorry, that was an accident." Wang Bo narrowed his eyes at Wang Li, chuckling. She fumed at him, "You dare to laugh!"

Wang Bo found the situation entertaining. When Wang Li stopped Silly Boy giving up his seat and chased away the crippled old man, it was because she could see he was a pickpocket, his shrieking and scolding just a distraction. This sort of cheap trick could fool Silly Boy, but not Wang Li—and so she'd chased him away. She didn't want him to take anything from this carriage, or more accurately, she didn't want Silly Boy to learn that there were thieves in the world after all, but would rather he indulged in his fantasy of

时候又很傻,她被傻小子一句话感动了,于是要充当保护神的角色。可是这可能吗?王丽被瘦子踩了一脚,又是瘦子疑心王丽要下手,也是从中作梗的意思。螳螂捕蝉,黄雀在后。因此王薄笑起来。

其实王薄早已看出这个刀疤脸是个角色,只是一时还不能确定是什么角色,小偷还是劫匪?但有一点可以肯定,他的注意力同样在傻小子的帆布包上,他不会允许任何人碰它。王薄在心里说,你也别碰,大家都别碰。

他决定成全王丽。

这是一个美丽的梦。

夜已经深了。车厢里人大都沉沉睡去,连过道上站着的人也在打盹。不时有人撞在别人身上,邻近被撞醒的人一下醒过来,转头看看,又继续打盹。大家都显得格外宽容。也有几个人没睡,仍在注视着傻根这边。他们是些悠闲的旅人,有足够的耐心等待什么事情发生。

王丽已经睡着了,头靠在傻根宽厚的肩膀上,像一只温顺的猫。傻根先前还试图挪开一点,可是挪一点,王丽的脑袋就跟一点。后来就几乎侧卧在傻根身上。傻根靠窗,已经挪不动了,就

innocence. Wang Bo knew that Wang Li could be tremendously clever at times, and completely foolish at others. Now, she'd been moved by a few words from this boy, and had cast herself in the role of his protector. But was this possible? And when the skinny man stepped on her foot—was that because he'd thought she was about to make a move, and wanted to thwart her plan? The praying mantis stalks the cicada, but behind it is a bird waiting to pounce. And so Wang Bo laughed.

Already, Wang Bo was certain that Scarface was no ordinary bystander—it was just unclear what his part would be in all this, bandit or thief. But one thing was certain: all his attention was on the foolish fellow's canvas bag, and he wasn't going to allow anyone to go near it. Wang Bo said to himself, *Then you'd better not touch it yourself—we'll all stay clear of it.*

He decided to go along with Wang Li's plan.

It was a beautiful dream.

Deep into the night, most of the carriage was sound asleep. Even those standing in the passageway would doze off, and from time to time collide with their neighbors, who'd wake up, look around, and slide back into sleep. Everyone was exceptionally tolerant. But there were also those who didn't sleep, whose attention was focused on Silly Boy. These were leisure-and pleasure-seeking travelers, patiently awaiting the expected incident.

Wang Li dropped off, her head pillowed on Silly Boy's broad shoulder, like a tender little cat. Silly Boy moved aside, but her head followed him, until she was practically lying on him and he was pressed against the window, with nowhere else to go. He looked at

冲王薄看，小心翼翼地说："要不咱俩换换？"其实傻根感觉挺好，肩上搭个年轻女子是个福气，可他又怕人家不乐意。王薄很宽容地笑笑，说："不用，让她睡吧。"口气就像是赏赐。傻根就有些受宠若惊，重新坐稳了，用肩膀和半个身子托住王丽，动也不敢动，唯恐弄醒了她。他不能辜负了人家的信任。如此坚持了个把小时，傻根很累了，也开始发困，就渐渐打起盹来，和王丽耳鬓厮磨，睡得又香又甜。

王薄没敢睡。

王薄不睡是因为身旁的刀疤脸没睡。

王薄试图和他聊聊，就问："先生到哪去？"

"前头。"刀疤脸爱答不理的样子，继续抽他的烟，地板上已扔了一片烟头。这家伙显得百无聊赖，不时翻看那本有半裸女人的杂志，光线不太好，看不清字，就只看封面和插图。一时又丢下，继续抽烟。刀疤脸精神好得很。王薄相信他在等待时机。他在心里想，你不会有机会的。他决心和他较较劲儿。尽管他觉得这事有点荒唐。荒唐就荒唐吧，人生在世，大约总会做点荒唐事的。

此后的三天三夜，车上人上上下下，最早一块上车的人大部

Wang Bo and gingerly asked, "Should we change places?" Actually, Silly Boy was enjoying this, having a young woman on his shoulder undoubtedly pleasurable, but he feared causing offense. Wang Bo smiled generously and said, "No need, let her sleep." His tone of voice implied this was a gift. Overwhelmed with gratitude, Silly Boy sat back more comfortably, supporting Wang Li with his shoulder and torso, afraid to move in case he woke her. He couldn't betray this man's trust. After an hour of this, Silly Boy was tired too, and began to nod off. Cheek by jowl with Wang Li, he entered into a deep, sweet slumber.

Wang Bo didn't dare to sleep.

Wang Bo had to stay awake, because Scarface was awake.

Wang Bo tried to engage him in conversation. "Where are you traveling to, sir?"

"Up ahead," said Scarface indifferently, still smoking. The floor was now paved with discarded butts. This chap seemed completely bored by his surroundings, preferring to flip through the pages of his girlie magazine. The light wasn't good enough to read by; he could only look at the pictures. After a while, he flung it down and lit another cigarette. Scarface was in good spirits. Wang Bo believed he was waiting for his chance, and thought, *That's not going to happen*. They'd go head to head. No matter how ridiculous this whole affair seemed—well then, let it be ridiculous. In this life, we all end up doing some ridiculous things.

During the three days and nights after that, people got on and off the train. The first batch of passengers were mostly gone, leaving only Silly Boy and those around him. None of them knew

分都下车走了，唯独傻根和他周围的几个人没谁下车。他们谁也不知道对方要去哪里，就这么死死随着。

王薄和王丽早已达成默契，两人轮流睡觉，不管傻根临时下车买东西还是上厕所。总有一人跟在后头。傻根已在他们严密监控之下。一次傻根下车买吃的，一群人围住一个食品车，傻根掏出钱买烧鸡，不知道一只手伸进他的帆布包。王丽看得清清楚楚，那人挤出人群正要离开，王丽高跟鞋一歪踩在那人身上，转眼间又从他裤袋里把钱掏了出来。傻根买烧鸡出来，王丽迎上去说看你把衣领都挤开了，不冷吗？就上去为他扣衣领整衣裳拉正了帆布包偷偷把钱塞了进去。傻根站得像根冰棍心里却热乎乎的眼泪几乎流出来，自从离开老家的村子，已经几年没有女人为他这样拉拉拽拽整衣裳了，就热热地叫了一声：“姐，你真好！”王丽说：“快上车吧，车要开了。”傻根在前头往车上跑，王丽的眼睛湿润了。这一声"姐"叫得她心里热热的血往上涌。

在这三天三夜里，刀疤脸一直有些漫不经心。还时常抽空打个盹，他不可能老是不睡觉。但只要傻根一动地方，他就会立刻醒来。他并没有急急忙忙跟着傻根，可是傻根下车买东西上厕所，却一直都在他的视野里。刚才在车下发生的一切，傻根浑然不觉，

where the rest were going, but they were determined to follow each other there.

Wang Bo and Wang Li fell into a rhythm early on, taking turns to sleep. Whenever Silly Boy left the carriage to buy something or use the toilet, one or the other would follow him. He was under their secret surveillance. Once, he'd gone for some food. As he stood in the crowd around the snack cart, reaching for money to pay for his roast chicken, he had no idea a hand was sidling into his canvas bag. Wang Li saw the whole thing, and watched the man squeeze out of the crowd ready to flee. She stretched out her high heeled shoe, to trip the man up and retrieve the cash from his pocket in a flash. When Silly Boy emerged with his chicken, Wang Li came up and said, *Look at you, your collar's wide open, aren't you cold?* And as she straightened his clothing, she slipped the money back into his bag. Silly Boy stood as still as an icicle, but his heart was warm, and hot tears almost trickled from his eyes. Since he'd left his home village, no woman had fussed over him like this. He said, thickly, "You're so good to me, like an older sister." Wang Li said, "Come on, the train's about to move off." Silly Boy ran ahead of her, and Wang Li's eyes glistened. "Older sister." Those words sent hot blood surging through her heart.

For three days and nights, Scarface seemed distracted. He did doze off now and then—no one could stay awake for all that time—but as soon as Silly Boy moved, he'd jolt awake. He didn't actually tail him, but tried to keep him in sight while he made his purchases or visited the lavatory. Silly Boy was completely unaware of the incident with the pickpocket, but Scarface had watched the whole

刀疤脸却从窗口都看到了。可他依然不露声色，掏出一支烟又抽起来。

这天傍晚，车到北京站。

傻根要转车到郑州，王丽热情地帮他买票。傻根和他们已经很熟了。傻根说姐太麻烦你了，王丽说你别乱跑就站在这里别动，对王薄说你看好他我去买票，就急匆匆去了。北京火车站很热闹，傻根的眼睛有些不够用，东看看西看看。有人聚堆说话，他也凑上去听听；看人扛个牌子接站，就上去摸摸牌子。王薄将他扯回来，说你别乱跑过会儿跑丢了！傻根就笑笑站住了仍是东张西望。王薄一边看住傻根，一边也在东张西望。看了几圈，没发现那个刀疤脸瘦子，心里便有些得意，估计这家伙看看无法下手，只好走了。王薄和王丽说好在北京下车的，他要去中国美术馆看看画展，离开画界几年，他想知道画界有什么变化。现在刀疤脸走了，就没人知道傻根身上带有钱，让他一人回去也可以放心了。

过了很久，王丽终于捏着车票回来，圆圆脸上汗津津的，头发凌乱。王薄打趣说遭抢啦？王丽说你倒清闲，买票差点挤死人，

thing from the window. His expression unchanged, he lit a cigarette.

On the third evening, the train arrived at Beijing Station.

Silly Boy had to change trains now for Zhengzhou. Wang Li enthusiastically offered to help him get his ticket. They were friends now. Silly Boy said, *Sister, I don't want to trouble you.* Wang Li said, *Stand right here, don't run around.* And to Wang Bo, she said, *Keep an eye on him, I'm going to the ticket office.* She hurried off. Beijing Station is a busy place. Silly Boy felt like he didn't have enough eyes to see everything around him. He stared at it all. When people gathered in conversation, he moved closer to eavesdrop; when he saw someone holding a welcome board waiting at the arrivals gate, he wanted to touch the board. Wang Bo pulled him back, calling, *Don't you get lost, running all over the place.* So Silly Boy stood still, laughing artlessly, goggling at everything. Wang Bo looked around too, but also kept one eye on Silly Boy. After some time, Scarface still hadn't shown up and he felt safer. That fellow must have seen there was no chance, and given up. Wang Bo and Wang Li had decided they'd break their journey at Beijing. He planned to see an exhibition at the National Art Museum—after so many years away from the scene, he wanted to know what the latest trends were. And with Scarface gone, no one would know how much money Silly Boy had on him. They could let him go off alone without worrying too much.

It was quite a while before Wang Li returned with the tickets in her hand, her round face glistening with sweat and her hair in a mess. Wang Bo teased, *What happened, were you robbed?* Wang Li

快上车吧时间要到了。拉起傻根就往站里跑,看王薄还站着就说你愣着干什么,快走啊!王薄疑惑说干什么?王丽说上火车啊去郑州。王薄说不是说好在北京下车的吗?王丽说我买了三张票,干脆送他到家。王薄说你疯啦?王丽说我没疯,你不去拉倒我自己去,扯起傻根转身就走。王薄眼睁睁看他们要进去了,突然喊一声等等我!拎起包追了上去。

他知道他拗不过王丽。

三人上了火车正在寻找铺位,一个小偷就盯上了傻根,手刚伸向他的帆布包,就被王薄一把捉住了。但王薄没有声张,只用力捏捏他的手腕。小偷赶紧溜了,他知道遇上了高人。傻根见王薄和那人拉了拉手,就说你们认识?王薄说认识。傻根说认识怎么没说话?王薄说他是个哑巴,刚才是用手语交谈。王丽捂住嘴笑,傻根却信以为真。

这次他们买的是卧铺票,傻根是第一次坐卧铺,稀罕得什么似的,这里摸摸那里摸摸,说真是不得了,火车上还有床,三下两下蹿到上铺说我就睡上头。王丽睡中铺,王薄睡下铺。安顿好东西,三人坐在王薄的下铺上吃了点东西喝点水,傻根说我要睡

said, *Very funny, I was almost squeezed to death in that crowd—now come on, it's time to get on the train.* Pulling Silly Boy along with her, she began striding to the platform. She called back at Wang Bo, who hadn't moved. *What are you doing, come on, stir yourself!* Wang Bo said, puzzled, *What are you doing?* Wang Li said, *Getting the train to Zhengzhou.* Wang Bo said, *Didn't we agree we'd stop in Beijing?* Wang Li said, *I've bought three tickets, we might as well take him all the way home.* Wang Bo said, *Are you crazy?* She replied, *I'm not crazy, but I'll go on my own if you don't want to come.* And with that, she took Silly Boy's arm and walked off. Wang Bo gaped at them with wide eyes before shouting, *Wait for me!* He grabbed his bag and dashed after them.

He knew he couldn't change Wang Li's mind.

As the three of them searched for their places on the train, a thief fixed his eye on Silly Boy—but as soon as his hand slipped into the canvas bag, Wang Bo had grabbed it. He didn't say anything, just pinched his wrist with bruising force. The thief slipped away as soon as he could. He knew he'd met his match. Silly Boy saw Wang Bo shaking the man's hand and said, *Do you know him?* Wang Bo said, *Sure, I know him.* Silly Boy said, *Then why didn't you speak?* Wang Bo said, *He's mute, we were speaking in sign language.* Wang Li covered her mouth and giggled, but Silly Boy believed every word.

They'd bought sleeper tickets. This was Silly Boy's first time in a bunk, and he seemed very taken by it, running his hands over everything and saying, *Incredible, a bed on a train.* A second later he'd bounded onto the highest bunk and said, *I'll sleep up top.*

觉了,王丽说你去睡吧睡一觉差不多就到郑州了。傻根爬上去躺倒,一会儿就睡着了。王丽松一口气,看着王薄说谢谢你。王薄说干吗要谢我?王丽说这事本来和你无关的,王薄说和你也无关啊,王丽说这是我揽下的事,王薄说分什么你的我的,你的事不也是我的事吗?王丽说到郑州咱们真的该分手了。王薄说你打算去哪里?王丽说先回陕西老家看看我弟弟,我已经五年没见他了。以后呢?以后再说,找个工作干干吧。王薄拉过她的手拍拍,没再说话。两人就这么牵着手,一动不动,心里都有些伤感。突然王丽火烫似的把手抽回,往旁边指了指,王薄转头看去,那个消失的刀疤脸瘦子正临窗站立,不禁吃了一惊,这家伙从哪里又冒出来的?

两人都有些紧张,看来这事没完。

王薄低声说别怕,有我呢。

王丽没吭声,王丽走神了。王丽突然有一种不祥的预感,心里有些发抖,悄声说:"这家伙会不会是冲咱们来的?"王薄一经提醒,心里也咯噔一下,说:"你怀疑他是公安?"王丽说:"没准。"王薄沉吟一下自言自语:"不会吧?"他想这怎么可能呢,几

Wang Li took the middle, and Wang Bo the lowest sleeper. After putting away their things, the three of them sat on Wang Bo's bunk to eat and drink. Silly Boy said, *I'm tired.* Wang Li said, *Go to bed, when you wake up we'll be almost in Zhengzhou.* Silly Boy climbed up and was asleep in a short while. Wang Li let out a breath and said to Wang Bo, *Thank you.* Wang Bo said, *Why are you thanking me?* Wang Li said, *This affair has nothing to do with you.* Wang Bo said, *You neither.* Wang Li said, *I took this on myself.* Wang Bo said, *Why fuss about whose affair it is, haven't your problems always been mine too?* Wang Li said, *When we get to Zhengzhou we really should split up.* Wang Bo said, *Where will you go?* Wang Li said, *First to my old home in Shaanxi to visit my little brother, it's been five years since I've seen him. And after that? I'll think about that later, find a job or something.* Wang Bo patted her hand and said nothing. Holding hands like this, the two of them sat motionless, their hearts melancholy. Suddenly, Wang Li's hand withdrew as if she'd been scalded, and she pointed urgently to one side. Wang Bo turned to look—and there was the skinny scarfaced man, standing by the window. He was startled. Where had this fellow come from?

The two of them grew agitated. This business wasn't over yet.

Wang Bo whispered, *Don't be scared, you have me.*

Wang Li said nothing, her thoughts wandering, a dark premonition causing her heart to tremble. She murmured, "This chap couldn't possibly be after us?" Wang Bo, suddenly alert, felt his heart thud. He said, "You think he might be the Police?" Wang Li said, "Could be." Wang Bo thought for a while, muttering to

年来他和王丽虽然作案多次，但从不固定一个地方，而且间歇很长，也没有引起多大动静，并没听说过悬赏捉拿之类的事，也就一直没有惊慌逃跑有意藏匿，倒是潇洒从容天南海北地闲荡，他们甚至没有过犯罪的感觉。至于这个刀疤脸瘦子，完全是偶然碰上的，怎么会是冲我们来的呢？

王薄这么说服自己，心里却不踏实，到底做贼心虚。他第一次有了罪犯的感觉。

这时王丽捅捅他："前头要到站了，要不你先走！"

前头是个小站，王薄往外看看，低声说："你呢？"

王丽往上铺看了一眼："我等等再说。"

王薄说："你还惦着这个宝贝啊？"就有些着急。

王丽说："……反正咱们迟早得分手，也许那人不是公安呢。"其实凭一个女人的直觉已让她断定，刀疤脸就是公安人员，而且是冲他们来的。

王丽的直觉没错。

刀疤脸确是公安人员，并且是个侦查英雄，他脸上的刀疤就是无数次和歹徒生死搏斗的见证。其实他身上还有多处刀伤。三年前，他奉命追踪这一对大盗，跑遍了全国各地，后来一直追到

himself, "Surely not?" It seemed impossible. He and Wang Li might have committed many crimes over several years, but they were all in different places, with long gaps in between, and none had caused much of a stir. They'd never heard of a bounty on their heads or anything of the sort. So instead of scurrying about in the dark or hiding, they wandered openly, without restraint, from north to south, not even thinking of themselves as criminals. So this Scarface showing up must be a coincidence. How could he possibly be after them?

Wang Bo tried to convince himself, but failed—as they say, the thief's heart is weak. For the first time, he experienced guilt.

Now Wang Li nudged him. "There's a station up ahead, why don't you go first?"

A tiny station, in the distance. Wang Bo eyed it. "And you?"

She glanced at the top bunk. "I'll think of leaving later."

"Can't bear to leave your little darling?" Wang Bo was growing anxious.

Wang Li said, "In any case, we'd need to split up sooner or later, even if that man isn't from the Police." But her female perception told her he was, and that he was here to arrest them.

Wang Li's intuition was never wrong.

Scarface was, indeed, a police officer—in fact, a hero of the detective squad. The scars were evidence of countless life-and-death fights with villains. There were many others on his body too. Three years ago, he accepted the task to track down this pair of outlaws, pursuing them across the entire country. Finally, he reached the great desert, but found it like seeking a needle in the sea, arduous

大沙漠。他像大海捞针,费尽艰难,虽没抓住他们却一步步逼近。当他在沙漠边缘的小站上猛然发现这一对男女时,他的心几乎要跳出来。他相信终于找到他们了。王薄和王丽的相貌还是三年前那个在宾馆被敲诈的处长提供的。一路上他巧妙地伪装着自己。离开沙漠碰上傻根,他本想顺便做些保护,没想到却撞上这一对大盗。但他们几天几夜的举动又让他疑惑不解。很显然,他们在保护傻小子。刀疤脸素以铁面果敢闻名,这次却变得犹豫不决。他一再拖延对他们的抓捕,连他自己都说不清为什么。挂在腰带里的手铐已让他摸得汗湿,却到底没摘下来。他又对自己说,再等等看,这挺好玩的,一对大盗保护一个傻小子不被人盗。他对自己说,你别乱来这不是看戏,你千山万水追捕了三年好不容易找到,可别让他们溜了,他们随时都有脱逃的可能。但接着他又为自己开脱,你真的确定他们就是你追捕了三年的大盗?天底下长相差不多的人多着呢,还是再等等看。他用种种理由说服自己延缓抓捕,其实他心里清楚,真正的原因是他动了恻隐之心,他觉得这一对男女挺可惜的,他们是大盗可他们在做一件好事,这不仅离奇而且还有点浪漫。他想成全他们。他们所做的事日后判

and unrewarding, fruitless even though his quarry seemed to draw closer step by step. When he came upon this couple in the small station by the desert, his heart almost leapt from his chest. He believed he'd finally tracked them down. Wang Li and Wang Bo matched the descriptions supplied by the division director who was cheated three years ago in that hotel. And so he tailed them, keeping himself in disguise. Seeing Silly Boy at the station, he'd decided to protect him as much as he could, not expecting this larcenous pair to turn up. Yet their actions over the previous days and nights had baffled him. They were obviously keeping watch over the foolish lad. Scarface was known for his iron will, but this time found himself hesitating. He delayed their arrest again and again, and was unable to explain why, even to himself. The handcuffs hanging from his waist grew damp with sweat from his fingering, but he never took them off. He said to himself, *Let's wait and see, this is fun, a pair of notorious thieves stopping a bumpkin from being robbed*. Then he thought, *Don't play the fool, this isn't a movie, you've been chasing these two over hill and dale for three years now, and finally you've got them within your sight, don't let them slip away, they could escape at any moment.* Next he tried to find a way out, asking himself, *Are you certain these are the ones you've been after these last three years? This world is full of people who look similar, why not wait a little longer?* He tried all kinds of reasons to persuade himself there was no rush, but he knew it was really because his compassion had been stirred. He pitied this man and woman. They might be wanted criminals, but they were doing a very good thing, also a strange thing with a touch of

刑时会对他们有利。他知道他在冒险，甚至在违反纪律。可他就是拿不出手铐。

王薄还在犹豫。

王薄觉得这么跑了怪对不住王丽，就说咱们一块逃吧，王丽说一块逃谁都逃不了，目标太大。王薄还在犹豫，王丽说快走，车要停了，什么行李也别带，装着下车买东西，别慌。王薄拍拍她的手，慢慢站起身，伸个懒腰，瞄了刀疤脸一眼，对王丽说我去买点水果，就慢慢往车门走去。车刚缓缓停下王薄就跳了下去。

但这时车上却突然出事了。

王丽对面上铺的一个男子本来一直蒙头睡觉的，就在列车即将停下的一刹那，突然跃起扑到傻根铺上，抓起他的帆布包滑下来就要逃，傻根仍在沉沉大睡，毫无知觉。王丽猝然间愣了一下，立刻明白发生了什么事，尖叫一声扑到那人身上，死死扯住他的衣裳说："你放下！"这一声喊惊动了刀疤脸也惊动了这个车厢里所有的人，都回过头看。王丽已死死抱住那人的腰，那人一时挣脱不了，拼命用胳膊肘捣击王丽，刀疤脸一个箭步跨来，正要扭住那人时，突然又冲出两个歹徒，原来他们是同伙。那个男子看

romance. He wanted to let them be. What they'd done here might be counted as a mitigating factor in their sentencing. He knew he was taking a risk, and probably breaking the law himself. But still he couldn't bring himself to use those handcuffs.

Wang Bo continued to consider his options.

Wang Bo thought running away on his own was unfair to Wang Li, so he said, *Let's escape together*. Wang Li said, *If we both try to run, neither will make it, we'd present too large a target*. Wang Bo hesitated again. Wang Li said, *Quickly, the train's about to stop, leave your luggage, say you're going to buy something, stay calm*. Wang Bo stroked her hand, stood up slowly and stretched, and glanced at Scarface. To Wang Li he said, *I'll go get some fruit*. And with that, he walked slowly towards the door. As the train came to a halt, Wang Bo leapt from the carriage.

Then everything happened at once.

The man on the top bunk opposite Wang Li had been asleep the whole time, his head covered. The instant the train stopped, he leapt across to Silly Boy's bunk, grabbed the canvas bag, slid down and tried to flee. Silly Boy didn't wake up, completely oblivious. In an instant, Wang Li realized what was happening. She shrieked as she flung herself at the man, clinging onto his shirt and shouting, "Drop it!" Her roar startled awake Scarface, and indeed everyone in the carriage. They all turned to look. Wang Li had her arms firmly around the man's waist, and he couldn't get away, frantically jabbing his elbows into her. Scarface shot forward like an arrow, but before he could grab the thief, two other bandits burst onto the scene from nowhere—part of the same gang. Unable to struggle

看挣扎不开,一甩手将帆布包扔给一个同伙,那人接过帆布包三跳两蹦冲下车去。王丽看帆布包已被抢走,撒手就要追,被歹徒一拳打倒在地。刀疤脸面对两个歹徒,毫无惧色,对方已各自亮出刀子,刀疤脸猛往下缩身,一圈扫堂腿将二人打翻在地,被闻讯赶来的两个乘警按住了。刀疤脸已飞身下车,王丽满脸是血也跌跌撞撞追了出去,一边大喊大叫:"抓贼啊!抓!……"样子凶猛得像一头母豹。

两人跳下车时,却见那个携帆布包的歹徒正在几十米外的地方狂奔,背后一个高大的汉子紧追不舍。眼看要追上时,歹徒好像回手一刀,高大汉子踉跄一下猛扑上去将歹徒压在身下,两人就在地上翻滚。这时列车上下无数人在呐喊助威,有几个人跳下车也追上去。刀疤脸最先赶到很快将歹徒制服,他发现被刺伤的高大汉子却是王薄,心里真是为他高兴。这时王丽也赶到了,看王薄一身是血抱住他大哭起来。王薄坐在地上脸色苍白,苦涩地笑笑说:"不要紧,肚子上……挨了一刀。"

刀疤脸把歹徒交给几个随后追来的乘警,掏出证件给他们看看,说请你们把这几个歹徒押走,一弯腰背起王薄,对王丽说你

free, the man flung the bag to one of his accomplices, who swiftly jumped off the train. Seeing the canvas bag gone, Wang Li let go of her prey and tried to pursue it, only for the bandit to punch her to the ground. Scarface confronted the two robbers without showing any fear, even as they produced their knives. He ducked down and skillfully swept an outstretched leg in a martial arts move, tumbling the two men. A couple of railway policemen, drawn by the row, arrived and grabbed hold of them. Scarface dashed off the train. Wang Li, her face bloody, was also stumbling out, screaming, "Stop, thief! Stop!" Fierce as a mother leopard protecting her cubs.

By this time, the bandit with the canvas bag was dozens of meters away, sprinting for dear life, hotly pursued by a well-built man. Just as he was about to catch up, the bandit seemed to attack with a knife, and the big man stumbled before flinging himself at his adversary, tackling him to the ground, where the two men grappled. Numerous people on and off the train were shouting threats and encouragement, and several had jumped from the carriage to join in the chase. Scarface arrived first and quickly subdued the bandit. He found the other man, bleeding from a knife wound, was Wang Bo. Scarface was happy for him. Wang Li caught up with them, and seeing Wang Bo covered in blood, hugged him tightly and burst into tears. He sat on the ground, his face ghastly pale, and smiled bitterly. "It's not important. Just one cut. My belly."

Scarface handed the bandits over to the railway police, showing them his identification, saying *Please arrest these robbers and take them away*. Then he bent over and scooped up Wang Bo onto his

在后头扶着,咱们赶快送他去医院!王丽从王薄怀里拿过帆布包,看看几捆钱还在,长舒一口气。她把帆布包交给乘警,怯怯地说:"这钱是十六号卧铺那个小伙子的,他吃了安眠药还在睡觉。等他醒来,请你们把钱还给他……还有,别告诉他刚才发生的事,好吗?"

乘警不解:"为什么?"

刀疤脸转脸熊他:"叫你别说你就别说,别问为什么!"说罢背起王薄大步朝站外跑去。

忽然乘警在后头喊:"姑娘,车上还有你的行李呢!"

王丽扭转头,一脸泪水,说:"不需要了。"

1998 年

back, and said to Wang Li, *Help support him from behind, we should get him to the hospital quickly.* Wang Li took the canvas bag from Wang Bo's arms and made sure the bricks of cash were all still there before she let out her breath. She handed the bag to a police officer and said timidly, "This belongs to the fellow in bunk sixteen. He's taken a pill and is still sound asleep. When he wakes up, please return this to him. And... don't tell him about what's just happened."

The railway policeman didn't understand. "Why not?"

Scarface turned fiercely on him. "The lady asked you not to tell him, so don't tell him, and don't ask why!" With Wang Bo on his back, he started striding towards the station exit.

From behind them, the railway policeman called, "Miss, your luggage is still on the train."

Wang Li turned around, her face streaked with tears, and yelled, "Never mind!"

1998

鞋匠与市长

鞋匠在这个巷口补鞋已有四十多年了。刚来时留个小平头，大家叫他小鞋匠，现在满脸皱纹，大家叫他老鞋匠了。

在几十年的时间里，不论春夏秋冬、风霜雨雪，鞋匠几乎没有一天不坐在这个巷口，晚上睡觉前，老鞋匠还在路灯下忙碌。早起晨练或者拿牛奶，出门往巷口看，老鞋匠肯定已坐在那里了，

The Cobbler and the Mayor

Translated by Florence Woo

The cobbler had been repairing shoes here, at the entrance of the alley, for over forty years. When he first arrived, sporting a crew cut, people called him the Little Cobbler. But now that his face was covered with wrinkles, he was known as the Old Cobbler.

Decade after decade, in every season, in wind, frost, rain, or snow, every day the cobbler could be found sitting at the entrance of the alley. Before turning in at night, you could see the old cobbler busy working beneath the streetlamp. And as you looked out the door into the alley when you went out for morning exercise or to pick up the milk, the old cobbler was sure to be sitting there already, as

感觉他头天晚上就没有回去过。

巷子里的人都和老鞋匠熟，家家户户都找他补过鞋。大家上下班经过巷口，总要和老鞋匠打个招呼。一些离退休的老人没事也常来这里坐一会儿，看看街景，打打牌，扯些闲篇，或者骂骂什么人。话题自然很广泛。老鞋匠很少插话。他不是那种健谈的人，只是低了头听。他手里永远在忙着。

忽然起了一阵风，飞起一些树叶。有人猛醒似的问老鞋匠，说鞋匠你找到三口井没有？大家愣了愣，哄地笑了。老鞋匠吃惊地抬起头，意思说你们还记得这件事呀，就有些窘，说我还没顾上去找。那人说都三十多年了，还没顾上，我看你也是扯淡。老鞋匠就低了头缝鞋，呐呐说，我总归要去找的。大家看出老鞋匠有些不高兴了，好像刚才的话伤了他。有人打圆场说，干脆让市长帮你打听打听算了，市长熟人多，见识广，你一个人哪里去找？老鞋匠说这事和市长没关系，这是我自己的事，我总归要去找的。气氛有点僵，这事再说下去就像揭人家短了。大家又哈哈几句，

if he had not gone home at all the previous evening.

Everyone who lived in the alley knew the old cobbler. Every family had had shoes repaired by him. Everyone on their way to work or home would say hello to him. Some retirees, with nothing else to do, would often come by and sit for a while, and watch people come and go, or play cards, or chitchat, or complain about someone or another. Naturally, they covered every topic under the sun. The old cobbler seldom joined in. He was not the talkative type. He would just listen with his head down. His hands were always busy working.

A wind picked up suddenly, blowing some leaves into the air. Someone, apparently reminded of something, asked the old cobbler, "Cobbler, have you found Three Wells yet?" Everyone startled, and broke out in laughter. The old cobbler lifted up his head in a shocked fashion, as if to say, *You still remember that?* Looking a bit embarrassed, he said, "I haven't had the time yet." The other man said, "It's been over thirty years and you never had the time to? I guess you aren't serious about it." At that, the old cobbler lowered his head to keep sewing, and, stammering, replied, "I'll go look for it eventually." The crowd saw that the old cobbler was a bit upset, as if the conversation had hurt him. To smooth things over, another person said, "Why don't you ask the mayor to ask around for you? He knows a lot of people and a lot of things. How would you go about looking for it all by yourself?" The old cobbler said, "This has nothing to do with the mayor. This is my business and I will go look for it eventually." The air became a bit tense, and continuing the subject would amount to ridiculing the old cobbler. The crowd joked

也就讪讪散去。

但没人相信他真的会去找那个叫三口井的鬼地方。老鞋匠说这话都三十多年了,至今还没动身,就说明他只是嘴硬,说过的话不好收回罢了。

其实巷子里的人还是不了解老鞋匠。老鞋匠并没有打消寻找三口井的念头。他只是有些后悔,不该把这件事告诉别人。当初为什么要告诉别人呢?有时候一个秘密只能属于自己,说出去别人也不懂,只会被人嘲笑。这事说起来的确有些荒唐。很多年前的一个黄昏,鞋匠正在低头补鞋,突然刮来一股风,一张小纸片飞旋着飘来,啪地贴在他额头上。后来的事就从这里开始了。当时他眯起眼拿下纸片,正要随手抛掉,却发现小纸片上有几个字,就不经意地看了一眼,"三口井一号"。鞋匠那会儿正好口渴,看到这几个字就笑了,好像那是一桶清凉的水。他犹豫了一下就没有扔,把纸片放到面前的百宝箱里。当时没有多想,收工时差不多都把它忘了。可是第二天上工时又看见了它,也是脑子闲着无聊,就一边修鞋,一边打量那张小纸片。他不知道"三口井一号"是什么意思,想来想去可能是个地名。但这个城市没有叫三口井

a bit more, and dispersed awkwardly one by one.

But no one believed he would really go look for that silly place called Three Wells. The old cobbler had been saying that for over thirty years and he still hadn't set off. That was proof enough that he was just too stubborn to take back what he had said.

In fact, the residents of the alley did not really understand the old cobbler. The old cobbler never stopped thinking about searching for Three Wells. He just regretted somewhat having told others about it. Why did he have to tell other people about it back then? Sometimes, a secret can only belong to oneself: no one else could understand it if you told them, and they would only laugh at you.

The whole thing was admittedly a bit absurd. One evening many years ago, as the cobbler was mending shoes, head down, a breeze suddenly rose up, and a small slip of paper flew twirling towards him. With a *smack* it stuck right against his forehead. That was the beginning of everything. He narrowed his eyes and peeled it off, and just as he was about to toss it away, he noticed a few words on the paper: "No. 1, Three Wells". The cobbler was feeling a bit thirsty right then, and he laughed as he saw those words, as if they were a bucketful of clear and cool water. He paused for a moment. Rather than throwing the paper away, he put it in the toolbox before him instead. He didn't make too much of it at the time, and by closing time he had almost forgotten about it. But the next day, as he got ready for work he saw it again. With nothing else to occupy his mind, he pondered over that slip of paper as he worked on his shoes. He did not know what "No. 1, Three Wells" meant. He thought and thought, and figured that it could be the name of a

的地方，附近郊县也没有，说明这个地方很远。那么三口井在什么地方，是在另一座城市，还是在一座县城或者一个小镇上？为什么叫三口井？是因为历史上那地方有过三口井吗？如果是，三口井现在还有吗？三口井是什么人凿出来的？为什么要凿三口井？还有，什么人写了这张小纸条？是男人还是女人？是写给别人的，还是别人写给自己的？这张小纸条是从哪里飘来的？是从这个城市的某个角落还是一个遥远的地方？这张小纸条是被扔掉的还是不小心丢落的，会不会因为它的失落而耽误什么事情？……总之在后来的日子里，鞋匠没事就琢磨这张小纸片，它激发了他无尽的想象力。他发现这张小小的纸片具有无限想象的空间，就像一个永远不能破解的谜。从此小纸片成了鞋匠生活的一个重要部分，使他原本呆板的生活充满了乐趣。鞋匠常常被自己感动，感动于自己对三口井一个个新奇的猜想。他发现自己除了修补破鞋，还有这等本事。每有一个新的猜想，他都会高兴半天。

小纸片伴随着他在巷口修鞋，伴随着他深夜回家，伴随着他入梦。鞋匠成了一个想象的大师。他越来越相信，"三口井一号"

place. But there was no such place as "Three Wells" in the city, or in the neighbouring counties. So it had to be a faraway place. So, where was Three Wells? Was it in another city? Or was it in a county seat somewhere, or a little town? Why was it called Three Wells? Was it because historically there were three wells there? If that's the case, are the three wells still there? Who dug the wells? Why did they have to dig three of them? Also, who wrote this slip of paper? Was it a man or a woman? Did this person write it for someone else, or did someone else give it to him? Where did this paper come from? Was it from a corner of this city, or from a distant place? Was this paper thrown away, or lost accidentally, and would its loss cause someone inconvenience? ...

In the days after that, the cobbler contemplated on this slip of paper whenever he could. It aroused his boundless imagination. He found that in this tiny little slip of paper was infinite space for imagination, like a riddle without an answer. From then on, the slip of paper became an important part of the cobbler's life, filling his hitherto dull days with delight. He was often fascinated by himself, fascinated by each novel idea he had about Three Wells. He discovered that, besides repairing broken shoes, he had this ability. Every time he came up with a new hypothesis, he would be excited for the rest of the day.

The little slip of paper kept him company when he was repairing shoes at his stall, kept him company when he went home late at night, kept him company as he drifted into his dreams. The cobbler became a master of imagination. He became firmer and firmer of the belief that "No. 1, Three Wells" was bound to him by some fate—

和他是有缘的，不然怎么会随风飘到自己面前呢。这事有点神秘。他想他应当去寻找那个地方，去看看那个地方。鞋匠常听人说起这个城市的许多风景，说起各地的名山大川，可他都没有兴趣。他只对三口井一号这个地方感兴趣，这个地方是属于他的，他必须找到它。这个念头日复一日的强烈。终于有一天，他把自己的秘密告诉了别人。这个奇怪的念头已经搅得他日夜不安，不说出来会非常难受。那天第一次向别人说起这件事时，鞋匠激动得满脸通红，他希望别人分享他的快乐。可他看到的却是惊讶的表情和嘲弄的大笑。他们一致认为鞋匠走火入魔了，一天到晚低头瞎寻思弄出病来了。有人说鞋匠你赶紧去找，那地方说不定有狗头金；有人说那里可能有个骚娘们在等着你。大家把纸条拿过来，嘻嘻哈哈研究，胡乱猜测一番，完全没个正经相。鞋匠窘在那里，他没想到大伙会这样，当时就后悔了。他知道他们并没恶意，可是他们不懂。鞋匠把纸条要回来，说我总归会去的。

这件事说过去就算了，巷子里没谁把它当回事，只是在几十年间，偶尔还会有人提起，也就是开个玩笑，但这并没有影响大

otherwise, why would it have flown to him on the wind? There was so much mystery in this. He thought he should go seek out that place, go have a look at it. The cobbler often heard people talk about the many sights around the city, the famous mountains and rivers all over the country; but he never took interest in any of that. He was only interested in this place called "No. 1, Three Wells". This place was his. He must find it. This thought grew stronger and stronger by the day.

Finally, one day, he revealed his secret to others. This strange idea had been worrying him day and night, and he had to let it out, else it would be unbearable. That day, the first time he brought this up with others, the cobbler's face was flushed with excitement. He had hoped that they would share his happiness. Instead, what he saw were expressions of shock and mocking laughters. They all agreed that the cobbler had gone mad, that he had spent so long in his own thoughts that something had gone wrong with him. Someone said, "Cobbler, hurry and go look for the place. There might be gold nuggets there." Another said, "A sexy lady could be waiting for you there!" They snatched the slip of paper from him, and laughed as they studied it, making random guesses, irreverent and not at all serious. The cobbler stood there, embarrassed. He would never have guessed that they would be like this, and he regretted it. He knew they meant no ill, but they just didn't understand. The cobbler took the slip of paper back, saying, "I'll go eventually."

It would have been well to just let this matter be. None of the alley residents really thought too much about it. Over the decades, someone would still bring it up as a joke every now and then, though

家的关系。鞋匠是个厚道人,巷子里居民把他当成自己人。巷子里姑娘晚上外出归来,远远看到鞋匠,心里就安定了,走近黑黑的巷子也不再害怕。有时居民也向鞋匠讨几枚钉子,借把锤子,老鞋匠从不拒绝。他的修鞋筐是个百宝箱,各种钉子、钳子、剪刀、鞋刀、锤子,什么都有,甚至还有个打气筒。他不修车,但备了一个打气筒,大家可以免费使用。鞋匠有人缘,活儿也干得好,面前永远摆着修不完的鞋子。有等着穿鞋的,坐在小凳子上等一会儿。不等着穿的,拿来丢在鞋摊上,该干啥还干啥去,约个时间再来取。当天修不完的鞋子,鞋匠晚上用小推车推回去,第二天又推回来接着修。大家不急,鞋匠也不急。时光就在这不急不忙中年年流逝,好像谁也没觉得,只看到鞋匠的头发渐渐花白了。

市长也是这里的常客,当然不是为了修鞋子,市长的鞋子几乎都是新的,他不能穿一双破鞋或修过的鞋子接待外宾、出席会议,那会有损于这个城市的形象。市长大多是傍晚的时候来。多半是成功地推辞了一次宴请,悄悄跑到小吃摊上吃一碗馄饨,然

this never affected their friendship. The cobbler was honest and kind, and the residents of the alley took him to be one of their own. If a girl was coming home late at night, she would feel at ease as soon as she spotted the cobbler from a distance, and would not fear walking into the dark alley anymore. Sometimes, a resident would go ask the cobbler for a few nails or to borrow a hammer. The cobbler never refused any request. His tool basket was a treasure trove. It had everything imaginable: all kinds of nails, pliers, scissors, shoemaker's knives, and hammers. There was even a pump. He did not repair bicycles, but he kept a pump for others to use for free. The cobbler was well-liked, and his workmanship was good. There was always a bottomless pile of shoes before him waiting to be repaired. Those who needed their shoes right away would sit and wait for a bit on the little stool; those who didn't would drop them off at the stall, go do whatever they had to do, and make an appointment to come pick them up. The shoes that didn't get repaired during the day the cobbler would put on a small cart and take them home, and bring them back the next day to continue. People were not in a hurry, and the cobbler was not in a hurry. Time passed by imperceptibly, year after year, in this unhurriedness. All they noticed was that the cobbler's hair gradually turned grey.

  The mayor was a regular here too. Obviously he wasn't there to get his shoes repaired. His shoes were almost all new. He couldn't wear a pair of old or patched-up shoes to meet with foreign guests or attend meetings; that would damage the city's image. The mayor mostly visited in the evenings. More often than not, he had just gotten out of a dinner invitation and had slipped off to the snack stall

后到老鞋匠这里坐一会儿。市长似乎更喜欢这种平民的生活方式。开会或者宴请，前呼后拥，官话套话客气话，累人。坐在老鞋匠这里，淹没在黄昏朦胧的街灯里，和老鞋匠聊一些鸡毛蒜皮，是一种享受。但市长时常会走神，有时突然就不说话了，看着街上的人流、车流、对街的楼房或广告牌，久久不语。每逢这种时候，老鞋匠就不打扰他，由他安静地待一会儿。他知道市长心里装着这个城市太多的事情。鞋匠时常觉得这孩子怪可怜的。

市长的家也在这条巷子里。他本来早就可以搬出去的，不知为什么一直没搬，仍然住在他家的几间老房子里。市长对这条巷子肯定是有感情的，因为他从小在这里长大。那时候市长家里很穷，小时候都是穿哥哥们穿过的衣服鞋子。那些鞋子都是经鞋匠修补过的，他记得那上头的每一块补丁，小时候的市长就接着穿。当然，他得为他改一改，市长的脚还太小。先把鞋子拆开，把鞋底割掉一圈，鞋帮也剪去一圈，然后重新缝好。小时候的市长爱踢足球，鞋子烂得很快，要不了几天就露脚指头。鞋匠就不厌其烦地为他修补，而且常常是不要钱的。市长出生不久，父亲就去

to eat a bowl of wontons. And then he would go to the old cobbler's stall and sit for a while. The mayor seemed to prefer this kind of down-to-earth life. Business meetings and dinners were full of fanfare, with a retinue about him speaking bureaucratese and formulaic pleasantries; and they were exhausting. It was a pleasure to be able to sit here at the old cobbler's, immersed in the faint glow of streetlamps, and chat with the old cobbler about inconsequential matters. But the mayor would often zone out and stop talking all of a sudden. He would stare at the foot traffic, car traffic, the buildings across the street, or the billboards, and stay silent for a long time. The old cobbler would not interrupt him, but let him sit for a quiet moment. He knew that the mayor held too many things in his heart about the city. The cobbler often thought to himself: *Poor child*.

The mayor also lived in this alley. He could have moved out long ago, but for some reason he never did. Instead, he stayed in the few old rooms owned by his family. Undeniably the mayor had an attachment to the alley, as he had grown up there. Back then, the mayor's family was very poor; as a child all he had to wear were clothes and shoes his older brothers handed down to him. The old cobbler had repaired each of those shoes. He remembered every patch on them. And the mayor, as a child, would continue to wear them. Of course, the cobbler had to alter them for him, since the mayor's feet were still too small. He had to first take the shoe apart, trim a round off the sole and a round off the upper, and then sew the two together again. The mayor liked to play football as a child, and his shoes wore through very fast. His toes would poke through in a matter of days. Tirelessly the cobbler repaired his shoes

世了，母亲领着三个儿子过日子，家里极其艰难。但那个年轻的寡妇坚持让三个儿子都上学。鞋匠只要看到她拎着一双破鞋子走来，就有些心里发慌。他和她几乎没说过什么话，鞋子就是他们的语言。送来一双破鞋子，取走一双修好的鞋，偶尔碰个眼神，寡妇转身就走。其实她比他还要心慌。那时鞋匠会偷偷从后面看她的背影，她的衣服很旧，但从来都很干净。她的腰很细，这么细的腰却要承担这么重的担子，让鞋匠感叹不已。以后市长上学经过巷口，鞋匠看到他的鞋子破了，就主动喊他过来，脱下鞋子缝几针再让他上学去，并且嘱咐说，以后鞋子破了自己来。小时候的市长，最尊敬的人就是鞋匠，他感到他像父亲；最佩服的人也是鞋匠，不管鞋子烂成什么样，到他手里都会焕然一新。市长时常赤着脚，一手拿着鞋底，一手拎着鞋帮来找他，鞋匠从不推辞，也不批评他。他喜欢这个孩子，这个孩子能把球踢到树梢那么高，巷子里所有孩子都不如他。他为这个孩子骄傲。他觉得他

for him, often for free.

Soon after the mayor was born, his father passed away. His mother had to raise her three sons alone under dire circumstances. But the young widow insisted that all three of her sons go to school. Every time the cobbler saw her walk over with a pair of torn shoes, he would feel a bit distraught. He almost never said anything to her—their only interaction was through shoes. She would bring him a pair of torn shoes and take away repaired ones; maybe her eyes would briefly meet his before she turned around and left. As a matter of fact, she felt more distraught than he did. In those days, the cobbler would secretly watch her from behind as she left. Her clothes were old, but were always immaculately clean. Her waist was very slim. How could such a slim waist carry such a heavy burden?—the cobbler would sigh as he wondered. Some time later, when the mayor passed by the front of the alley on the way to school, if the cobbler saw that his shoes were falling apart, he would call him over, take his shoes off, and put a few stitches in before letting him go off to school. He also told the boy, "In the future, come on your own when your shoes are broken."

When the mayor was little, the cobbler was the man he respected most. He considered him his father. The cobbler was also the man he admired most: no matter how tattered a shoe was, in his hands it would become as good as new. Often, the boy would come to the cobbler, barefoot, carrying the sole of a shoe in one hand and the upper in the other. The cobbler never refused to help, nor did he ever judge him. He liked the boy. This boy was able to kick a ball as high as the top of the tree; none of the other children in the alley

能把球踢到这么高也有他一份功劳，因为市长的鞋子是他特制的。市长的那双破球鞋本来是从哥哥们手里传下来的，鞋匠给重新换了底和帮，底用平板车外胎割制而成，帮用平板车内胎缝制，弹性十足，这么结实的鞋子，市长也就穿个把月，他就一次次给他重换底帮，其实是完全重做，已经面目全非。这双鞋子穿了三年。后来家里条件好一点了，母亲才给他买了一双新球鞋。但那双鞋一直没舍得扔，由母亲为他保存着。后来母亲死了，由他自己保存着。

市长大学毕业后又回到这座城市，从小职员干起，然后是科长、处长、副市长、市长。以前是骑自行车上班，后来坐小汽车。小汽车停在巷口鞋摊不远处，市长从巷子里走出来，一路和人打着招呼，到巷口向老鞋匠点点头，上车去。他和老鞋匠之间的感情几十年都没有变。老鞋匠目送他上班的目光，像看着自己的儿子。老鞋匠为他高兴。自从他当市长，这个城市每年都发生着巨

could do as much. He was proud of the boy. He felt that he deserved some credit for the boy's ability to kick a ball that high, because he had made those shoes especially for him. That tattered pair of running shoes was a hand-me-down from his older brothers. The cobbler had replaced both the soles and the uppers. The soles were cut out of the tire of a flatbed truck, and the uppers were sewn from the truck's inner tube. This made the shoes flexible and resilient. But even such a sturdy pair of shoes would only last a month or so before the cobbler had to replace the soles and the uppers again. In reality, he was making a new pair, as the shoes were already unrecognizable from the original. And thus the mayor was shod for three years. It was only later on when his family had a bit more money that his mother bought him a new pair of running shoes. But he could not bear to throw the old pair of shoes away, and had his mother keep them for him. When his mother passed away, he kept them himself.

After the mayor graduated from university, he returned to his hometown and started his career as a minor clerk. He went on to be section chief, department director, deputy mayor, and then mayor. At the beginning, he went to work on a bicycle, but later on he took a sedan. The sedan would stop not far from the shoe stall at the entrance of the alley. The mayor would walk out from the alley, greeting people along the way, nod at the old cobbler at the entrance of the alley, and board the sedan. The affection between him and the old cobbler remained over the decades. When the old cobbler watched him go to work, it was like watching his own son. The old cobbler was happy for him.

大的变化。马路变宽了，汽车变新了，楼房变高了，空气变好了，城市变绿了，人们的衣着变鲜亮了，人人红光满面，来来往往的人都像遇着了什么喜事。就连他的鞋摊子也发生了变化。以前摆放的都是些破破烂烂的鞋，发出一种混合着脚臭和汗馊的气味。现在看不到那样的鞋了。至多就是哪里裂开了，缝几针就好，再不就是姑娘们来换高跟鞋底。男人们的皮鞋没人打铁掌了，至多打一块皮掌，美观又大方。偶有人送一双破破烂烂的鞋子，老鞋匠居然如获至宝。这才像个修鞋的样子，这才能显示他的手艺。

老鞋匠喜欢破鞋子，越破越好，他的职业就是对付破鞋子。可如今满大街锃亮的皮鞋、美观的休闲鞋，每每让他有些不安，常常让他感到眼前的日子有些不真实。有时候老鞋匠会问市长，不会有啥事吧？市长笑起来，会有啥事啊？老鞋匠看住他，说没事就好，千万别出啥事。市长说你觉得会出啥事？鞋匠放低了声音，人家说眼下当官是个危险的行当。市长说你老放心。鞋匠就很高

Ever since he became mayor, the city saw great changes every year. The roads became wider. The cars became newer. The buildings became taller. The air became cleaner. The city became greener. People's clothes became brighter in colour. Everyone's faces glowed, and every passerby looked as if they had an occasion to celebrate. Even the old cobbler's shoe stall had changed. In the past, the shoes piled before him had been all tattered and torn, emitting an odour of feet mixed with acrid sweat-smell. But now, such shoes were nowhere to be seen. At most, the shoes had a tear somewhere, and could be fixed with a few stitches. Or some girls would come to get the heels of their high-heels replaced. Men no longer came to get metal heel-plates. At most, they came to have a leather sole put on for the elegant and classy look. Once in a while, when someone brought over a pair of tattered shoes, the old cobbler would feel that he had received the most precious treasure. This was what shoe-repair should be about. This was what could showcase his skill. The old cobbler liked tattered shoes; the more they fell apart the better. His profession was to deal with tattered shoes. But now, the streets were filled with shiny leather shoes and smart-looking walking shoes. The sight disturbed him, and often made him feel that these days were not entirely real.

Sometimes the old cobbler would ask the mayor, "Is everything going to be all right?"

The mayor would laugh and say, "Why wouldn't it?"

The old cobbler would gaze at him and say, "Well and good then. Let's hope nothing will happen."

The mayor would say, "What are you thinking could happen?"

兴，说我放心。

当然也有让老鞋匠不高兴的事，隔些日子就会有不相识的人，提着烟酒找到老鞋匠，请他向市长转交一些上告信、申诉书之类的材料。不知道他们怎么打听到这个老鞋匠和市长的关系不同一般。老鞋匠当然不肯收，既不收烟酒也不收材料。他说我和市长没关系。但事后他总会告诉市长，说你哪里肯定不对头，老百姓找到一个鞋匠转交材料算咋回事？市长点点头说我知道了。也不知他采取了什么措施，反正这类事渐渐少了。

其实老鞋匠并不像市长那样关心这个城市的事情，他只关心他的鞋子。面前摆放的鞋子不像以前那么破了，也不像以前那么多了。有时候他甚至会有闲着的时候，这让他有点失落，觉得该歇歇手了。他已经在这个巷口坐了几十年，一个人大半辈子坐在同一个地方，需要极大的定力。大多数时候他都是安心的，安心坐在巷口，安心补鞋。可他自己知道，内心也有不安定的时候。

The cobbler would lower his voice and say, "People say, these days it's a dangerous business to be a government official."

The mayor would say, "Don't worry, sir."

The old cobbler would then cheer up and say, "I won't."

Of course, there were also things that made the old cobbler unhappy. Every now and then, some people he didn't know would come to him, cigarettes and liquor in hand, asking him to relay things like petitions and appeal letters to the mayor. It was unclear how they found out that this cobbler had a special relationship with the mayor. The old cobbler, of course, would refuse everything, taking neither the cigarettes and liquor nor the letters. He would say, "I don't have any connections with the mayor." But he would always tell the mayor afterwards, "There must be something wrong with you. Else why would regular people ask a cobbler to pass letters on to you?" The mayor would nod and say, "All right, I see." He then must have done something, because this kind of incident grew less and less frequent.

The old cobbler did not care about the city as much as the mayor did. He only cared about his shoes. The shoes laid out before him were not as torn as they were before, nor were they as numerous as before. There were even times now when he had nothing to do. This made him a bit dejected, feeling that perhaps he should give it a break. He had already sat at the entrance to this alley for decades. For a man to spend most of his life sitting in one place requires great willpower. Most of the time he was content, content with sitting at the alley entrance, content with repairing shoes.

But he himself knew that there were restless moments in his

每当看到巷子的人进进出出,特别是一些人提着旅行包出差去,老鞋匠总是很羡慕的。他知道他们去过很多地方,他也想出去一趟。他的要求并不高,只想在哪天动身,去寻找那个叫"三口井一号"的地方。只要能找到那个地方,这一生就没有缺憾了。那是积攒了一生的心愿,积攒了一生的思念。随着年岁的增长,那个叫"三口井一号"的地方,就像他的梦中情人,几乎夜夜和他相会。那张小纸片一直被鞋匠藏在箱子里,他不愿意再让人看到,也不想再被人议论。那是他心中的圣土不能被人糟蹋了。在过去的岁月里,他一直珍藏着这个心愿,并没有急着去寻找,是因为他不想过早地看到那个地方,如果过早看到了,就不会再有猜想,那么后半生干什么呢?他要慢慢地充分地去想象它,享受想象的快乐。"三口井一号",这地名实在美妙而神秘,他曾把它想象成一座古镇上的一条古街,古街上有三口古井,古井周围有参天的银杏树,树下常有一些白须飘拂的老人坐在石凳上呷茶谈古,纹枰论道。古井有湿漉漉的井台,幽深的井口,清凉的井水,不时有年轻女子来打水,担着两只桶,桶和她的腰一同闪摇,两只奶子一跳一跳的。他想象那女子是个未嫁的姑娘,或者是个少妇,

heart. Every time he saw people go in and out of the alley, especially when they were carrying bags to go on a business trip, the old cobbler felt envious. He knew they had been to many places. He wanted to travel, too. His expectations were not high: he just wanted to leave, one day, to go seek the place called "No. 1, Three Wells". If he could find this place, he would have no regrets in life. This was the wish he had kept all his life, the yearning he had kept all his life. As the years went by, the place called "No. 1, Three Wells" became like the lover in his dreams, meeting him in a tryst every night. The little slip of paper was kept hidden in the box. He did not want it to be seen again, and he did not want it to be talked over again. It was the holy land in his heart; he must let no one trample on it. Through all these years, he cherished this dream in his heart, but was in no hurry to go on his search. That was because he did not want to see that place too early. If he did, he would have nothing left to imagine about, and what would he do with the rest of his life, then? He wanted to fantasize about it, slowly, fully, enjoying the pleasure of imagination.

"No. 1, Three Wells". A truly beautiful yet mysterious place name. He had once imaged it as an old street in an ancient town. There were three old wells on the old street, and around the old wells were gingko trees that reached the skies. Often, old men with flowing white beards would sit on stone stools under the tree, sipping tea, reminiscing, playing a game of *go*. The wellheads were wet and slippery, the mouths of the well dark and deep, the water cool and fresh. At times, a young woman would come to fetch water, carrying two buckets. The buckets were swaying this way and that, like her

也许是个寡妇。然后，又沿着每一种可能想象下去，比如长相、年龄、性情、住处、家人……"三口井一号"具有无限的可能性，具有无限的想象空间。三十多年了，老鞋匠仍然无法穷尽它，想象如深山密林中的小径，随便踏上一条，就能没完没了地走下去。市长当然也知道他的这个心愿，知道他要去寻找一个叫"三口井一号"的地方，但市长从来没有问过，就像不知道一样。可有时他会对着低头补鞋的老鞋匠久久打量，似乎要破解这个老人。应当说他对这个老人是了解的，从他少年时鞋匠就进入了他的生活，那时他只知道他是个善良的手很巧的鞋匠，是个雕像一样永远坐在巷口的可亲近的人，是个只知低头干活很少说话甚至有些木讷的人。后来他听说了那张小纸片的事，说实话当时他很震惊也很感动。显然他一直没有真正懂得他。一个人要懂得另一个人，不是一件容易的事。

后来市长才真正体会到，其实一个人要真正弄懂自己同样不是一件容易的事。那是他出事以后才慢慢明白的。在副市长、市长的位子上，他曾顶住了几百次行贿。他曾以为他有足够的定力，可以顶住任何诱惑，可以做一个好市长。但在某一天夜晚，他却

hips; her breasts were bouncing up and down. He imagined that the woman was an unmarried girl—or maybe she was a young mother, or maybe a widow. Then, he would imagine along the line of each possibility, such as her looks, her age, her personality, her house, her family... "No. 1, Three Wells" contained infinite possibilities, infinite space for imagination. It's been over thirty years, but the old cobbler still could not exhaust it. His imagination was like forest paths in the hills—go on any one of them, and you can walk down it forever.

The mayor, of course, knew about his dream, that he wanted to seek a place called "No. 1, Three Wells", but he never asked about it, as if he didn't know. But there were times when he would size up the old cobbler, mending shoes with his head down, for a long while, as if he wanted to solve the mystery that was the older man. By any account, he should understand this old man. The cobbler had been part of his life since he was a boy. Back then, he only knew him as a kind, skilled cobbler; an agreeable man who sat, like a statue, always at the front of the alley; a man who only ever buried his head in his work, speaking little, to the point of being taciturn. When he heard about the little slip of paper, he was, in truth, both amazed and moved. Apparently he had never truly understood him. It is not easy for a man to really understand another.

Only later on did the mayor realize that it was no easier for a man to understand himself either. He only came to this realization slowly after he got into trouble. As deputy mayor and then mayor, he had resisted hundreds of bribes. He once believed that he had sufficient self-control to hold out against any temptation, to be a good mayor. But one night, he accepted a hundred thousand *yuan*

接受了不该接受的十万块钱。此前有几次行贿人送来的钱都超过百万，他都顶住了，可这十万块钱却让他栽了跟头。

市长出事了。这个城市几乎所有的人都不相信，市长怎么能出事呢？市长在任期间干了那么多大事，干了那么多好事，怎么突然就出事了呢？区区十万块钱算什么？他们甚至认为市长即使受贿起码也应在百万以上，十万块钱太丢份了。十万块钱毁了一个市长，他们由衷地为他惋惜，然后就愤怒地咒骂那个行贿的家伙，那个家伙成了这个城市的公敌。

老鞋匠差不多是这座城市最后一个知道这件事的人。出乎意料的是，老鞋匠表现得异常平静。他听说后仍然每天补他的鞋，一句话也不说，只埋头补鞋。那几天几夜，他几乎没有休息。面前堆放的那些鞋子，终于让他补完了。那天补完最后一双鞋，交到主人手上，然后他收拾好鞋摊，推着那辆破旧的手推车离开巷口，离开巷口的时候，他往这条巷子注视了好一阵，还伸了个懒腰，好像这一生的活儿终于干完了。

后来这个巷子的人再也没有看到老鞋匠。

that he should not have accepted. Before this, people had come to him with bribes exceeding a million, and he had resisted. But before this mere a hundred thousand, he stumbled.

The mayor got into trouble. Almost everyone in the city was in disbelief. How could the mayor have gotten into trouble? He had done so many great things, so many good things, during his term as mayor. How could he have gotten into trouble all of a sudden? A hundred thousand was nothing! They even believed that, had the mayor accepted a bribe, it should have been over a million; a hundred thousand was beneath him. A hundred thousand *yuan* ruined a mayor. They sincerely felt sorry for him, before starting to curse angrily the lowlife who bribed him. That fellow became the public enemy of the whole city.

The old cobbler was almost the last in the city to find out about this. To everyone's surprise, he was extraordinarily calm about it. After he heard the news, he continued to repair his shoes, day after day, burying himself in his work without saying a word. He barely rested through those days and nights. The pile of shoes before him were finally all repaired. One day, he finished mending the last pair of shoes. He handed them back to their owner, and then he packed up the shoe repair stall and left the entrance of the alley, pushing the old, rickety push-cart before him. As he left, he gazed back towards the alley for a long time, and stretched deeply, as if he had finally finished his life's work.

After that, no one in the alley saw the old cobbler again.

The old cobbler had left the city to seek "No. 1, Three Wells".

He finally went. He had already waited for thirty years. If he

老鞋匠离开这座城市,去寻找"三口井一号"去了。

他到底上路了。他已经等了三十多年,再不上路就走不动了。

他是空身去的,身上只背了个小包袱,里头包了几件替换衣裳。他不打算再补鞋了。他已经干了一辈子。他把手推车推进了垃圾堆,然后一身轻松地离开了这座城市。

老鞋匠没有任何线索,走一处打听一处。

他到过很多大城市,走过很多小县城,去过很多小乡村。鞋匠走了两年多,走了几千里路,终于某一天在一个遥远的偏僻的山凹里,他打听到了"三口井一号"。他知道他会找到的。

三口井是这座山凹小镇的名字。那天他风尘仆仆走进小镇的时候是在黄昏。小镇不大,只有百十户人家,横竖两条街,街面上铺着青石板,街两旁有很多参天的银杏树。他看到了三口井,三口井有湿漉漉的井台,井口有很多凹口,那是打水的绳子几百年勒出的岁月留痕。他看到一些年轻女子来打水,来来去去,桶都是木桶,很粗。女子个个细腰丰胸,走起路来一摇一颠的,很好看。她们打满水,陆续挑往四处去了。小镇上到处炊烟袅袅,

had waited any longer, he might not be able to walk anymore.

He left with nothing but a small bundle on his back, a few changes of clothes wrapped in a piece of cloth. He did not plan to repair shoes anymore. He had already done a lifetime of that. He pushed his push-cart into the garbage pile, and left the city free as a bird.

The old cobbler had no leads to go on. He just asked around as he went.

He passed through many big cities. He walked through many towns. He visited many little villages. The cobbler walked for over two years and covered thousands of miles. Finally, one day, in a remote, hidden hollow surrounded by mountains, he got an answer to his inquiries about "No. 1, Three Wells".

He knew he would find it.

Three Wells was the name of the town in the valley. It was evening that day when he entered the town, travel-worn. The town was not big, home to only a hundred families or so. Two black slate-covered roads ran through it, crossing perpendicularly; on either side of the roads stood many gingko trees reaching to the skies. He saw three wells. The three wellheads were wet and slippery. There were many notches on the mouths of the wells, markings of time etched by ropes dragged up and down to fetch water over hundreds of years. He saw some young women coming to fetch water, walking from every direction. The buckets were all made of wood, thick and solid. The women all had slim waists and ample chests; as they walked they swayed this way and that, and were very pleasant to look at. They filled their buckets and went away one by one. There was smoke coming out of every chimney in the town, and the

一股股饭的清香弥漫在小镇上,到处一派古雅祥和的景象。这样的场景他曾想到过,果然眼见成真,让鞋匠十分欢喜,也十分熟悉。

但当他按门牌找到"三口井一号"时,却让他吃了一惊,原来他发现这里是座监狱,一座很大的监狱。高墙铁网,戒备森严。老鞋匠打了个冷战,以为自己眼花了。可是擦擦眼再看,还是座监狱。没错。监狱坐落在镇子南端,紧靠着大山,大山下还有一座很大的农场。

老鞋匠盯住监狱大门看了很久。他觉得很沮丧,这个结果不在他的想象之中。他什么都想到过,就是没想到会是一座监狱。

现在他知道了自己的想象力还不够,想了三十多年,还是没有想透。后来他回到镇里,找到一家最便宜的客栈,他觉得很累很累。客栈里已住了一些客人,也都风尘仆仆的样子,多是些老人、妇女和孩子。不用问,他们都是来探监的。老鞋匠忽然心有所悟,什么也没说,住下了。一夜无话。

第二天正好是探监的日子。老鞋匠也随着他们去了。进了大门,在值班室做登记。老鞋匠报出市长的名字,他预感到他会在

sweet fragrance of cooked rice filled the air. All he saw around him was quaint and peaceful. This was a scene that he had visited in his mind before. Seeing that it was real, the cobbler was delighted, and he felt a sense of familiarity.

But when he followed the street numbers to "No. 1, Three Wells", he received a shock. It turned out to be a prison, a very large prison. It was surrounded by high walls and wire fencing, and was heavily guarded. The old cobbler shuddered, thinking that his eyes had deceived him. But when he rubbed his eyes and looked again, it was still a prison. There was no doubt about it. The prison was located at the southern end of the town, leaning right against a tall mountain. At the foot of the mountain was also a large farm.

The old cobbler fixed his eyes on the gates of the prison and stared at them for a long time. He was crestfallen. This was not the ending that he had envisioned. He had thought of all possibilities, except for it being a prison.

Now he knew that he had not been imaginative enough. He had thought about this for thirty years, and still he failed to arrive at the right answer. So he returned to the town, and looked for the cheapest inn. He felt immensely drained. There were already some guests in the inn, all looking travel-worn, mostly older people, women, and children. It went without saying that they were here to visit someone in the prison. The old cobbler suddenly thought of something. He said nothing, but took a room. And the night went by.

The next day happened to be visitation day. The old cobbler went along with the crowd. He passed through the gates and went to register at the office. He said the name of the mayor. He had a

这里。不知为什么，自从看到这座监狱，他就预感到这里有玄机。果然值班人查了查，说有这个人，你是他什么人？老鞋匠说是他街坊。那人很和气，说你要见他吗？老鞋匠摇摇头，说麻烦你告诉他，有个老鞋匠在外头等他，一直等到他出来。值班人员目送他走出监狱大门，有些不懂。他不知道这个老人究竟是谁。

老鞋匠回到镇里，仍住那家小客栈。一路走来时，他的心态已经很悠然了。他发现很多家这样的小客栈，小客栈是这座山凹小镇的一大景观，仅半条街就有十七家之多。入住的都是些老人、妇女和孩子。他们都是来探监的。他们走了很远的路，鞋子都走坏了。

他在心里想，看来还得重操旧业。

从此，这个小镇子上有了一个鞋匠。

镇上的人说，三口井早该有个鞋匠了。

三口井常有一些远方来探监的人。

他们都是些老人、妇女和孩子。

他们的鞋子都走坏了。

2001 年

feeling he would be here. For some reason, as soon as he saw this prison, he had a feeling that there was something special about it. Indeed, the clerk looked him up, and said, "Yes, he is here. What is your relationship to him?" The old cobbler said, "I was his neighbour." The clerk asked genially, "Do you want to see him?" The old cobbler shook his head and said, "Please, tell him that there's an old cobbler waiting for him outside, waiting until he comes out." The clerk on duty, puzzled, watched him walk out of the gates. He could not tell who this old man really was.

The old cobbler returned to the town and stayed at the same little inn. As he walked, he felt a load taken off his mind. He discovered many little inns just like his; they were a sight of their own in this little town in the valley. There were no fewer than seventeen of them on just half a block. People staying there were old people, women, and children. They were all here to visit someone in the prison. They had walked a long way, and their shoes were worn through.

He thought to himself, "Looks like I have to pick up the old trade again."

From then on, this town had a cobbler.

The townsfolk said, "We should have had a cobbler long ago."

Three Wells often had people who came from afar to visit prisoners.

They were old people, women, and children.

Their shoes were all worn through.

2001

斩　首

已是仲秋，夜晚有些凉了。路边的草丛里，有虫子在喊："冷啊——冷啊——"

囚车一直往北走。

马队夹着囚车过来的时候，虫子立刻敛声，它们不知道发生了什么事。尽管没有人喊马嘶，扑扑通通的声音还是显得动静很

Decapitation

Translated by Shelly Bryant

It was mid-autumn, and the nights were cool. Insects cried in the grass by the side of the road, "It's cold."

The death cart was heading north.

When the contingent of mounted troops rolled this way, with the death cart between them, the insects immediately stopped crying, uncertain what had happened. Even though the troops did not yell nor the horses neigh, the thumping of the wagons and hooves seemed loud. The sounds were depressing, hasty, and a

大。那声音沉闷、急促，还有些慌张，愈显出夜的深邃和寂静。

匪首马祥坐在囚车里，看不清身体的轮廓，只是黑糊糊一团。其实他披着一件棉袄，却敞着怀。马祥心里很热。

这是一条古驿道，因为年久失修，坑坑洼洼的不好走。囚车每颠一下，那团黑影就滚动一下，东倒西歪的。马祥突然凶恶地叫起来："慢一点，老子要散架啦！"老刘忙从后头赶来，低声吆喝赶车的士兵："扶住车把，稳住！"

囚车一直往北走。

囚车过去后，路边草丛里虫子又喊起来："冷啊——冷啊——"

匪首马祥依然牛气。甚至比被捉住前还牛气。囚车要载他进京，赶秋斩。这是他没想到的。

当了二十多年土匪，天天都想到过死，这没什么好怕的。他设想过各种死法，比如抢劫失手被人打死，仇家跟踪暗杀，被同伙投毒或者背后捅一刀，抓住被绞死，用棍子打死，用石头砸死，按在水里淹死，枪决，刀劈，千刀万剐，油炸火烧，总之不得好

little flustered, emphasizing the depth and silence of the night.

The chief bandit, Ma Xiang, sat in the death cart. The profile of his body could not be seen clearly; he was just a black mass. He was wearing a cotton-padded jacket, but it was unbuttoned. He felt very warm.

This was an ancient post road, and long overdue repairs left potholes, which made traveling it bumpy and arduous. Every time the death cart shook, the dark mass was tossed about. Ma Xiang suddenly yelled fiercely, "Slow down, my bones are pulling apart!"

Liu rushed from the back, and cried out to the soldier driving the cart in low tones, "Hold onto the handlebar and steady the cart!"

The death cart continued rolling toward the north.

After the death cart passed, the insects in the grass by the road started crying again, "It's cold."

The chief bandit, Ma Xiang, was still proud. In fact, he was more arrogant now than before he was caught. The death cart was taking him to Beijing in time for an autumn execution, contrary to Ma Xiang's expectations.

He had been a bandit for more than twenty years and was used to thinking of death every day. It was nothing frightening. He had thought of various ways to die, such as being killed when a robbery went wrong, being followed by an enemy and assassinated, being poisoned or stabbed in the back by his own accomplices, being caught and hanged, beaten to death with a rod, smashed by rocks, drowning as his head was held under water, executed by shooting or by knife, hacked to death, fried in oil, or burned by fire... One way or another, it would be a violent death. He had not thought about

死。但没想过死在什么地方,那好像不是什么问题。既然是太湖土匪,大约也就死在太湖一带,大不了弄到苏州、无锡,规格就不低了。可现在要去的地方是京城,天子脚下,说不定还能进金銮殿,见皇上一面,得个御批。然后押出午门,最不济也要到菜市口。那可是大英雄和大清朝臣砍头的地方。当土匪当到这个份上,不仅可以,而且很可以了。

什么叫正果?这就叫正果。

但马祥也有不满意的地方,就是一路押解他总赶夜路,白天反倒睡觉。这让他不爽。好像这是件见不得人的事。让沿途百姓看看热闹不是很好吗?既显着官家威风,又显着他马祥气派。站在囚车里,脚上有镣,脖子上有枷,背后插一根亡命牌,上有"斩首"二字,面不改色,让大伙见识见识什么叫好汉,起码可以说道几十年。

马祥想不明白。

马祥为此和官兵闹了几天,大骂老刘是个蠢猪。老刘是这一队官兵的头儿,不知是个什么鸟官。可他好脾气,任马祥怎么骂,

where he would die, because it did not seem to matter. Since he was a bandit from Taihu, he thought he would probably die in that area. At the most he would be executed in Suzhou or Wuxi; that would mean he had sort of got people's attention. But now he was going to Beijing, which was the imperial city of the Son of Heaven. He might even be able to enter the throne room and see the emperor and get a royal assent. Then he might be taken out the Meridian Gate of the Forbidden City, at least to Caishikou, the food market, to be executed. In fact, that was the place where all great heroes and courtiers of the Qing Dynasty were beheaded. To be given such a high honor as a bandit was considered pretty good.

What was accomplishment? This was accomplishment.

But Ma Xiang had his disappointment too. They seemed to be always hitting the road at night and sleeping during the day. This upset him. Was this a disgraceful event? It would be good if the common people got to see the death cart along the way. It would make the government look authoritative and Ma Xiang impressive. He would stand in the death cart, with fetters around his ankles and wood shackles around his neck, a death card stuck to his back with the word *Decapitation* written on it. He would put on a straight face, allowing the people to take in the face of a hero and giving them something to talk about for several decades.

Ma Xiang did not understand.

He had quarreled with the officers over that, calling Liu a stupid pig. Liu was the head of this team of officers and men. What sort of an officer was he? But he had a good temper. No matter how Ma Xiang scolded him, he never got angry, and he even waited on

就是不生气，还一路小心伺候，都是他亲自端吃端喝。马祥知道他们不敢把他怎么样，进京赶秋斩，不能拉个死人去。马祥叫骂没用，干脆绝食。这下老刘慌了，苦劝马祥说，兄弟你得吃饭，饿死了我可担不起。还解释说事关重大，你是朝廷钦犯，白天走路怕人劫了，我就是个死罪。我家上有老娘下有妻子什么什么的。马祥就不好说什么了。马祥也是个孝子，可惜老娘上吊死了。

还是出事了。

那夜三更天，马队走到一片野洼，突然发现前头站着一排人，黑暗中一动不动，堵在走道上。

那一刻，老刘的头发都竖起来了。

官兵一阵骚动，都拔出刀枪。碰上劫道的了。他们怕的就是这个，选在夜里走还是没能躲过。马祥是匪首，经营太湖二十多年，盘根错节。他手下有许多人，虽然打死不少，还是有一些逃跑了。看来，他们是救他来了。也许他们已跟踪了几天，根本就没有躲过他们的眼睛。这片野洼前后几十里不见村庄，周围还有些河汊，芦苇很深，选在这地方再合适不过。

匪首马祥也知道是怎么回事了。但他并不吃惊，他知道他们

the condemned man with care, bringing him food and water himself. Ma Xiang knew why they did not ill-treat him; they could not bring a dead man to Beijing for execution. Since his scolding did not bring forth results, he started to starve himself. Panicked, Liu tried to persuade Ma Xiang to eat, telling him how he could not bear the responsibility for Ma's death, adding that this was very important, as he was a criminal pursued by imperial order. If they traveled by day and lost the prisoner in an ambush, he would have to face the death penalty. Liu told him he had an old mother and wife or something at home. When Ma Xiang heard that, he could not argue. He too, was a filial son, but unfortunately, his mother had hanged herself.

Even so, something did happen.

Around the midnight that day, the contingent came to a wild, low-lying area. They suddenly discovered a row of people standing in front, motionless in the dark and blocking their path.

At that moment, Liu's hair stood on end.

There was a disturbance among the officers and men, and guns and knives came out. These men were hijackers. Fearing this, Liu's troop had chosen to travel by night, but they were still unable to avoid it. Ma Xiang was a chief bandit and had been in control of the Taihu area for more than twenty years. He had established a great, tangled network of connections and had many people under him. A great number of them had been killed, but there were still some who had escaped. It looked like his rescuers had arrived. They might have shadowed the caravan for days and nothing escaped their eyes. There were no villages within a dozen miles of the wilderness area,

会来。

老刘一马当先，厉声喝问："你们要干什么？"

黑影中一个说："请你们放人。"

老刘说："大胆！马祥是朝廷钦犯，知道劫囚车是什么罪吗？"

那人说："死罪。"

老刘说："知道死罪，还不快滚？闪开！"

一排黑影不动。

一阵野风刮来。老刘挠挠头皮，回头看看他的士兵，看样子都准备好了，在等他的命令。老刘拔出腰间的刀，寒光一闪。

这时候，匪首马祥在囚车里说话了："兄弟们，你们回去吧，老婆孩子在家等你们呢。"

一阵沉默。

此时旷野的风刮得呜呜咽咽的，像哭泣。

然后，一排黑影墙一样塌了下去。所有马祥的兄弟都冲囚车跪下了。

囚车一直往北走。

两天后，马队到达一个叫左驿的地方。老刘决定在此休整一

and it was surrounded by river branches. There were deep reeds all around, making it an ideal place to carry out something of this sort.

Ma Xiang knew what was going on, so he was not surprised. He had known they would come.

Liu took the lead, shouting harshly, "What do you want?"

Someone in the shadows said, "Please, release him."

Liu said, "How dare you? Ma Xiang is a criminal wanted by the imperial government. Do you know the punishment for hijacking the death cart?"

That person answered, "The death penalty."

Liu said, "If you know that, then get the hell out of here!"

The row of shadows did not budge.

A wild gust of wind blew their way. Liu scratched his head and looked back at the soldiers. They looked ready, waiting for his orders. Liu pulled out the sword from his waist, and a cold light glinted.

At this point, the bandit, Ma Xiang, spoke from the death cart, "My brothers, go home! Your wives and children are waiting for you."

It was silent. Only the wind in the wilderness was whimpering, like someone crying.

Then the row of shadows fell like a wall. Ma Xiang's brothers knelt, facing the death cart.

The death cart continued traveling north.

Two days later, the contingent reached a place called the Left Post. Liu decided to rest for the whole day there. All the way, they had been highly nervous which, coupled with the lack of sleep, left the officers and Ma Xiang exhausted.

天。一路上神经高度紧张，加之睡不好觉，官兵和马祥都很疲惫了。

左驿自古就是皇家驿站，坐落在大运河东岸，故而称为左驿。千百年下来，左驿已由一个单纯的驿站，演变成一座运河重镇。镇上有上万人口，街巷纵横，商家林立，十分繁华。

但古驿站依然保留着使用着，并且是左驿的中心建筑。驿站有三进院，左右两侧还有旁院，院角矗一座钟鼓楼，可以在上头观敌瞭哨。平日，驿站有三十多人的常年驻军，还养几十匹善于奔跑的良马。驿站接待官府信文邮差，也接待过往官员，自然也接待押解粮草、囚犯的官兵。住在这里极为安全。

马祥被关进了地牢。

马祥没想到，这一关就是几个月。

头一天是驿站的士兵给他送饭。这马祥能理解，老刘和押解他的士兵们在休息，暂把他交给驿站管。可是第二天、第三天，一连多天都是由驿站的人给他送饭。马祥就纳闷了，不是说只休整一天吗？怎么不走啦？老刘他们呢？

马祥向驿站送饭的士兵打听，那小家伙神色慌张，连一句话

The Left Post had been a rest stop for imperial messengers since ancient times. It was located on the east coast of the Grand Canal, giving it the name Left Post. Over thousands of years, the Left Post had been transformed from a simple post station into an important canal city. The city had a population of tens of thousands, with streets running freely and businesses standing in great numbers. It was extremely prosperous.

The ancient post station, the central building in the Left Post, was still being used. The post station was a three-section compound, with courtyards on both left and right sides. In the corner of the court stood a bell tower, where one could watch the enemy's moves and send out warnings. On an ordinary day, there were more than thirty base troops stationed at the post station, with over a dozen good horses which could run if necessary. The post station had hosted postmen delivering official mail and, naturally, officers and men who were passing by, escorting supplies and prisoners. It was a very safe place to stay.

Ma Xiang was confined to the dungeon. To his surprise, he was imprisoned there for a few months.

Soldiers at the post station brought Ma his food on the first day. He thought Liu and his men must be resting and had handed him over to the post station temporarily. But on the second and third day, and for the next few days after that, his food was served by soldiers from the post station. Ma Xiang was puzzled. Weren't the officers going to just rest for a day? Why weren't they leaving? Where were Liu and his men?

Ma Xiang tried to find out what was going on from the soldier

也不说。

匪首马祥断定出事了。

可是会出什么事呢？火并！这是他最容易想到的。就是说老刘和他的马队和驻防驿站的士兵发生了冲突，并且吃了大亏，不然老刘怎么不见了呢？可他们都是官家人，有什么理由火并？何况老刘脾气并不暴。

要么，就是老刘把自己移交给驿站，带着他的马队去别的公干了。这倒有可能。据说官府传送文书，也是一站一站移交的，换人换马，奔下一站。如果是这样，那就是老刘和他的马队已经离开左驿。可他们怎么不打个招呼就走了呢。

匪首马祥忽然有点思念他们。老刘人不错，像个邻家大哥。官身不由己，吃这碗饭也不容易。

匪首马祥心情不好起来，感觉失了一个朋友。落到一群陌生人手里，谁知会怎样呢。

隔天，那个小士兵又来送饭。马祥再次打听，究竟地面上出了什么事。问话的时候，匪首马祥甚至和蔼地笑了一下，他怕吓着他。小士兵十七八岁的样子，看上去还是个孩子。但小士兵不

who brought him his food. The fellow looked flustered and would not utter a single word.

Ma Xiang was convinced something had happened.

What could have happened? Factional fighting was the first thing that came to his mind. A conflict might have erupted between Liu's group and the soldiers on garrison duty at the post station. Liu's group must have lost. Otherwise, why would they have disappeared? But they all belonged to the official family, so why would they fight each other? Moreover, Liu was mild-tempered.

It might also be possible that Liu had handed him over to the post station, then led his men away to fulfill another duty. He had heard that when messengers delivered documents, they went from one station to another, changing people and horses to rush to the next station. If that was the case, Liu and his men had already left the Left Post, but why did they not at least say something to him before leaving?

Ma Xiang suddenly missed them a little. Liu was a nice person, almost like a neighborly big brother. An official was not free to do whatever he wanted. It was not an easy livelihood.

Ma Xiang was in a bad mood, feeling like he had lost a friend. He had fallen in the hands of a group of strangers, and now he was not sure what would happen.

The next day, the same soldier brought him his food. Ma Xiang again tried to find out what had happened outside his cell. When he was questioning the soldier, he even put on a friendly smile, not wanting to scare the fellow, who seemed like a kid of about seventeen or eighteen years old. But the young soldier would not

搭理他,连正眼看一眼都不敢,放下饭碗,锁上门转身就跑。马祥听到他沿台阶往上爬的时候,好像还栽了一个跟头。

现在马祥有点明白了,看来这事还是和自己有关,也许是自己的案子有了变化,比如不送京城了,准备就地正法。不然那小士兵不会吓成那样。

这事有点气人。堂堂大清朝,怎么说话不算话呢。说好进京砍头的,半路上就把老子弄死,窝囊。

匪首马祥在地牢里大叫起来:"哎嗨嗨——送我进京!"但叫了半天,没人理他。马祥盯住上头那个巴掌大的小窗口看,连个麻雀也不见。

隔天送饭,果然换了人,是个系着围裙的伙夫,除了一碗饭,还加了一碗豆腐。临死前,给点好吃的,这是惯例,马祥懂。他问伙夫,我哪天砍头?伙夫笑笑,说伙计你急什么?吃吧。明天还是我给你送饭。

总不会吃肥了再砍吧。

匪首马祥没有吃肥,也没有砍头。

后来伙夫又给他送来一床棉被。地牢很小,就像个地窖,不

answer his questions and did not even dare look directly at him. He put down the food, locked the door, and turned on his heels. Ma Xiang even heard the soldier taking a tumble as he climbed the stairs.

Ma Xiang somehow took it to mean that the matter had something to do with himself. Maybe there was a change in his case, and instead of going to the capital, they were carrying out the execution on the spot. Why else would the young soldier be so scared?

That was a little frustrating to Ma Xiang. How could the great, dignified Qing court not keep its word? The plan was to go to Beijing for the execution. How could they kill him when he was halfway there? How depressing!

Ma Xiang started yelling in the dungeon, "Hey — get me to the capital!" He got no response, despite yelling for a long while. He stared at the window, which was the size of his palm, and did not see so much as a sparrow.

The next day, it was a different person who brought him his food, a cook wearing an apron and carrying a bowl of rice and a bowl of tofu. Ma Xiang understood that they were probably feeding him better before his death. This was the usual practice. He asked the cook when his execution date was. The cook smiled and asked him why he was so anxious. He told Ma Xiang to eat and said he would be the one bringing food the next day.

Were they fattening him up before beheading him?

Ma Xiang did not fatten up, nor did he get beheaded.

Later, the cook brought him a quilt. The dungeon was very

算太冷。只是憋闷得厉害。

转眼深秋。地牢上那个巴掌大的小窗口，总泛着阴阴的光。一片落叶，遮住半个窗户。地牢里光线更暗。不时有秋雨淅沥，溅进来凉凉的。

马祥已明白，变故和自己也没有关系。世上肯定发生了什么大事，顾不上他了。看来，秋斩是赶不上了。

匪首马祥便有些惆怅。说不定这座地牢会是自己最后的归宿。他并不怕死，但死在这个地方，实在有些不甘心。哪怕提上去，拉到左驿街头砍头也行呀。

伙夫仍然来送饭，开始是一日两送，后来改成一日一送，再后来两日一送，甚至三日一送。奇怪的是匪首马祥并不觉得饿。他盼他来地牢，只是希望看见一个人，一个活物。

匪首马祥太寂寞了。地牢里几乎分不清白天黑夜，没有尽头的死一样的寂静，让他感到恐惧。马祥一辈子没怕过什么，现在他知道了，人在世上总会有一怕。其实马祥还有一怕，只是过去从不愿承认，就是怕毛毛虫。现在他承认了。

冬天是悄无声息来到的。

small, like a cellar. It was not too cold, but was extremely stuffy.

Soon, it was late autumn. The palm-sized dungeon window constantly glimmered with faint light. A fallen leaf covered half the window, dimming the limited light in the dungeon. Sometimes, there was the patter of autumn rain, cool raindrops splashing through the small opening.

Ma Xiang was now aware that the change had nothing to do with him. There must be big changes in the world, so he was left there unattended to. It looked like they would not make it in time for an autumn execution.

Ma Xiang felt a little disconsolate. This dungeon might be his last home. He was not afraid of dying, but he felt a little unwilling to die in this place. It would be even worse than being dragged up from the dungeon and getting beheaded in the streets of the Left Post.

The cook brought him his food, as usual. At first, it was two meals a day, then it decreased to one meal a day. Later, it fell to one meal every two days, and then all the way to one meal in three days. The strange thing was that Ma Xiang did not feel hungry. He looked forward to the cook's visit, because he just wanted to see another person, something alive.

Ma Xiang was extremely lonely. In the dungeon, he could barely make out day or night. An endless quietness like death terrified him. He had not been afraid of anything in his life, but now he realized that every person living in this world must fear something. Actually, Ma Xiang had another fear that he had never acknowledged. He was afraid of caterpillars. He admitted it now.

那天,他昏昏沉沉蜷缩在被窝里,醒过来时,往小窗口看了一眼,突然发现那上头落了一层薄薄的雪。

匪首马祥这才感觉到冷。他虚弱得厉害,只能偶尔爬起来坐一坐,大部分时间是躺着的。地牢里很潮湿,那条薄薄的棉被湿漉漉的。还有,就是臭。大小便都在里头。以前伙夫还来帮他清理一下,现在已有很多天没有清理了。记忆中,那老家伙好多天没来过了。也许来过,马祥不知道。

落雪的天气让匪首马祥有点高兴,甚至有了一点饥饿的感觉。他微微抬起头,居然发现旁边放了一碗饭。既然没死,就得吃。马祥爬过去,端起饭往口里扒。饭太硬,又是冷的,很难下咽。可他还是坚持吃完了。旁边还有一碗水,他端起来喝了几口,太凉。再说,也得留一点。万一伙夫不再来了呢。

匪首马祥告诉自己,得坚持下去。都坚持几个月了,无论如何得坚持下去。他不知道等待自己的会是什么,坚持下去有什么意义,坚持和等待成了一切。他已经不再猜测上头发生了什么事,反正和自己无关。他只是觉得这件事太操蛋。什么大不了的事,居然比老子杀头还当紧。

Winter arrived quietly. That day, he was curled up sleepily in his quilt. When he awoke, he glanced at the little window and discovered that a thin layer of snow had fallen on its top.

Ma Xiang finally felt cold. He was very weak, and he could only drag himself to a sitting position once in a while. He spent most of his time lying down. It was very damp in the dungeon, and his thin quilt was wet. And there was the stench. He disposed of all his bodily wastes in the small dungeon. At first, the cook helped him clean up the waste, but it had been left uncleared for many days now. In Ma's memory, that old fellow seemed to have disappeared for many days. He might have come, but Ma Xiang was not sure.

The snowy weather made Ma Xiang a little happy, and he even felt some signs of hunger. He lifted his head slightly and discovered a bowl of rice beside him. Since he was still alive, he thought he should eat. He crawled towards the bowl and lifted it, shoving the rice into his mouth. It was too hard and cold, and not easy to swallow. Ma Xiang forced himself to finish the whole bowl. There was also a bowl of water beside him. He drank a few sips. It was too cold. He decided that he should save some water anyway, in case the cook did not return.

Ma Xiang told himself he had to persevere. He had already done so for months now, so he had to go on, no matter what. He had no clue what awaited him and what it might mean to hold on, but persevering and waiting was everything now. He stopped guessing what had happened above ground, since it had nothing to do with him anyway. He just felt the matter was too screwed up. What could be so important that it was even more critical than

匪首马祥胡乱想了一会儿,昏昏沉沉又睡去了。马祥一辈子也没睡过这么多觉。

他梦见自己又上了囚车,还是老刘和他的马队押解。马祥抖擞精神笑了。

囚车一直往北走。

此时,正有一人一骑离开京城,往南星夜驰奔,古驿道上的落雪被踏得梨花四溅。

当初老刘押解囚车到达左驿的当夜,忽然传来一个惊人的消息:革命党人在武昌造反!这事非同小可,老刘决定不再贸然进京,只在原地等候消息。果然又传来新消息,各省纷纷宣布独立。正当大家惊魂未定时,老刘接到命令,让他把匪首马祥交给驿站看押,带上他的马队去山东护送一个官员秘密回京。老刘带上马队匆匆走了。

老刘进京复命后,又奉命和他的马队驻扎在京郊一处驿站,随时候命。一连多日,各种消息不断传来,大厦将倾,人心惶恐。一些马队的士兵偷偷离营走了。老刘没有追究,和剩下的十几个弟兄坚守在驿站。如此过了一个多月,忽然又传来孙中山在南京

beheading him?

Ma Xiang's mind wandered aimlessly for a while, then he drifted to sleep again. He had never slept so much in his life.

He dreamt that he boarded the death cart again, escorted by Liu and his men. He perked up and laughed.

The death cart continued its northward journey.

At that moment, a figure was riding a horse out of the capital, rushing southward into the starry night. The snow on the ground of the ancient post road was splashed in all directions as the horse galloped past.

On the night Liu brought the death cart to the Left Post, shocking news had reached him: *revolutionists were rioting in Wuchang!* This was a serious matter, and Liu decided he was not going to enter the capital without careful consideration. He chose to wait for news at the post station. More news came. The provinces were declaring their independence one after another. Just when everyone was badly shaken, Liu received orders to leave Ma Xiang in the custody of the post station and bring his contingent to Shandong to secretly escort an official back to the capital. Liu left hastily with his men.

After Liu fulfilled his duty in Beijing, he received orders to station himself and his men at a post station in the Beijing suburbs and remain on call. For several consecutive days, all sorts of news flowed in. The situation was getting hopeless, and terror was spreading. Some soldiers in Liu's contingent secretly abandoned the camp. Liu did not pursue the matter, but held his ground with the remaining dozen or so officers and men at the post station. More

就任临时大总统的消息。又过一个多月，皇上宣布退位。至此，老刘才彻底死了心，当即解散马队弟兄，一个人连夜奔左驿来了。

这些日子，他其实一直惦着匪首马祥。

大清国灭亡，老刘悲喜交集。皇上退位那天夜里，他和弟兄们面向京城磕了三个头，大哭一场，然后才各奔东西。这一路来，老刘还在不断流泪。但马祥逃过一死，又让他高兴。他和马祥并无交情，可他觉得和马祥是一段奇缘，既然天意不让他死，自己就应当去救他。只是一路都在担心，马祥有没有福气熬到这一天。也许他在地牢里早已死了。天下大乱，驿站的人肯定早就跑光了，谁还顾得上他。

老刘到达左驿，坐下那匹红鬃马居然倒地死了。他知道它是累死的。

驿站果然人去房空，只剩下一个老伙夫在睡大觉。老伙夫是当地人，留下看房院，却不知道该怎样处理匪首马祥。他不敢放他，更不敢也无权杀他，就慢慢消磨时日吧。也许他活不了几天了。

老刘一把揪起伙夫，厉声问道："马祥还活着吗？"

than a month went by, and the sudden news of Sun Yat-sen being established as the interim president in Nanjing arrived. Another month or so went by, and the emperor announced his abdication. Thus, Liu gave up completely and disbanded the contingent of officers and men, then rushed to the Left Post alone.

In fact, he had been thinking about Ma Xiang all this time.

The destruction of the great Qing Dynasty brought Liu mixed feelings. The night of the emperor's abdication, he and his men kowtowed towards the capital three times, cried to their hearts' content, then parted ways. Liu wept the whole way, but Ma Xiang had escaped death, and that brought him joy. He was not friends with Ma Xiang, but he felt he was bound to the latter by a strange fate. Since providence had saved Ma from death, Liu felt obliged to go rescue him. He worried all the way there, because he was not sure if Ma Xiang had survived this long. He might have died in the dungeon long ago. There was great disorder in the world, and all the people at the post station must have already escaped. Who would care about Ma?

When Liu reached the Left Post, the chestnut horse he was riding fell over, dead. He knew it had been worked to death.

The post station was abandoned, except for an old cook snoring in his sleep. The cook was a local who had been left to look after the place, but he did not know what to do with the bandit, Ma Xiang. He did not dare to release or kill him, and he had no authority to kill him anyway, so he decided to let him be. He thought Ma Xiang might not last much longer.

Liu seized the cook and asked him harshly, "Is Ma Xiang still

老伙夫眨巴眨巴眼，认出老刘，说你是说那个匪首？忙掏出钥匙，说你自己……去看吧。

老刘伸手抓过钥匙，直奔地牢。

老伙夫随后收拾点东西，匆匆离开了驿站。他真的不知道那个匪首是活着还是死了。他非常害怕，还是一走了之。

老刘打开地牢的门，一股恶臭立刻扑鼻而来。他顾不上这些，冲黑暗中大喊："马祥！马祥！"没人应声。

老刘心头一沉，估计有些不妙。忙摸索着寻找，渐渐看到墙角躺着一团黑影，抢过去就摸，却摸到一只手，有些温乎乎软绵绵的。还活着！老刘心头一喜，这小子总算没让我白跑一趟，立刻又喊又摇："马祥！马祥！……"

马祥终于被他摇醒了。

他听到有人在叫他，声音有些遥远，还有些熟悉。他慢慢睁开眼，看到一个人影正俯在面前，却看不清脸。

老刘兴奋地大叫："马祥！兄弟！你还活着呀！"

马祥终于听清楚了，是老刘！他有点不相信自己的耳朵，嗫嚅道："你……真是老刘！"

老刘说："马祥是我！你还活着太好了，我还以为你死了

alive?"

The old cook blinked a few times, then finally recognized Liu. "You mean the bandit?" He quickly fished out the key and said, "Go look... for yourself!"

Liu snatched the key and rushed to the dungeon.

Meanwhile, the old cook packed his belongings and left the post station in a hurry. He really did not know if the bandit was alive or dead. Terrified, he decided to flee.

Liu opened the door to the dungeon and his nose was assaulted by a nauseating stench. He had no time to think about that, but shouted into the darkness, "Ma Xiang! Ma Xiang!"

There was no answer.

Liu's heart dropped. He thought things were not well. He fumbled around and slowly made out a dark mass lying in the corner near the wall. He rushed over and reached out his hands to grasp him. He found a hand, which felt warm and soft. He was still alive! Liu felt sudden joy. This fellow would not let his trip be a futile one. He started shouting and shaking, "Ma Xiang! Ma Xiang!"

Ma Xiang was finally jerked out of sleep.

He heard someone calling his name, but the sound seemed faraway, and a little familiar. He slowly opened his eyes and saw the shadow of a person kneeling over him. He could not make out the face.

Liu yelled excitedly, "Ma Xiang! Brother, you're still alive!"

Ma Xiang finally heard everything clearly. It was Liu! He could not believe his ears. He stammered, "You're... really Liu?"

Liu said, "Yes, it's me. It's so good you're still alive. I

呢！"说着把马祥拦腰抱起，马祥张手也抱住了老刘，两个人都呜呜地哭起来。马祥说老刘哥……你去了哪里，咱们……不是说好……只休整一天的吗，这会儿啥都误了……赶不上秋斩了……老刘说傻兄弟咱们不去京城了，没人砍你的头了，大清朝完蛋了皇上宣布退位了。匪首马祥大吃一惊松开手说老刘哥你可不能瞎说，大清朝……怎么完蛋了呢皇上怎么会退位你说这话也要杀头的。老刘说马祥兄弟，我不是瞎说，皇上真的退位了……现在是民国了！

马祥目瞪口呆坐在那里，居然没觉得欣喜。原先他还在心里抱怨，世上出了什么鸟事，会比砍头更重要。现在看来，这事比砍头重要多了，江山易手，改朝换代，简直是天大的事啊！

匪首马祥被老刘背出地牢，在驿站精心调养了一个多月，才逐渐恢复。这期间，都是老刘在照顾他。老刘居然会烧菜，会熬汤。

终于该分手了。老刘问马祥："你准备去哪里？"

马祥其实已想了多天，他说："我准备留在左驿。家里没人了，不想再回太湖。回去了那帮弟兄还会找我。"

老刘有点意外。以他的身份，在左驿能混得下去吗？可他

thought you were dead!" As he said this, he threw his arms around Ma Xiang. The latter returned Liu's embrace, and the two men sobbed uncontrollably. "Liu... where did you go? Didn't we agree... to just rest for one day? Everything has been delayed... we can't make it to an autumn execution..."

Liu answered, "Don't be silly! We're not going to Beijing. Nobody is going to behead you. The great Qing Dynasty has fallen, and the emperor has given up the throne."

Ma Xiang released him in shock. "Liu, don't talk nonsense! How can the great Qing Dynasty collapse? How can the emperor abdicate? Talking such nonsense will also cost you your head!"

Liu said, "I'm not kidding. The emperor has really abdicated. It's the Republic of China now."

Ma Xiang sat dumbstruck and speechless, but he did not feel joy. He had just been complaining to himself a little earlier, *What the hell in the world could be more important than an execution?* Now he realized that this event really was more important than an execution. The country was changing hands, and the old dynasty was replaced with a new one. This was an incredible event!

Liu carried the bandit out of the dungeon on his back. Ma stayed at the post station for more than a month, building up his health and slowly recovering. During this time, Liu took care of him. The old soldier actually knew how to cook and make soup.

Soon, it was time for them to part. Liu asked Ma Xiang, "Where do you want to go?"

Ma had actually been thinking about this for days. He said, "I plan to stay in the Left Post. I don't have any family, and I don't

没说。

马祥问老刘:"你呢?"

老刘苦笑了一下:"回家。我家在天津,还有一大家人呢。来左驿的时候经过天津,没顾上回家打个招呼,这些日子他们肯定急坏了。"

匪首马祥眼睛湿润了,说老刘哥,你其实不适合当兵。

老刘哈哈大笑起来,说马祥你错了,我其实是个职业军人,当了半辈子兵了。

马祥说老刘哥你以后还会当兵吗?

老刘摇摇头,忽然眼角闪出一点泪光。

当天,两人洒泪告别。

马祥果然在左驿定居下来。

他在运河边搭了一个草棚,开垦荒地。一个人干。刚开始,他不怎么会干。但他坚持下来,很快开出一大片荒地。

左驿没人去招惹他。大家很快就知道了他的身份。

后来,马祥娶了一个逃荒的女人做老婆。以前他曾有过很多女人,但他一直没有娶过老婆。那时他觉得像他这样的人不应当娶老婆。这个逃荒的女人很争气,一连给他生了七八个孩子。

feel like going back to Taihu. I'm afraid my gang of brothers will look me up."

Liu was a little surprised. Given Ma Xiang's identity, would he be able to survive in the Left Post? But he kept silent.

Ma Xiang asked Liu, "What about you?"

Liu smiled sadly, "I'll go home. I live in Tianjin, and I have a big family. On my way to the Left Post, I passed Tianjin, but I had no time to greet my family. They must be waiting anxiously for me now."

Ma Xiang started tearing up as he said, "Actually, being a soldier doesn't suit you."

Liu broke into laughter. He said, "Ma Xiang, you're wrong. I'm a professional soldier, and I have been one for half my life."

Ma Xiang asked if Liu would continue to be a soldier. Liu shook his head, and a tear flashed at the corner of his eye.

That day, they wept as they parted.

Ma Xiang did in fact settle down at the Left Post. He built a straw shack on the side of the canal and developed the waste land with his own hands. At first, he did not know what he was doing, but he persevered, and very quickly, he had cultivated a big patch of land.

Nobody bothered him at the Left Post, for they had early on learned about his identity. Later, he married a woman who had fled from the famine. He had had a lot of women in the past, but had never taken a wife. He had not thought he was fit to marry back then. This woman did not let him down, blessing him with seven or eight children.

再后来，马祥在镇里驿站旁边买下宅基，盖了院房阁楼，马家成了左驿一个大家族。

匪首马祥终于老得不能动了。他时常坐在阁楼上泡一壶茶，慢慢喝，久久看着驿站那片青砖灰瓦的三进院落。

驿站很破旧了，屋脊上长了很多茅草，有麻雀在上头寻草籽吃，小脑袋一动一动的。

外一篇

公元二〇〇一年，左驿有个叫小鱼的惯偷被判了死刑。小鱼并没有人命，但因为偷盗曾六次进宫，屡教不改，才判了极刑。

宣判后小鱼没有上诉，却提出愿意捐献文物，希望能够减刑。按照他的要求和指点，法官从他家阁楼夹墙里取出一只木箱子，打开看里头有三样东西：脚镣，木枷和亡命牌，亡命牌上有"斩首"二字。小鱼说这是他曾祖父留下来的，小鱼说曾祖父还传下话说，咱们家欠上天一个命债，这东西早晚还用得着。法官哭笑

Much later, Ma Xiang bought a homestead beside the post station in town and built a house. The Ma family established itself as a big family in the Left Post.

The chief bandit finally grew so old he could not move. He usually sat in the loft drinking his tea slowly, gazing at the three-section compound built with black bricks and grey tiles at the post station.

The post station had become dilapidated, and its ridges were covered with thatched grass. Sparrows searched for grass seeds on top of the buildings, twitching their little heads this way and that way.

Another Story

In 2001 A.D., there was a habitual thief called Xiao Yu who was given the death sentence at the Left Post. He did not commit murder, but he was put in prison six times for theft, and was thus finally given the death penalty for being incorrigible.

After the sentence was passed, Xiao Yu did not appeal, but said he was willing to donate some cultural relics in hopes of reducing his sentence. According to his demands and instructions, the judge retrieved a wooden box from the wall in the loft at his house. When the wooden box was opened, there were fetters, wooden shackles, and a death card with the word *Decapitation* written on it. Xiao Yu said that these were left behind by his great grandfather. His great grandfather had left word that their family owed Providence a life debt and that these things would come to good use one day. The judge did not know whether to laugh or cry. He

不得，说你指望用这个减刑吗？小鱼笑了，小鱼说无所谓，我也就是说说，主要是想叫你们把东西取走。取走这些东西马家后人就清净了。几辈人了，我家老听到半夜里脚镣响。

法官听得毛骨悚然，训斥他说你胡说什么！但还是请来文物专家鉴定。文物专家摸摸看看，说这是晚清的刑具，有一点价值，但文物价值不大。

小鱼还是被枪毙了。

2004 年

asked, "You're hoping for a lighter sentence with these?"

Xiao Yu laughed and said, "It doesn't matter. I'm only offering this casually. The main idea is for you all to take these things away. Once we've gotten rid of them, the descendants of the Ma family will have peace. For generations, we've been hearing the sound of shackles in the middle of the night."

The judge was absolutely terrified after hearing that and reprimanded him, "What nonsense are you babbling about?"

In the end, the judge still asked a cultural relic expert to appraise the things. The expert touched and examined them, then concluded that they were instruments of torture used during the late Qing Dynasty and had some value, but not much, in terms of cultural relics.

Xiao Yu was executed before the firing squad.

2004

临 界

跑啥呢?

街坊都这么说,不是你干的你怕什么?不跑啥事没有,一跑就可疑了,不抓你抓谁?

有人当面问四毛,四毛你傻不傻,你打人了吗?

四毛说,没打,我和人家无冤无仇的,我真的没打,是别人

On The Verge

Translated by Shelly Bryant

"Why did you run away?"

The neighbors all said, "Nothing would have happened if you didn't take flight. It looked quite suspicious, you running away. Who else would they go after?"

Someone asked Simao to his face, "Are you nuts? Did you fight with someone?"

Simao said, "No, I didn't, honestly. I had nothing to do with them. It wasn't me. I didn't know them at all."

打架，我不认识他们。

没打你跑啥？

我怕溅身上血。

或者问，四毛你偷人家啦？

四毛说，我没偷，真的没偷！

没偷你跑啥？

四毛说我害怕。

街坊说，东西不是你偷的，你怕啥？

四毛说，我怕说不清。

处长说，什么说不清？就是你偷的！只是没抓到证据罢了。

一日，四毛从拘留所出来，街坊围上去打听，说四毛，听说你摸人家女人屁股？

四毛红了脸分辩说，不是我，我是那样人吗？

处长说不是你是谁？看你就像个流氓！

四毛说肯定不是我，我看到前头一个人摸的，是个五十多岁的老头。用左手，左撇子。人多拥挤，女人转身时，他已经溜了，可巧我走到那女人后头，女人转头看见我，我怕误解，转身就跑，

"Then why on earth did you run away?"

"I was afraid of the blood."

Or when asked, "Did you steal from someone?"

Simao would reply, "No, I didn't. Really, I didn't."

"Then why on earth did you run away?"

"I was afraid."

The neighbors asked, "What were you afraid of if you didn't steal?"

"I was afraid I couldn't explain it."

The division head at the detention centre said, "You can't explain it? Then it must have been you. It's just that we haven't got enough evidence yet."

One day when Simao was released from the detention centre, the neighbors gathered around him, asking, "Is it true that you touched a woman's ass?"

Flushing, he protested, "I told them it wasn't me. Do I look like someone who'd do that?"

The division head said, "Who else could it be? You look like a rogue."

Simao said, "Definitely not me. I saw a man over 50 do it, with his left hand. He's a lefty. It was crowded and when the woman turned around, he slipped away. Unluckily I was right behind her and afraid she'd mistaken me for the man, so I turned and ran. I only got a few steps away before I was caught."

The division head said, with obvious contempt on her face, "Who'd believe that?"

刚跑十几步就被警察逮到了。

处长说谁信？处长说这话时，一脸鄙视，然后转身走了。她嫌四毛一嘴臭豆腐味。

四毛冲处长喊：真不是我，处长，你得相信我！我摸那干啥？

处长离他几步远又转回头，不是你为啥让你蹲拘留所？

四毛说，那女人冤枉我，不信你问张警官。我这不是放出来啦？

处长说，那是张警官包庇你！

邻居们围着议论，将信将疑。按说四毛没这个胆，他不是那种胆大妄为的人，只是太好奇。大街上发生什么事，比如打架、偷窃、撞车、耍流氓，这么说吧，凡是出了事有人围观，四毛必定凑上去看一看，发现真的出事了，立刻撒腿就跑，一边跑一边回头看，一副惊慌失措的样子。就凭他这么一点胆子，应该不会摸人家屁股。但谁知道呢，这家伙四十多岁了，至今仍是单身，熬不住了呢？

四毛曾和一个打工的农村女人同居过一段时间。后来那女人把两个孩子也从老家接来了，接来就接来吧，四毛有父母留下的

Then she turned and left, frowning at Simao's breath, which smelled of stinky tofu.

Simao cried out, "Hey, it's really not me! You've got to believe me! Why would I touch her there?"

The division head, a few steps away from him, turned around and said, "Why were you detained if it was not you?"

Simao protested, "The woman wrongly accused me. You can ask Officer Zhang if you don't believe me. You see, I'm out now, right?"

She replied, "That's because Officer Zhang always shows you favor."

The neighbors all gossiped about it, not quite convinced, saying that Simao was not the type who'd be bold enough to do such a thing, that he was merely curious. Whenever there was a crowd on the street watching whatever occurred—say, a fight, a theft, a car crash, some sexual harassment—Simao would surely go to have a look, then immediately run away when things went awry. He'd keep looking back while running away, all in a panic. Timid as he was, he wouldn't be bold enough to touch a woman's ass. But then, who could tell? What if he couldn't contain himself? After all, he was a single man over forty.

Simao once lived with a country woman who came to the city to work. Later, she brought two kids from her hometown. He was fine with that. He had plenty of room for them all, since his parents had left him with an old three-room flat. Actually, he was quite pleased to get a woman along with two kids—a really good bargain—

三间老瓦房，反正也住得下。四毛很高兴，讨个女人带俩孩子，这便宜大了。就托片警张磊帮忙，把两个孩子从农村转来上学。当时张磊不想接招的。他警告四毛说，这事不靠谱，你们不是合法夫妻，同居就同居了，这种事民不告官不究的，我也理解你一个人不容易。可增加两个孩子，又是吃饭，又是上学，你又没个正经收入，拿什么养活他们？你得想清楚了。四毛就求他，说张警官，咱们是从小的同学，这个忙你一定得帮，你知道我找个女人不容易，不帮孩子，女人肯定待不住。张磊说这女人到底怎么回事？在老家有丈夫吗？四毛说他们离婚了，她拿离婚证给我看的。以前的丈夫是个恶人，横行霸道，还打老婆，一打就打个半死，头发薅得快成斑秃了，头皮上都是血疤。张磊看他说得可怜，加上两个孩子上学不能耽误，就出面帮助联系了借读。但张磊对他说，四毛你往后得正经干些事了，有了女人又有了孩子，不能老干那些偷偷摸摸的事，丢人现眼还犯法。四毛很想说我从没干偷偷摸摸的事，你抓过我无数次，哪一次坐实过？可他咂咂嘴没有分辩，他在求他办事，不能惹他生气。

so he asked the community police officer Zhang Lei to help transfer the two kids from the rural area to the city for schooling. At the time, Zhang Lei was quite reluctant to help out, warning Simao, "This sounds absurd. You're not legally married to this woman. It's OK that you live together as long as no one sues you. I understand that it's not easy to live life alone, but without a regular income, how can you manage to feed two extra mouths, plus their schooling fees? You need to think straight."

Simao begged him, saying, "Officer Zhang, you have to help me this time. We were classmates since we were children. It's not easy for me to get a woman, and she won't stay if I don't help with her kids."

When questioned about the woman and whether she had someone at home, Simao said, "She's divorced. She showed me the certificate. Her ex-husband was a hooligan, impulsive, and often beating her half to death. You can see the scars on her head where her hair was pulled out in the fight."

Zhang Lei pitied him then, and agreed that the two kids needed schooling, so he helped put them into a local school. Then Zhang warned Simao, "Now with a woman and two kids living with you, you need to stop these offenses. It's shameful and illegal."

Simao would have liked to say that he'd never done anything like that, and that there was never any evidence of him doing so, though he'd been detained dozens of times. But he simply licked his lip without protesting, afraid of irritating Zhang while asking him for a favor.

四毛和张磊是小学同学，可他从来不喊他名字，都是称呼张警官。他一直怕他，从小就怕。张磊当了警察更怕。准确地说，所有的警察四毛都怕，看见警察就出虚汗，看见警察转脸就跑，完全不由自主，两条腿根本不听招呼，就是猛跑。就因为这样，四毛老是被当成嫌疑犯，不知被抓了多少次。其中张磊抓他最多。张磊并没有因为四毛是同学就不抓，该抓时坚决抓。但让张磊恼火的是，这么多年，抓四毛无数次，居然没有一件事能够坐实。有些事能弄清，比如抓到了真正的小偷，或弄清打架的是一伙小流氓，和他没什么关系，也就放了。可有些事你永远都搞不清，人家东西真少了，真正的小偷又没有抓到，抓到可疑人四毛，可四毛矢口否认，身上又没有赃物，折腾几天，只好疑罪从无，放了完事，但又没法真正排除怀疑。比如摸人家屁股，女人咬定是他，可女人并没有看到，也没有证人。但没有证据并不一定不是他，伸手缩手之间，一秒钟的工夫，没人看到也很正常。总之，四毛牵扯的都是些似是而非、没头没脑的案子，终于一件事也落

Simao and Zhang Lei had been classmates in primary school, but Simao always addressed Zhang as Officer Zhang. He had been afraid of Zhang since childhood, and more so after Zhang Lei joined the police. Actually, Simao was afraid of all police officers. He'd sweat at the sight of an officer and immediately run away for no reason at all, just dashing off as if his legs were not under his command. Because of this, he had always been taken as a suspect and was picked up numerous times, mostly by Officer Zhang.

Zhang didn't have a soft spot for Simao for the sake of old times. In fact, what annoyed Zhang most was that, over the years, he had no hard evidence whatsoever against Simao. In some cases, Simao was released because the real offenders were caught, clearing him as a suspect. In other cases, he had to be set free after a couple of days because there was insufficient evidence. For instance, when something got stolen and the real pickpocket was on the run, Simao became the suspect, but he denied everything and nothing could ever be found on him. After days of futile inquiry, he had to be set free, presumed innocent but not really cleared of suspicion. Or perhaps a woman was sure that he had touched her ass, but she didn't see it with her own eyes, and there was no witness either. The thing was, the lack of evidence did not entirely acquit Simao of the accusation. It was quite normal that no one saw exactly what happened, since it usually happened in a matter of seconds. Anyway, Simao tended to be involved in such minor offenses, but nothing could ever be confirmed, so Zhang Lei was furious each time he released Simao, blaming him for making trouble. Simao always ended up

实不下来。所以每次放他，张磊都一肚子火气，说四毛你不是添乱吗？弄得四毛直向他道歉，说张警官你看，又让你白抓了，对不起对不起。张磊心里窝囊不说，所里所外都有人怀疑他包庇四毛。每次四毛弓着腰快步蹿出派出所，张磊都想冲上去踹他一脚。

其实四毛比张磊更窝囊，一次次无端被抓，虽然最后都放了，但并没有彻底洗刷罪名，很多次都是让他回家等候调查。就是说，四毛虽然是自由的，却是个背负着许多悬案的人。更为麻烦的是，这类悬案还在不断发生。比如有人在街上被自行车撞了，肇事者却跑了，恰好四毛骑车经过，忙上前扶起老人，老人却说是他撞的。这种事太普通了，媒体经常报道，四毛就摊上好几次，叫警察来也说不清，围观者也说是他撞的，不然你扶他干什么？不是心虚吗？老人要住院，要索赔，四毛叫天天不应，只好自认倒霉。或三百五百，或一千两千，最多的一次赔了一万。四毛没什么钱，平时就是靠打些零工，早晚捡些垃圾卖点钱。那次赔一万，可把他难坏了。同居女人让他不要赔，说不是你撞的，干吗要赔？四

apologizing, "Sorry, sorry, Officer Zhang. Your efforts are wasted again."

Quite humiliated and suspected of shielding Simao on top of it, Zhang Lei felt like kicking Simao's ass as he scurried out of the detention centre, back hunched.

Actually, Simao was even more humiliated that he had never been cleansed of those accusations, even though he was repeatedly set free after being detained for no reason. Most of the time, he was told to wait at home for further inquiry. In other words, he was free, but remained a prime suspect in numerous open investigations. To make matters worse, similar cases kept popping up. In a bicycle hit-and-run case, Simao happened to ride by and stopped to help the elderly victim, only to be accused of the offense by the old man. Things like this were frequently reported on the news. Simao was involved in a couple of such cases and failed to explain himself in the presence of the police, while the onlookers blamed him, asking why he came to help if he had a clear conscience. Simao had to yield to his bad luck, paying the victims' claims or medical costs, from 300 or 500 *yuan* to 1,000 or 2,000 *yuan*, with the highest being 10,000 *yuan*. Simao was stuck, especially on that occasion when he was demanded a compensation of 10,000 *yuan*, since he didn't have much money and lived on odd jobs or picking up junk for resale. The woman living with him asked him not to give the victim any money, wondering why he felt he had to do so, if he was not the one who knocked the old woman down. Simao replied, "What could I do, since the old woman was so sure I was the offender?"

毛说不是说不清吗？那老太太咬定是我撞的，有什么办法？女人说你这人怎么这样，叫你赔你就赔啊？不赔！看他们能把你怎样？四毛说不赔不行，她两个儿子很厉害的，再说老太太也可怜，听说骨头都撞断了，看样子很疼的。女人就跺脚，说你这人！你拿啥赔人家呀？四毛也正为难，说真是的，拿啥赔呢？四毛在屋里转了几圈，说把电视机卖了吧，两个孩子立刻冲上来护住，说卖了电视机俺们看啥呀？就哭了。四毛只好松手，再说这破电视看了多年，经常要拍几下才出图像，卖也只能当废品卖，几十块钱的事，不解决问题。四毛站在房子中央，四处寻看，实在没什么值钱的东西，又到院子里回头打量这三间老瓦房。女人忙跟出来，心里直发毛，她担心四毛把房子卖了，卖了房子就无处落脚了。她愿意和四毛同居，主要是看中他有三间瓦房，人也实在，如果没有了房子，人实在管个屁用！还好，四毛打量半天，没说卖房子，说把门窗卖了吧。女人这才注意到，这座房子的门窗有些特别，全是雕刻花鸟什么的，只是很破旧了，说这能值钱吗？四毛

She said, "Nonsense! How come you just did as you were told?"

Asked what the old woman would do to him if he refused to give the money, Simao replied that her two sons were quite tough, and she had broken bones and looked miserable. His woman was mad, saying "nuts" and asking him what he could use for compensation. Simao was worried too, asking himself, "Indeed, how can I pay it?"

He paced up and down in the room, and finally settled his eyes on the dilapidated TV set, saying, "Let's sell it off."

The two kids rushed forward, clenching the set, whining that they would have nothing to watch if it were sold. Simao had to let it go, saying that the TV set would sell for next to nothing, since it was too old to show proper pictures without him giving the set a few knocks. He then added, "Anyway, it just won't do with such a small sum of money."

He stood in the middle of the room, looking around, but couldn't find anything valuable. Then, he stepped out of the room, taking a close look at each of his three rooms. His woman hurried out with him, fearing that he would sell the flat, leaving her and her kids homeless. She agreed to live with him in the first place mainly because he had a flat with three rooms, and besides, he was a kind man. But if the flat were gone, what the hell use was it that he was kind?

Fortunately, Simao looked for a while, then suggested selling the doors and windows of the rooms. It was then that she noticed

冲她点点头，很骄傲地笑了，说值钱呢。原来，这三间老瓦房原是一座大院的一部分，解放前属于一个资本家的，解放初给他分了。四毛的爹娘分得这三间房。院子的其他房屋分给了好多户，这几十年都陆续拆了、毁了。上世纪八十年代，又在原地建了两座五层高的楼房。现在独有四毛的三间老瓦房还存着，夹在两座楼房之间。所以四毛没有秘密，有什么事，邻居们从楼上都看得一清二楚。

四毛的三间瓦房高大敞亮，门窗都是金丝楠木做的，上有很多精致的雕刻。前几年一个文物贩子发现了，要四毛把门窗卖给他。四毛没答应，说好好的门窗拆了卖掉，这座房子就残了，我不能卖。文物贩子死缠烂打，价钱出到两万，说还可以另外给你买一套新门窗安上。四毛犹豫了一下，还是没舍得卖。事后听说，这套门窗可以卖到五万。现在急等用钱，四毛顾不得了，找到那个文物贩子，说两万就两万，你再给我买一套门窗安上，这套老门窗就归你了。谁知文物贩子听说四毛撞了人急等钱用，就拉下脸说，现在行情不行了，我正要洗手不干。四毛就求他，说好歹帮我个忙，人家老太太急等救治呢，这可是积德的事。文物贩子这才改口说，你要卖，我只能出一万，新门窗你自己买。四毛一

the doors and windows were carved with patterns of birds and flowers, looking somewhat distinct, if worn-out. When she asked if the doors and windows could sell for a good price, Simao smiled and nodded proudly, saying the three tiled rooms were originally part of a big house, owned by a capitalist before Liberation. Afterwards, it was divided between different families, among whom Simao's parents got three rooms. Over the years, the rest of the rooms were either torn down or destroyed. In their places two five-story buildings had been erected, leaving Simao's three rooms stuck in between. Simao had no secrets, since his neighbors could see whatever happened in his house from their windows high above.

Simao's three rooms were spacious and well-lit, with doors and windows made of silkwood carved with exquisite patterns. A couple of years earlier when a cultural relics monger asked Simao to sell him the doors and windows, Simao didn't agree, saying the rooms would be incomplete without them. The monger pestered him, offering a price of 20,000 *yuan*, plus a new set of doors and windows to replace them. Simao hesitated, but didn't sell. Later he was told they could sell for up to 50,000 *yuan*. Now he was urgently in need of money, so he went to the monger, ready to accept the previous offer. But the monger, knowing what had happened, made a face and claimed that he was going to quit the field because of the sluggish market. Simao then begged him for help, saying it would be kind of him to do so, since the old woman was in hospital awaiting treatment. The monger then offered 10,000 *yuan* cash, without the addition of new doors and windows. Simao was shocked, reasoning that the original

听傻眼了，说你以前不是出到两万吗？还说给我买一套新门窗，人家说值五万呢！文物贩子说，谁说值五万你卖给谁去，我只能出一万，还未必能出手。四毛气得转脸就走。刚到家，被撞伤的老太太两个儿子正等在家里拿钱，一听四毛没筹到钱，不由分说就打，连扇几个耳光，鼻子都打出血来了。四毛欲哭无泪，只好转身再找文物贩子。不料那家伙又压价了，只肯出八千。四毛说我真想杀了你。文物贩子笑道，你现在不卖，明儿来只能出六千，卖不卖由你。四毛央求半天没用，还是八千块成交。四毛把八千块如数交给人家，答应剩下的两千半个月内筹齐，老太太两个儿子才勉强同意。门窗被文物贩子拆走，三间瓦房留下几个大窟窿，要多难看有多难看。同居女人一直埋怨，说门窗拆了，刮风下雨咋办？四毛只好到处捡了些破木条、塑料布，随随便便钉上完事，说凑合住吧。

但没过半个月，又出事了。忽然一天，一个五大三粗的男人找上门来，抓住四毛就打，四毛一边招架一边说别忙别忙，你是谁呀，我可认识警察。那男人并不怕，说你别拿警察吓唬我，我经常蹲局子，认识的警察比你多。四毛说我不认识你，干吗要打我？男人说打的就是你，你睡了我老婆，不打你打谁？四毛有点

offer was 20,000 *yuan* plus a new set of doors and windows, and that they were now worth 50,000 *yuan*. The monger told him to sell them to whoever offered 50,000 *yuan*, but that he could offer no more than 10,000. Angry and dejected, Simao went back home, only to find the two sons of the old woman waiting there for their money. On hearing that he failed to raise the amount, they gave him a good many slaps to the face, making his nose bleed. Helpless, Simao went to the monger again, who reduced the price one more time, offering just 8,000 *yuan*. Simao felt like killing him, but the fellow said he would only offer 6,000 *yuan* the next day, and less the day after, so Simao could take it or leave it. After repeated begging and bargaining, Simao had to agree at 8,000 *yuan*, all of which he gave to the two sons, promising to give the remaining 2,000 within half a month. They grudgingly agreed to this arrangement. The doors and windows were then torn down, leaving ugly holes in the walls. His woman complained about what they would do in case of rain or wind. Simao went to pick up some planks and plastic cloth to cover the holes, then settled in, more or less.

Things went awry again only two weeks later. One day, a robust man went to his door and beat Simao the moment he saw him. Defending himself and trying to scare the man off, Simao said that he had friends at the police station. The man was not afraid, saying he knew more police officers than Simao did, since he was often in prison. Simao protested, saying he didn't know the man and asking what was meant by the beating. The man said he beat Simao for sleeping with his wife. When it started to dawn on Simao what

明白了，说你们不是离婚了吗？我见过离婚证的。男人说离了婚还是我老婆，她是在我蹲局子时候离婚的，不能算数。正在这时，女人回来了，女人在外头打了一份工，就是扫扫大街。进院看到男人，一时吓得两眼发直，说你你你……男人推开四毛，冲过去一把揪住女人头发，说娘们！你跑到这里就以为找不到你啦？说着就往屋里扯。四毛愣在门外，脑子里一团乱麻，不知道该怎么办。屋里并没有争吵声，四毛猜想他们也许在协商什么，就坐下来等候消息。可不大会儿，屋里传来铁床的猛烈摇动声，女人杀猪样嚎叫，说你这个畜生，咱们不是夫妻了，你不能这样！……后来，四毛听到男人一声虎啸龙吟，然后安静下来，只有女人嘤嘤的啜泣声。

后来，男人就住了下来。房间是由男人分配的，他们一家四口住两间，四毛住了一间。这个男人的出现，让两个孩子非常高兴，女人似乎也渐渐高兴起来。男人承诺说不会再打她了。女人答应和他复婚，说两个孩子不能没有爹。一到晚上，一家人就围在一起吃饭，吃完饭挤在一起看电视。忽然图像没有了，男人就嘭嘭拍几下，还骂骂咧咧，厉声说四毛！你狗日的啥破电视？赶明儿去买个新的来，这让人怎么看！四毛像个老鼠，躲在另一个

had happened, he protested that the couple had divorced and he had even seen the certificate himself; the man replied that she remained his wife, since they got divorced when he was in prison, invalidating the proceedings.

They were arguing when the woman returned from her job sweeping the streets. At the sight of the man, she was so frightened that she became tongue-tied. The man pushed Simao away and rushed to pull the woman's hair and drag her into the room, shouting, "You bitch! You think I wouldn't find you if you ran away?"

Simao was stunned. He stood outside the room, not knowing what to do. There was no quarreling inside the room. Simao assumed that they were talking, so he sat down to wait. Soon, he heard the clanking of his iron bed and the woman's howling and crying, "We are not husband and wife any more! You can't do this, you brute!"... Then everything became subdued after one huge sigh from the man. The only remaining sound was the woman's weeping.

After that, the man stayed, with the four of them in two rooms and Simao in another, as stipulated by the man. The man's arrival made the two kids happy, and the woman seemed to be happy too. He promised not to beat her again, and she agreed to remarry him, saying the two kids needed a father. At night, the four of them sat at the table for dinner, then huddled before the TV when they were done. When there was no picture on the TV, the man would knock on the set, shouting at Simao, "What the f**k kind of junk have you got here? Go get a new one tomorrow!"

房间啃干馒头，他完全成了局外人，还是女人有点看不下去，送过来半碗青菜汤。对男人的叫骂，他不敢应声，他知道应一声就会招打。可他心里充满了悲伤和愤懑。这样过了十几天，还是邻居们发觉异常，赶紧报告片警张磊。张磊急忙赶来，问明情况，毫不客气地把他们赶走，四毛才重新成为自己房子的主人。

可是，当他们一家四口在张磊严厉的目光中惶惶然离开的时候，四毛并没有想象中的兴奋，而是显得很麻木，事后也没有对张磊说一句感谢的话，之后好几天都没有出门。

四毛像变了一个人。以前他不爱喝酒的，现在经常一个人在家喝酒。喝醉了就哭。他不知道这辈子怎么啦，咋会赶上这么多倒霉的事。

其实这一切早就开始了。四毛知道，他这半辈子，就没有开好头。

上小学六年级时，班里不时发生学生少铅笔的事，开始是一个人少，后来是几个人少，还有一次居然有二十多个同学少了铅笔，而且是同一天。以前有同学零星少铅笔时，四毛就害怕，一直埋头不吭气，脸红红的，他特别怕同学怀疑自己。那时张磊是班长，已经显出特别有正义感。每次都认真追查，还向老师汇报

Like a frightened rat, Simao hid in his room, nibbling stale bread. Pitying him, the woman brought him half a bowl of vegetable soup. Now an outsider in his own home, he didn't dare to respond to the man's barking, knowing that he'd get a good beating if he did, but he was filled with sorrow and indignation. A few weeks later, when the neighbors realized something was wrong, they reported it to Officer Zhang, who came to chase the family away after some inquiry, finally returning the house to its rightful owner.

But Simao was not as thrilled as one might expect when the four scurried off under Zhang Lei's glare. Rather, he was quite numb, not saying even a word of thanks to Zhang. He remained indoors for a few days after that.

Simao then turned into an entirely different man. He had never enjoyed drinking before, but now he often drank alone at home. He cried when he got drunk, not knowing why he was so ill-fated as to get involved in so many unpleasant things.

Actually, it had all started early on in life. He really did not have a good start in this world.

Back in his sixth year of primary school, there was a time when his classmates kept finding that their pencils had gone missing. At first, one was reported, then a few, and then over twenty in a single day. In previous cases when some of his classmates found their pencils missing, Simao kept quiet, lowering his head and turning red in the face, afraid of being suspected. Zhang Lei was the class representative back then, and already demonstrated a strong sense of justice. He made a thorough investigation each time and reported the

说，四毛最值得怀疑，因为四毛一直红着脸大喘气，还建议搜查一下。老师倒还沉着，并没有搜查，在班里讲话时，也没有认定是四毛偷了铅笔，只是多看了四毛一眼，然后对大家进行了一番教育，最后说如果哪位同学拿了别人的铅笔，可以交给老师，以后不犯这个错误就行了，老师一定替他保密。老师走后，班里气氛就有些怪怪的，大家都在偷偷观察，看谁从教室里单独出去了。四毛没想那么多，因为紧张，直想尿尿，就慌慌张张跑出教室，去了一趟厕所。回来时却发现，所有同学都在看着他。四毛更加慌张，脸涨得像猪肝，结结巴巴说，我……刚才……上厕所的。班里同学哄地笑起来。四毛知道糟了，这趟厕所去得不是时候。他和张磊是同桌，回到座位时，张磊小声问，你交给老师啦？四毛连忙摇头。张磊着急道你赶快交给老师呀，老师会给你保密的。四毛抬头看看，所有的目光仍在盯着他，于是一下大哭起来。

这件事不了了之，因为它实在太小。

一个月后，当几乎所有人都把这事忘了的时候，班里突然又少铅笔了，并且是一天里少了二十多支，另外还有二十多个同学的课本被人用刀划烂。一切都表明，这是一次预谋已久的行动。就是说这是一个极聪明的偷窃和恶作剧者，他懂得试探，懂得潜

matter to the teacher, saying that Simao was the prime suspect, since he was always gasping and his face turning red. Zhang suggested a search. The teacher was wise enough not to do so, merely casting a meaningful glance at Simao and telling the class to hand the pencils to the teacher, and she would keep the secret if the perpetrator promised not to do it again. When the teacher left the room, the entire class got a bit tense. Everyone was secretly watching to see who would leave the classroom alone. Not thinking much of it, Simao hurried to the washroom to pee, mostly out of nervousness. Coming back he saw everyone staring at him, putting him in more of a panic. His face turned crimson as he stuttered, "I... went... to the washroom... just now."

The class guffawed, alerting Simao to the fact that he had gone to the washroom at a terribly inconvenient time. When his deskmate, Zhang Lei, asked if he had handed in the pencils to the teacher, he shook his head. When Zhang urged him to do so, since the teacher would keep his secret, he looked up and found the whole class fixing their eyes on him. He burst into tears.

Eventually, the case was dropped, being too small for anyone to bother about.

A month later, when virtually everyone had forgotten about it, more pencils were found missing, over 20 in a day. In addition, over twenty students' textbooks were cut into shreds. It was evident that it was a pre-meditated move made by a mastermind thief and prankster who knew when to hide, when to tempt fate, and when to make a sudden move for sensational effect. Now things were getting

伏，懂得冷不丁出手，懂得制造轰动效应。这下问题严重了。

　　第二天，当警察出现在教室里的时候，四毛彻底崩溃，惨叫一声逃出教室，并且从此失踪。四毛的爸爸天天到学校要人。学校急了，警察也急了，大家都外出寻找。张磊带着同学也到处寻找，找遍了大街小巷，但没有踪迹。直到半年后，四毛的爸爸才在另外一座相邻的城市找到。当时，四毛正在那个城市的郊区垃圾场，头发蓬松，衣衫褴褛，就像从来没洗过脸，也没洗过澡，浑身又脏又臭，脸上还多了几道伤痕。四毛的爸爸走到跟前并没认出来，倒是四毛先认出了爸爸，丢下手里的垃圾袋，拔腿就跑。他怕爸爸会打他。他一直生活在恐惧之中，他不知道该如何向爸爸解释自己没偷，不知道向老师同学如何辩白。他逃到另一座城市，就是不想再见到任何一个认识他的人。当爸爸意识到他就是四毛时，赶忙飞奔追去，追出二里地，终于喘吁吁抓到他，却不敢相信眼前这个瘦弱不堪、脏得像乞丐的孩子是自己的儿子。那一刻，他没有责怪儿子，父子俩抱头痛哭。那一年，四毛才十二岁。四毛母亲去世早，只有父子俩相依为命。回来后，爸爸曾劝四毛再去上学，转个学校也行。但一说上学，四毛就浑身发抖，

serious.

The next day when the police arrived at the classroom, Simao collapsed and rushed out with a terrible cry. He did not come back. Every day Simao's father went to the school to pick up his son. The school and the police all grew anxious and went to look for him. Zhang Lei likewise went with his classmates to search all the streets and alleys, but to no avail. It was only half a year later that Simao's father finally found him in a neighboring city, where he had been living in a landfill site on its outskirts. He was unkempt and haggard, with a few scars on his face, and all in rags, as if he had never washed his face or taken a bath. He was completely filthy and stinky. His father did not recognize his son, even when the boy was standing before him. Instead, upon seeing his father, Simao dropped his garbage bag and rushed away, afraid his father would beat him. He had been living in constant fear, not knowing how to explain to his father or teacher and classmates that he didn't steal any pencils. He had fled to another city because he didn't want to see anyone who knew him.

Realizing who the boy was, his father rushed after him and caught him two miles away. Gasping, he couldn't believe the dirty, fragile boy standing in front of him like a beggar was his own son. Without blaming him at all, the father held his son tight, both of them weeping. Simao was only twelve that year. His mother had died when he was small, and father and son had no one but each other. Returning home, Simao's father tried to persuade him to go back to school or be transferred to another campus. Whenever he

两眼惊恐,爸爸终于放弃。

四毛从此失学。

开始的一段日子,四毛很少出门,只把自己关在家里,他还是怕碰见老师同学。爸爸在一家国营企业当工人,收入不高,却也稳定,爷儿俩吃饭没有问题。爸爸特别疼爱儿子,他知道儿子胆小,不想让他再受委屈,不上学就不上学吧。但他又担心儿子闷在家里会得自闭症,就对四毛说,爸爸相信你没干坏事,别人说什么都没用,你也不用老关在家里,该玩就出去玩,只要注意交通安全就行。这让四毛松了一大口气,爸爸的信任让他如释重负。后来很多年,每当别人误解自己时,四毛总是这样安慰自己:爸爸相信我。他在街上游荡时,做过无数好事,捡了钱交还失主,搀扶老人过马路,在公共汽车上让座。每做一件好事,心里的阴影就会少一片,他想证明给爸爸也证明给所有人看,四毛是个好孩子。

但四毛的努力,并没有阻止厄运一次次降临。

四毛十六岁时,爸爸在工厂一次燃气大爆炸中丧生,四毛接班进了工厂。可他干了不到十年,又成了下岗工人。四毛文化低,

heard the word "school," Simao trembled all over with terror in his eyes. His father had to give up.

From that time on, Simao did not go to school.

At first, he rarely went out, locking himself at home, afraid of meeting his teacher or classmates. His father worked in a state-owned enterprise, with a regular though moderate income that was sufficient to feed the pair of them. His father was fond of him. Knowing his timidity and not wanting him to be hurt again, he agreed to let him quit school, but he worried that Simao might suffer from autism. He told the boy that regardless of what other people had said, he believed in him. He urged his son to go out and play, but to watch out for traffic.

His father believed he had done nothing wrong. Simao was quite relieved to have his father's trust. That was how he comforted himself whenever he was misunderstood later in his life: *My dad trusts me.* When he was hanging out on the streets, he did numerous good deeds, such as returning a lost wallet to its owner, helping old people cross the street, or giving his seat on the bus to the weak or the sick. With every good deed he did, he felt he was stepping a little out of the shadow. He would like to prove to his father and everyone else that he was a good boy.

Sadly, his efforts didn't prevent bad luck from coming to him again and again.

When he was 16, his father was killed in a gas explosion in the factory. He took his father's place and worked there, but was laid off after ten years. He didn't have much education, and being

又一无所长,从此失业,只能靠打零工捡垃圾维持生活。四毛很坚强,仍然坚持管闲事,做好事。他一直记得爸爸的话,相信自己是个好人。

但随着一次次被抓,一次次被人误解,四毛的信心已在不知不觉中一点点动摇。因为事实证明,光是爸爸相信自己没有用,自己相信自己也没有用,别人说什么反而是有用的,不然自己怎么老是无辜被抓呢?虽然每次都被无罪释放,但有相当一部分案子是因为没有证据,并没有彻底还他清白。他始终生活在被怀疑的目光中。比如楼上那个处长鄙视的目光,时常让他无地自容。处长是个四十多岁的单身女人,她在公司里其实是个科长,公司内外的人叫她处长,完全是因为她仍保持着处女之身。当然,是不是处女别人无从得知,都是她自己说的。她对此毫不掩饰,时常炫耀自己谈过很多对象,没一个男人能入她法眼,所以一直保持着处女之身。大家叫她处长,她不仅不生气,还十分骄傲,经常感叹世风日下,说现在的年轻人不懂自重,许多女孩子上中学就失身了,不把贞操当回事。处长每说到这事,都是痛心疾首。有一次还毛遂自荐,要去一所中学上道德课,被校长婉言谢绝了,

unskilled, he was out of work from then on, making his living by doing odd jobs or reselling old junk. He was tough, persevering and continuing to do good deeds, and believing that he was a good man, as his father had said.

However, after being constantly caught and misunderstood, Simao was almost imperceptibly shaken in his belief. It had been proven that his father's trust and his own belief alone were not enough. What mattered was what others said. Otherwise, why was he always picked up for no reason? Though he had been released and declared not guilty, he was not completely clean, since some of the cases remained unsettled for lack of evidence. He was living under ongoing suspicion. The contemptuous look from the division head upstairs, for instance, always made him ashamed.

The division head was a single woman over forty. She wasn't actually a division head, but people in and out of the company all addressed her as "division head", since she was still a virgin. It was clear that nobody knew for sure whether she was a virgin, but she claimed to be one. She was always boasting about how many men she dated and how unworthy they were in her eyes, saying that was why she remained a virgin. When addressed as "division head," she was not the least bit angry. Instead, she was quite proud and often sighed, saying that young people today didn't think much of self-respect, and that many girls had lost their virginity even when they were in secondary school, as if virginity meant nothing to them. When it came to this topic, she was always lamenting over the loss of innocence. She even offered to give moral lectures in a secondary

因为校长觉得她脑子有病。邻居们对她更没有什么好印象,邻家什么事她都要掺和一下,还特别希望把事情闹大。楼上楼下邻里之间,夫妻之间,父女之间,母子之间,有时会为一些琐事争执几句,其实不算什么,过后就好。可处长只要听见了,立刻就报警。本来没事的,反倒弄出事来了。连两条狗打架,她也要打110。有一次张磊闻讯赶来,他怕伤到人,却发现不是狗打架,而是两条狗在交媾,张磊就很生气,说你懂不懂啊?处长说它们怎么能在大庭广众之下做这事呢?张磊说你说应该在哪里?邻居们都笑起来。处长指着张磊,又指指围观者,说你们全是流氓!

邻居们并不和她计较,都知道她谈过很多对象,高不成,低不就,受过不少刺激,据说有一次趁去外地出差的机会,差点自杀。但没人敢问她。她变得越来越古怪,只是有些事古怪得太离谱。比如她只要在家,大门经常是虚掩的,却又拒绝任何邻居进门。夜里睡觉时,她也会把门留一道缝。曾有邻居提醒她关好门,不然太不安全,结果被她奚落一顿:"你会来我家偷东西吗?"邻居惊诧不已,后来向别人说起,所有人都不懂。但不知道什么原因,小偷就是没去过。倒是别人家时不时有小偷光顾。这的确是

school only to be turned down by the headmaster, who believed she was out of her mind. The neighbors were not welcoming either, since she often nosed into whatever happened in other families, expecting to stir up a tempest in a teapot. It was no big deal for neighbors, couples, fathers and daughters, or mothers and sons to quarrel from time to time, but she would report it to the police and make a scene out of nothing. She even called 110 over a fight between two dogs. Zhang Lei, who rushed over, afraid that the dogs would hurt someone, was extremely angry when he found that it was not two dogs fighting, but mating. When questioned, the division head protested, asking how they could do such a thing in public. When Zhang Lei retorted, "Where do you think they should do it?", the neighbors laughed. She pointed at Zhang Lei and then the onlookers, calling them all hooligans.

The neighbors were not bothered by her, knowing that she was quite hurt after having so many dates but being too choosy to secure a good match. It was said that she almost committed suicide when she was on a business trip out of town, but no one dared to ask her about it. She turned increasingly odd, and many other things turned unexpectedly weird. For instance, she would leave her door open when she was home, but she would not let anyone in. She would even leave the door unlocked at night. When one of the neighbors reminded her to lock the door, saying it was unsafe not to, she mocked, "Will you come to my home to burgle?"

Shocked, the neighbor shared the story with the others, but no one understood why she behaved this way. Strangely enough,

一件奇怪的事。后来大家猜测，门开一道缝，可能是为了偷听人说话、争吵什么的，也方便快速出门。她不是一向爱管闲事吗？

但终于有人光顾处长的家了。不是偷东西，而是强奸！

这事震惊了整个小区，整条街道。

据处长后来描述，那家伙是在半夜过后推门进来的，当时屋里亮着灯，她一向是开着灯睡觉的。当她被惊醒时，屋里已是一片漆黑。那人肯定先把灯关了。她首先闻到了一股男士的香水味，随后感到一个高大而强壮的人，他仍然穿着上衣。她在触碰之间，感觉到是那种很高档的西服，脖子上还系着领带。他压在身上很沉很强烈，一只手捂住她的嘴，她憋得喘不过气，浑身一点力气也没有，只能软绵绵地任他摆布。那人刚出门，她就尖叫起来。不大会儿，她从窗口看见一辆黑色的轿车，一轰油门就开走了。路灯下可以看到那辆车很气派，让她猛然想起，那是她曾经见过的一辆豪华奔驰车，那辆奔驰车已跟踪她半个多月了，只是当时没有在意，也没留意车牌号，但肯定是一辆奔驰。

派出所很快成立了一个专案组，张磊任组长。在现场查看时，没有发现任何有价值的线索，没有搏斗的痕迹，也没有犯罪嫌疑人遗留的物品。这能说得通，处长的门是敞着的，又是在睡梦中

burglars never went to her place, but only to others' from time to time. The neighbors later assumed she left the door open to overhear others' talks or quarrels so she could go out more quickly to broadcast her findings, since she was such a busybody.

Finally, someone did go to her place, not for burgling, but for raping. The case shocked the entire neighborhood.

According to what she later said, the perpetrator went to her home after midnight. It had been bright, since she always kept the light on while sleeping, but it was dark when she woke up. The man must have turned off the light. She could smell the cologne the man wore and felt that he was a big, strong man wearing a good quality suit and a tie. He pushed himself heavily onto her, covering her mouth with one hand. She felt choked and extremely weak, and was completely at the man's mercy. The moment the man stepped out the door, she started screaming. Then from her window, she saw a black car dash away with a roar. The car under the lamppost reminded her of a Benz limousine she had seen following her for more than two weeks. She had not paid attention before and could not remember the plate number, but she was sure it was a Benz.

The local police station set up a special task force to look into the case, and Zhang Lei was the leader. There was no valuable clue or sign of fight at the scene, nor anything left behind by the suspect. It made sense, as the chief's door was open and she was unable to fight in her sleep, then was coerced and her mouth covered. The police were stuck when they started to collect other evidence. In a

被偷袭,且在强力压迫和捂嘴的情况下,完全失去了反抗能力,没留下搏斗痕迹和物证,也很正常。接下来的取证又遇到麻烦。按要求,受害人既然报案受到性侵犯,就有义务配合法医进行身体检查,以便提取体液,确定受伤害的程度和证据。但处长死活不去。张磊一再做工作,说只有这样,才能尽快破案,希望您能理解。张磊特意用了"您"字。不料处长还是不同意,她说我洗过澡了,没有什么狗屁体液!她一直处在狂怒之中,大骂张磊是个笨蛋,说我已经把罪犯描述得够清楚了,还要我出洋相吗?不去!但这件事必须做,因为牵扯到最重要的物证。张磊以足够的耐心,继续劝说,最后处长还是没去,但弯腰从床下扯出一条枕巾甩给他,突然失声痛哭道,你看那个王八蛋干的!

张磊小心用镊子捡起,立刻就闻到一股很亲切的臭味。另外两个女警也闻到了,其中一个刚出门就小声说:怎么像腐乳的味道?张磊一转脸,别瞎说!心里却想,怎么不是内裤?

检测结果很快出来了,那上头并没有男性体液,发出臭味的的确是腐乳,俗称臭豆腐,上头黏得一塌糊涂,起码需三块腐乳才能糊成这模样。问题是,枕巾上怎么会有臭豆腐?这么说,那个家伙不仅是个色情狂,难道还是个变态狂,对臭豆腐有特殊的

rape case, the victim was required to do a physical checkup to obtain her body fluids as evidence and to specify the extent to which she had been hurt, but she categorically refused to go for the check. She gave the officer a resounding no, saying she had taken a shower and there was no f**king fluid inside her. No matter how patient Zhang Lei was as he explained why it was necessary for her to cooperate and how helpful it would be for them to crack the case if she could be more understanding, she obstinately refused. In a rage, she cursed Zhang Lei as an idiot, claiming she didn't want to be further embarrassed and she had given a clear enough description of the criminal. But with even greater patience, Zhang Lei kept on persuading her to submit to the checkup, since it could produce the most important evidence. In the end she pulled a pillowcase from under her bed and threw it to Zhang Lei, crying, "See what the bastard has done to me!"

Zhang Lei picked up the pillowcase with tweezers and smelt a familiar, stinky smell. The other two policewomen smelt it too and murmured as they left, "Why does it reek of stinky tofu?"

Zhang Lei told them to shut up, thinking to himself, *Why not underwear, but a pillowcase?*

The result soon came out, saying that there were no male body fluids on it, but only stinky tofu. It was quite a mess, and would require at least three pieces of stinky tofu to make it that smelly. The thing was, how did the stinky tofu get onto a pillowcase? Did that mean the guy was not only an erotomaniac, but also a freak with a particular taste for stinky tofu? But based on what the

嗜好？可根据处长的描述，那家伙平常是个体面人，怎么会迷恋臭豆腐呢？两个女警察提出自己的疑问，张磊说这不奇怪，人都有一好，还有人喜欢臭脚丫子味呢。

根据处长提供的线索，张磊很快确定了侦破方向，就是先把全市的黑色轿车特别是奔驰车调查清楚，逐个摸底排查车主人。工作量当然很大，可张磊很兴奋，很久没有破大案了，以前光是四毛那些破事，已经牵扯他太多精力，而且劳而无功，一件事都没有落实，让张磊觉得自己特别无能，特别没面子，也特别憋气。

第二天刚上班，张磊就给两名女警察分别派了任务，准备分头行动。可正要出门，处长打来紧急电话，说要撤案。张磊一愣，问她为什么？处长什么也不说，咔嚓就挂了电话。

张磊像被打了一闷棍，不知这个古怪的女人怎么啦，一定又有什么意外，就和两个女警察迅速赶到她家。处长说你们来干什么？我不是撤案了吗？张磊说为什么？处长说不为什么。张磊说你撤案总得有个理由吧？处长说没有理由。张磊说没有理由就不能撤案。处长说不是说民不告官不究吗？张磊说这已经是一个刑事案件，你撤不撤案都得办。处长大喊一声：蠢猪！

张磊没有理她，带着两个助手走了。他决心要把这个案子办

division head had said, the fellow seemed to be a decent-looking person. How could such a man be obsessed with stinky tofu?

The two policewomen continued this line of inquiry. Zhang Lei replied that nothing was strange about that, as there were even people obsessed with the smell of stinky feet.

Based on the division head's description, Zhang Lei quickly specified the direction of the investigation—that is, he had to sort through all the black limousines in the city, especially every Benz, to locate the owners. It was a lot of work, but Zhang Lei was excited, since it was a big case. He was tired of the minor cases involving Simao, which meant much work but little results, making him feel incompetent and aggrieved.

The next morning when he finished assigning jobs to the two policewomen and started to get to work, they got an emergency call from the division head saying she had decided to withdraw the case. Asked why, she said nothing, but hung up.

Shocked and not knowing what had happened to this odd woman, Zhang Lei hurried with the two policewomen to her house. The division head asked why they came again, now that she had dropped the charge. Asked for a reason for the withdrawal, she said there was none. When Zhang Lei said without a proper reason, the case could not be withdrawn, she retorted, *doesn't the rule say the authorities shall not inspect a case if the victim or witness does not file a report?* As Zhang Lei told her a criminal case had to be investigated, whether a petition for withdrawal was filed or not, she let out a curse, *you stupid pig!*

到底,他要看看那个衣冠楚楚的禽兽到底是一个怎样的变态狂。

但一个月后,张磊失望了。他和专案组排查了市里所有的黑色轿车特别是奔驰车,也曾经发现了七八个嫌疑人,但最后都一一排除了。

案子走进死胡同,张磊才慢慢回想到一系列问题:处长对犯罪嫌疑人的描述是否真实可信?不让检查身体是想遮掩什么吗?次日突然要求撤案有什么隐情?但枕巾上粘着的腐乳,又说明那天夜里在她身上的确发生了什么事。

张磊决定重新开始。为了减少动静,他没带两个女警察,只以片警的身份,悄悄走访了小区居民,打听那天夜晚大家是否听到了什么,看到了什么。结果有几家相近的邻居反映,半夜过后时,确实听到了处长的尖叫声,但没有听到有人逃跑的声音,更没有看到有什么黑色汽车。小区在城市的一个角落,本来大白天汽车就少,半夜过后就静如荒野,如果有汽车加油门逃离,应当有人能听到声音的。结合前些日在全市对奔驰轿车的排查,基本可以肯定,那天晚上犯罪嫌疑人并没有开车。那么,处长所描述的那个体面人是否虚构,也同样值得怀疑了。现在不能排除附近乃至小区有人作案的嫌疑了。

Ignoring her insults, Zhang Lei left with the two policewomen, resolved to bring the fact to light. He wanted to find out what kind of a pervert that perpetrator was under the guise of a gentleman.

But after one month, disappointment came to grip him. Zhang Lei and the special task force had looked into all black limousines, especially every Benz. There were seven or eight suspects, but were all had been excluded after further inquiry. The case came to a dead end, but a chain of questions occurred to Zhang Lei: Was the division head's description of the criminal true and reliable? What was she hiding by not doing the physical checkup? Why did she suddenly withdraw the case? What on earth happened to her that night, with the pillowcase covered with stinky tofu?

Zhang Lei decided to start afresh. To keep off the radar, he didn't take the two policewomen with him. He went to the neighborhood and asked around about what they heard or saw that night. The neighbors close by said that they did hear the division head's scream, but did not hear anyone run away, let alone notice a black car. The neighborhood, in this corner of the city and with few cars in the daytime, was even quieter after midnight. Someone would have heard it if a driver stepped on the gas and fled. Given the investigation the police did of all the Benz limos, it would be safe to say that the suspect didn't drive a car that night. Was the man the division head described a mere fictional figure? It was possible that someone in this or neighboring communities may have committed the crime.

Thinking of this, Zhang Lei got a little excited again. He was

张磊想到这些，心里咯噔一下，他有些兴奋，因为距破案近了一步。但又有些隐隐的担心，一个模糊的预感袭上心头。

张磊带着复杂的心情走进四毛的家。

四毛正在吃晚饭，晚饭出乎意料的丰盛，一碗红烧肉，半只烧鸡，两个素菜。张磊笑道，四毛，改善生活了吗？没见你这么舍得吃过啊。四毛哈哈大笑，说我想明白了，人不能太亏待自己。四毛正在独自喝酒，举起酒杯说，张磊，喝一杯？张磊稍感意外，今天怎么直呼其名啦？忙推辞道，我还在上班时间，不能喝酒的。四毛说，你想喝我也不会给你喝。我怕牵连你。说着喝空杯中酒，收好酒杯。他看张磊要说什么，一抬手止住他，说你现在什么也别问我，我要吃饭了，等我吃完饭咱们再谈。张磊心想这家伙今天怎么像个大爷，平日胆小如鼠的样子不见了。就坐在那里没动，说行行，你吃饭，我坐会儿。四毛慢悠悠起身，从哪里端来一碟腐乳放桌上，看了张磊一眼，重新坐好，拿起馒头就吃起来。夹一筷子红烧肉放在嘴里，又夹一点腐乳抹在馒头上，一咬一大口。张磊看到那碟腐乳，心里跳得有点慌，这让他想起处长的枕巾，但他又告诫自己，别大惊小怪，这东西很多人都爱吃，自己也爱

getting closer to cracking the case, but he was worried too, enveloped by a vague instinct. With mixed feelings, he walked to Simao's house.

  Simao was having his dinner. The portion was unexpectedly large: a bowl of stewed pork with soy sauce, half a roasted chicken, and two dishes of vegetables. Seeing this, Zhang Lei smiled and said, "Simao, did you come into some money? I've never seen you have such a big meal."

  At this, Simao laughed, saying that he had finally come to understand that one should treat oneself properly and nicely. Holding his glass, he asked Zhang Lei if he'd like to join him for a drink. Zhang was slightly surprised that Simao addressed him by his name. He quickly explained that he couldn't, since he was on duty. Simao then said he would not ask Zhang to drink with him, for fear of getting Zhang involved. He finished his drink and put away the glass. Sensing that Zhang Lei had something on his mind, he raised his hand and stopped Zhang from asking more questions, saying that it was time for his dinner and whatever it was could wait until he was done. Surprised that Simao behaved like a master and not as timidly as he always had before, Zhang Lei sat tight, saying it was fine for him to wait. Simao then slowly went to fetch a dish of stinky tofu. Casting a glance at Zhang, he sat down and started to eat, a mouthful of steamed buns covered with stinky tofu, then a mouthful of pork. Seeing the dish of stinky tofu, Zhang Lei grew uneasy, thinking of the division head's pillowcase, but he reminded himself that he shouldn't be startled, since many people enjoyed eating that dish. In fact, he himself loved it too, and he had seen Simao eat it

吃，以前也见四毛吃过的，这不能说明什么。可心里还是在想，难道是四毛干的？四毛刚才说，我想明白了，人不能太亏待自己。那神情有点邪，不像单说吃饭的事。

四毛吃得很慢，很多，已经吃下六个馒头还在吃。张磊被他吃得不耐烦了，说你是不是准备三年不吃饭了？四毛也不理他，直到吃下八个馒头，咕咚咕咚喝下一瓷缸子水，才抹抹嘴起身说，走吧张磊。张磊心里有点数了，却明知故问，去哪里？四毛说我跟你走啊。不知是因为激动、不安还是慌张，张磊突然有点语无伦次，说四毛……你……这个……先坐下……四毛又重新坐下，说张磊你这次可以立功了，以前你抓我那么多次都是白抓，这次不让你白抓。张磊说四毛你啥意思啊？四毛笑道，张磊你还装傻，不就是处长的案子吗？是我干的。张磊猛然站起身，脸色都变了，真是你干的？四毛点点头，是我。我干的。怎么啦？

张磊突然吼道：你混蛋！

四毛长舒一口气，说张磊，你根本就不懂，当一回真混蛋，我心里有多畅快，多舒心！多恣儿！我终于不再被人冤枉了，那女人也该懂得，什么叫没有尊严了！

before; it really amounted to nothing. But he couldn't help wondering whether it was Simao who did it. When Simao said that one should treat oneself nicely, he didn't seem to be referring to meals alone. Something seemed strange about him tonight.

Simao ate slowly, and he ate a lot. He had finished six steamed buns and was still eating. Zhang Lei got impatient, asking if he was going fast for three years after this. Ignoring the comment, Simao kept eating until he finished eight steamed buns and a huge mug of water. Then, he wiped his mouth, stood up and said, "Let's go."

Zhang Lei was somewhat clearer now, but he still asked, "Where to?"

Simao said, "I'll follow you."

Zhang Lei was suddenly tongue-tied, partly from excitement, and partly from uneasiness. He stuttered, "Simao... you... well... sit down..."

Simao resumed his seat and said, "You can claim credit this time, at long last. In the past, your efforts were all in vain. This time, you will not detain me for nothing."

Zhang said, "What do you mean?"

Simao smiled at him. "You're acting dumb, Zhang Lei. Aren't you here for the division head's case? I did it."

Zhang Lei stood up immediately, his face turning pale, and asked, "Was it truly you?"

Simao nodded, "Yes, it was me. So what?"

Zhang Lei suddenly shouted, "You bastard!"

Simao let out a sigh of relief, saying, "You don't understand how pleased, satisfied, and thrilled I am by being a bastard for

张磊似乎还存着侥幸，说四毛你可别开玩笑，这事要蹲监坐牢的。你和我开玩笑的对不对？

四毛说，我没开玩笑。我说的是真的。你拿出本子来，我知道你们要做笔录的，我告诉你整个过程。

张磊有点木呆了，一时没动。

四毛催促说，记，记，快呀！

张磊渐渐恢复了平静，掏出本子和笔。好，你说吧。脸色却十分难看。

那晚我去了，是后半夜。我带了几块臭豆腐，想抹她一嘴的。平日看见我，她就会捂嘴，我问她怎么啦，她说你太臭了，一嘴臭豆腐味。我打算抹她一嘴，看她还说不说我嘴臭。她的门开一道缝，一推就开，屋里亮着灯。开始我有点害怕，怕有什么机关或者阴谋。但没有。我走进卧室，看她躺在床上，似睡非睡、似醒非醒的样子，只是脸色很憔悴，显然是长期失眠造成的。发觉我进来，她居然一点都没有惊慌，还冲我笑了一下。这么多年，我是第一次见她笑的模样，当时我手里还拎着几块臭豆腐。我看了看小塑料袋，心想算了，别抹了。往一张笑脸上抹臭豆腐，有

once. Finally, I am not wronged anymore, and the woman will know what it means to lose one's dignity."

Still Zhang Lei seemed to cling to some hope. He said, "Simao, don't you toy with me. You might end up in jail. You're kidding with me, right?"

Simao was serious. "No, I'm not kidding. I mean it. Take out your notebook now. I know you need to record everything. I'll tell you the whole story."

Zhang Lei was stunned. He did not move.

Simao urged him to write the story down.

Resuming his composure, Zhang Lei took out his notebook and started to make a record, quite embarrassed.

I went to her place that night, taking a few pieces of stinky tofu to put into her mouth. Whenever she sees me, she always covers her nose and says that I smell of stinky tofu. I intended to put the tofu into her mouth so that she would not dare say this to me any more. Her door was open a crack. I pushed it and saw that the light was on. I was a little scared at first, afraid of traps or schemes, but there were none. I walked into her bedroom and saw her lying on her bed, half awake and half asleep, looking very pale from insomnia. Seeing me, she was not panicked at all, but smiled at me. It was the first time I saw her smile. Looking at the small plastic bag in my hand with the stinky tofu in it, I said to myself, "Just leave it at that." I felt bad to throw stinky tofu at a

点说不过去。我转身要走。可她突然掀开被子，跳起来一把抱住我，我这才发现她是裸睡的，浑身一丝不挂。别看她平日脸上干巴巴的，没想到身子却又肥又白。她紧紧搂住我，又亲又摸，好像我是她久别的男人，完全不是她平日最憎恨的小偷、流氓。我有点犯糊涂了，这女人怎么啦？是不是认错人了？我赶忙大声说我是四毛！你弄错了吧？那女人说我不管你是谁，进了我的屋就是我男人！说着就把我往床上拉。那一刻，我有点明白了，这女人是真熬急了，她平日留着门，原来是等野男人的！不管这个男人什么身份，什么年龄，什么品行，只要是男人，她都会接纳。这女人真是疯了，她的又白又肥的身子紧紧贴着我，弄得我浑身起火。我还真是动心了，这便宜不捡白不捡。就一下抱住，想亲她一下，可我一看到她那张已经变形的马脸，兴致又突然消退了，特别想到十几年来她对我的轻蔑、鄙视和羞辱，一腔怒火又爆发了，和这样一个女人上床，恶心不恶心？而且天知道，上完床会发生什么事？她会告我强奸！这种女人，没什么事干不出来。她从来只想她自己的感受。我不能让她迷惑了，我不能上她的当。我那会儿居然想得很明白，上床是成全她，不上床才是折磨她、

smiling face, so I turned to leave. But she jumped out of her bed and held me tight. That was when I noticed she was naked. Her body was plump and white, though her face was dry. She held me in her arms, touched me, and kissed me, as if I were her man, whom she hadn't seen for a long time, and not a thief or rogue she hated.

I was puzzled and thought she must have mistaken me for someone else, so I cried out, "I'm Simao. Are you mistaken?"

She said, "I don't care who you are. You're in my room, so you're my man."

On saying this, she dragged me into her bed. Then I was aware that she was indeed thirsty. She had left the door open for a man, any man, regardless of his age, position, or character, so she could get laid. The woman was crazy. When she pressed her plump, white body against me, I was aroused, taking it as a good deal for me. I held her and tried to kiss her, but when I saw her twisted face, I lost interest, especially when I thought of all the insults, contempt, and humiliation she had inflicted on me all these years. I was outraged and disgusted at the idea of sleeping with this woman. Besides, who knew what would happen afterwards? She could sue me for rape. She's the kind of woman capable of anything. She's only concerned about her own feelings. I couldn't be seduced and swallow the bait. I was exceptionally clear-minded then, knowing that me getting into her bed was a victory for her,

惩罚她,哈哈!她口水、泪水全流出来了,发情呢,她多难受啊!哈哈哈哈……

张磊听得目瞪口呆,甚至都忘了记录,说四毛,这么说,你没强奸她?

四毛收住笑,擦擦笑出的眼泪,说我还强奸她?是她差点把我强奸了!

后来呢?

哪还有后来?我一把把她推到床上,就跑了。

那……你拿的臭豆腐呢?

别提!推推拉拉中,塑料袋破了,几块臭豆腐全沾到她身上了,我身上也沾了不少。

这回轮到张磊在心里笑了。因为他发现案情比他预想的要轻得多。可他还是有些不解,处长自始至终都没说四毛的名字,这是为什么?

张磊犹豫一阵,他很想和四毛探讨一下这个问题,又觉得以四毛现在的角色,不适合问他。

但四毛察觉到了,四毛说你在想那个女人为何不揭发我?

为什么?

while leaving it would be to inflict torture and punishment. How much would she suffer, with her mouth watering and tears all over her face! She was flirting and hollering. Hahaha...

Dumbfounded, Zhang forgot to take notes. He said, "Simao, are you saying that you didn't rape her?"

Simao stopped laughing. Wiping his tears, he said, "Me rape her? It was she who almost raped me."

"Then?"

"Then what? I pushed her onto the bed and ran away."

"Then... what about the stinky tofu you took there?"

"Well, in the jostle, the plastic bag broke and a few pieces got onto her, and me as well."

Now it was Zhang Lei's turn to smile in his mind. The case was far simpler than he thought. But he still couldn't figure out why the division head refused to give Simao's name.

Zhang Lei hesitated, eager to talk about it with Simao, but feeling it inappropriate to do so, considering the role Simao played in the case.

Perceiving his hesitation, Simao asked, "Are you wondering why the woman didn't give away my name?"

"Yes. Why?"

"Embarrassment and shame. She was ashamed to say she had been raped by Simao. She was under the illusion that she was a woman of dignity and could only be raped by someone who drove a

她怕丢人。她要是说被四毛强奸了，怕有失身份，她一直有个错觉，认为自己是个有身份的人，要是被强奸，也只能被开奔驰、宝马的人强奸。这女人就是太假了。

可她可以不报案啊？

当时她是气昏了头，恨死我了。她其实一直在幻想，在等待被人强奸，但应当是有身份的人。结果等了那么多年，我去了，也是饥不择食的意思，可我却没领这个情，还不把她气死？她报案后又冷静下来，一想这件事还是不能说出真相，不然丢人就丢大了。所以，她后来干脆要求撤案！

哎！张磊有些吃惊，说这些都是办案秘密，你怎么都知道啊？

四毛笑了，说张磊，你以为现在社会还有啥秘密？很多秘密都是自以为别人不知道，其实人家早就知道了。

张磊突然沉默了，低下头咂咂嘴，又抬起头，长叹一口气：四毛，对不起，那件事……我早该向你承认的。

四毛装傻，哪件事？

就是小学六年级时，铅笔……都是我偷的。

四毛愣了愣，干笑了一下，说其实……我早就知道。那天中午，你把铅笔埋在校门外的小树林里，我平日就喜欢到那里撒尿，

Benz or BMW. The woman is simply too pretentious."

"But she could have chosen not to report it to the police in the first place."

"She must have been mad at that time, and hating me to the core. She had been dreaming of being raped by some well-established man for years, only to see me there in her room. With no better option, she came onto me, but was rejected. Can you imagine how enraged she was then? After she reported it to the police in her fury, she calmed down. Knowing that it would be too shameful for her to tell the truth, she asked to withdraw the case."

"Ah?" Zhang Lei was a bit startled, asking how Simao knew this, since it was all confidential information.

Simao smiled and said, "Zhang Lei, how could you think there are any secrets in today's society? Many secrets are secrets only to the person himself, but not to others."

Zhang Lei was suddenly quiet. Lowering his head, licking his lips, then raising his head again, he said with a deep sigh, "I'm sorry, Simao. That thing... I should have admitted it earlier."

Simao played dumb. "What thing?"

"The thing in sixth year of primary school. The pencils... I stole them."

Simao paused, gave a dry chuckle, and said, "Actually I knew. That afternoon when you were burying the pencils in the bush outside the school gate, I saw you when I went there to piss. When

无意间看到了，等你走后，我还去扒开数了数，是二十二支铅笔。我没吭声，又埋上了。

当时，你为什么不揭发我？

我没想揭发你。我知道你肯定是闹着玩的，不是真想偷人家东西。如果我真的揭发了，也肯定说不清楚，大家会认为是我埋上又诬陷你的。

张磊又沉默了一阵，说是的。当时我肯定不会承认，会说你诬陷我。我还记得，当时为了不露马脚，还故意让老师同学怀疑你。你知道的，我从小就想当警察，那时认为警察就是抓小偷的，就琢磨要想抓住小偷，就得了解小偷，可怎么了解呢？干脆就做一回小偷，才能知道小偷的行为、心理。那时想法很简单，一开始的确是自己的一个游戏。可一旦真做了小偷，我才知道，心理是会变化、会扭曲的。我也没想到，那件事会带来那么严重的后果，害得你担了小偷的罪名，还失了学。这么多年，我一直有一种负罪心理，也一直想老实告诉你是我偷了铅笔。可我居然没有勇气。一个做了警察的人，承认少年时代偷过东西，真的需要很大的勇气。这件事一直像山一样压在我心里，就拼命工作，证明我是个好警察。我每一次抓到你，都心惊胆战，唯恐你真的做了

you left, I went to uncover them and counted, 22 altogether, then buried them again without telling anyone."

"Why didn't you give me away?"

"I didn't think of that. I knew you did it for fun, not for real stealing. If I gave you away, people might think I had buried the pencils to frame you. Anyway, I can never explain myself clearly."

Zhang Lei remained quiet for a while and agreed. "You're right. I would not have admitted it and would have said I was wrongly accused by you. To keep from giving myself away, I remember I purposefully led our teacher and classmates to suspect you. You know that I'd always wanted to be a policeman, and I believed that a policeman's job was to catch thieves. Then I thought I needed to know more about thieves if I wanted to catch them. But how? I decided to understand a thief's behavior and thinking by becoming one. It was a simple idea, just a game in the beginning, but my mind changed when I started stealing. I didn't expect it would have such severe consequences, giving you the reputation of a thief and putting you out of school. For all these years, I have felt guilty, wanting to tell you that I was the one who stole the pencils, but I didn't have the courage to do so. For a policeman to admit to stealing in his childhood takes great guts. It was like a weight on my conscience, so I worked super hard to prove that I was a good policeman. Every time I caught you, I was worried that you were truly a thief, a rogue, or a bad guy. I'd feel even more guilty if you

小偷、流氓、坏人。那样，我的负罪心理会更重……没想到，你到底还是……

四毛长长地吐出一口气，说张磊，三十年了，你总算给了我一个公道。可我不想把一生的不幸都归咎于你，我会对自己的行为负责，我不后悔。说着站起身，把双手伸出去。眼里却噙着泪水。

张磊说干什么？

四毛说，铐上啊！

张磊起身，摸摸腰间的手铐，又放下了，说算了吧。就这么跟我走吧。放心，你的处罚不会太重。

四毛说，别！你不要包庇我。我希望判个十年八年的，心里就踏实了，里头肯定比外头省心。

但这件事最终还是不了了之。原因是问询多次，处长坚称是一个穿西装开奔驰的人强奸了她，说四毛完全是瞎编，根本就没去过她家！办案的一个重要原则是重证据而不轻信口供，现场确实没有过硬的证据，四毛还是老一套：疑罪从无，释放回家。

这个案子有两年了，至今没破。

四毛很苦恼，经常上诉，并且得了忧郁症。

半年前，张磊离开警察队伍，只身去了深圳。据说，是去做

were. But after all, you still end up..."

Simao let out a long sigh and said, "Zhang Lei, you've finally given my innocence back, after thirty years. I don't want to blame my life of bad fortune on you. I will be responsible and not regret what I've done." Standing up, he reached out his hands to be cuffed, with tears in his eyes.

Zhang Lei asked, "What are you doing?"

Simao said, "Letting you cuff me."

Zhang Lei stood up, took out the cuffs, then put them back. He said, "You just go with me like that. Rest reassured, the penalty will not be heavy."

Simao said, "Please don't show me favor this time. I hope to be sentenced to eight or ten years in prison. I would feel more settled in there than out here."

But the case was dropped in the end, because the division head insisted that she was raped by a man in a suit driving a Benz, that Simao was making up a story, and that he had never been to her home. One of the fundamental principles in criminal investigation was to base it on evidence instead of testimony. Since there was no hard evidence at the scene, the same thing happened to Simao once again. He was released and presumed not guilty.

Two years later, the case remained unsettled. Simao was troubled and kept appealing to the court. He suffered from depression. Half a year ago, Zhang Lei quit his job and left for

生意了。

而处长从那件事以后，不知怎么迷上了臭豆腐。她经常会买一罐腐乳提在手上，招摇过市，逢人就说，这东西还真是美味！说着打开盖子，用指头抠出一块腐乳，你尝尝，不骗你的！对方赶忙躲开。处长哼一声，把整块腐乳抹进嘴里，咂巴着踉跄而去。突然碰上四毛，见他垂头丧气的样子，便乜斜着眼嘲笑：四毛，你告不赢的。

四毛便显得很茫然。

他一直在想，是不是还得干点什么？

2011 年

Shenzhen to start a business there.

The division head became obsessed with stinky tofu after this incident. She would often take a jar of it and go through the streets, telling everyone she met on the way how tasty it was. Saying this, she would open the lid, take a piece out of the jar, and urge others to have a taste. "I am not kidding," she would say. When they hurried away, she would put the whole piece into her mouth, smack her lips, and swagger off. When she ran into Simao and saw how depressed he was, she would squint at him, saying mockingly, "Simao, you will never win the case."

Simao was puzzled, completely at a loss.

He kept thinking, *What more do I need to do?*

2011

附录 | Appendices

评论

赵本夫论[1]

吴秉杰

一

先从本夫的获奖小说《卖驴》说起。这部在1981年获奖的短篇中自然也有当时的政治形势的影响,例如孙三老汉担心农村改革开放的政策有变,引出"卖驴"的反复等。本夫在他以后的创

---

[1] 本文略有删节。

Critique

On Zhao Benfu[1]

By Wu Bingjie
Translated by Mark McConaghy

1

Let us start from Zhao Benfu's award winning work "Selling Donkeys." This 1981 short-story was naturally influenced by the political circumstances of the time, for example in the way that Old Sunsan worries about the changing policies regarding the reform and opening of the countryside, which gives rise to the repeated instances of "selling his donkey." In later discussions regarding his

---

[1] This critique is slightly abridged.

作谈中几次说到这获奖作品，主题浅显，写得不算好。但我觉得这是作者以后对创作有了更高的要求，本夫的这篇处女作叙事通透自然，有传奇性因素（如大青驴把孙三老汉带到火葬场和"神鬼鞭"等），实际上在同期获奖小说中属比较出色的作品。至于政治背景那是当时创作不可避免地共有的。对于中国的一些观念、语言及社会现实的生存状态，或许具有一百年启蒙和四百年法制历史的外国人一辈子都难得搞明白，因此不需要太重视外国人在这方面的评价。重要的是本夫的这篇小说已有两方面与众不同——

第一，它是一篇"喜剧"，而不是当年流行的"悲剧"，或由悲剧转化为正剧（《班主任》《在乡场上》等）。《卖驴》一开始便拥有一些荒诞的色彩。

第二，它又随之引入了某种心理学的因素。人的心理学和一部分驴的心理学相得益彰。这种独特的视角及其潜在的含义，对于作家的创作而言，恐怕总是有机地、不可分割地结合在一起的。

本夫还有一篇小说《"狐仙"择偶记》，写到了男女情事、人

work, Benfu has said many times that this award winning work had a superficial theme and that it was not written particularly well. But I feel that this criticism reflects the greater demands the author would come to place on his work. This work, the first one he would ever write, has a natural, clear, and fluent narration, with some legendary elements (for example, when the Black Donkey takes Old Sunsan to the crematory and that "Genius Whip," etc.). In reality, out of all the award winning works of that time, it is a rather outstanding one. As for its political context, that was something that none of the works of the time could avoid. Foreigners, with their one hundred year old history of enlightenment and four hundred year old history of the rule of law, will perhaps find it forever difficult to understand certain Chinese concepts, terms, and social conditions of subsistence. As such, we should not put too much emphasis on their criticisms. What is important is that this work of Benfu's already has two dimensions distinct from its counterparts.

First, the work is a "comedy" and not, as was popular during those years, a "tragedy," nor is it a tragedy that turns into a serious drama. "Selling Donkeys" from its very beginning possesses absurdist coloring.

Second, it also introduces some psychological elements. Human psychology and the psychology of the donkeys complement each other brilliantly. This unique perspective and its implicit meanings are always organically and indivisibly intertwined in the author's work.

Benfu also has a fictional work "A Fairy Fox Seeks a Spouse", which writes about affairs of love between men and women, the

伦大欲，并没有涉及多少性描写，却在当年引起了是否"低俗"的巨大争议。这在几十年之后完全"低俗化"的时代回头再看，简直不可思议。实际上本夫的"狐仙择偶"却是有着"严肃"主题的。在这部轻喜剧般的小说故事中，黑嫂与丈夫的关系，坚持侍奉瞎眼的婆婆不改嫁，和应付、拒绝手握大权的支书老石，最后选择了有志气、不吃救济的老弯，表明了一种对传统道德的坚守和价值观。而价值观的追求，又是本夫以后创作上固执而一以贯之的课题。

小说创作总不免要受时代生活的制约。文变染乎世情，兴废系乎时序。在新时期之初，短、中篇小说发展迅猛，长篇则要滞后一些。在反映与反应、再现与表现、灯与火之间，短篇似乎更倾向于后者，这可能也是后人一再说短、中篇小说在艺术水准上要比长篇高的原因。其实不尽然，长篇相对于短篇应有不同的艺术要求和标准，而那些取代长篇要担任时代"书记员"的短（中）篇创作，多数也并没有真正能够留存下来。江苏省自高晓声以降

great desire within human relations. Though it doesn't contain many sexual descriptions, in the year of its publication it generated a tremendous debate regarding whether or not it was a vulgar work. When looked upon from our current age, in which everything has become vulgarized, this debate is almost unimaginable. In reality, Benfu's "A Fairy Fox Seeks a Spouse" had a very "solemn" theme. In this lightly comedic story, there is the expression of a set of values: the safeguarding of traditional morals. This is seen in the relations between Hei-Sao and her husband, Hei Sao's refusal to remarry amidst her continued care of her blind mother-in-law, her rejection of the powerful party secretary Lao Shi, and in the end her choosing of the courageous and self-reliant Lao Wan. The pursuit of values is the persistent subject that courses throughout Benfu's later works.

The creation of fiction tends to be constrained by the life of one's era. Writing is intertwined with the world, its rise and fall linked with the course of time. At the beginning of the Post-Mao era short stories and novellas developed swiftly, while novels lagged behind. Between reflection and response, expression and representation, light and fire, short stories were seemingly more prone to the latter. This is perhaps why people would later say that short and medium length stories of the time had a higher level of artistic accomplishment than novels. However this is not completely correct. Novels should have different artistic demands and standards than short stories. Most of the short stories and novellas that sought to replace novels in acting as the "archivists" of the age were not able to truly last. After Gao Xiaosheng, Jiangsu province failed to

或许并没有出多少有代表性的乡土作家，但本夫就其短、中篇和长篇创作所依托的生活题材、人生内容，尤其是思情和感悟而言，则绝对可列入有代表性的乡土作家，且是有独特追求的一个。他的短篇也写乡土美、人情美和乡土人情风俗的特殊性（《进城》《西瓜熟了》《羊脂玉》）；写乡村陋习及其带来的困苦矛盾（《月光》《雪夜》《水蜜杏》）；写新的时代生活的变化（《祖先的坟》《远行》）；也有乡土人物、乡土纪事（《老槐》《枯塘纪事》），这中间比较好的作品既有时代的印记，又似可越出特定时代，有更普遍、持久的涵义。如《远行》，兼得声情并茂与含蓄隽永，其细微处语言的表现力，堪称短篇中的精品。接近九十年代，本夫的短篇小说由乡村、小城镇生活渐渐地也发展到了城市，如《安岗之梦》《带蜥蜴的钥匙》《夏日》《收发员马万礼的一天》《寻找月亮》《鞋匠与市长》《洛女》《临界》等。他写城市生活较之乡土小说显得不是那么有把握，有些犹疑，感情也不再单纯，不但常联系起乡镇生活写城市，如《寻找月亮》《洛女》；而且经常地表现出一

produce many representative *xiangtu* (native) authors. Yet if we consider the subject matter and contents, especially in terms of feelings and ideas, in Benfu's short, medium, and long-form novels, then we can absolutely consider him a *xiangtu* author of representative value, one with a distinct pursuit. His short stories all write of the natural and human beauty of his native land as well as the distinctiveness of the local social customs ("Entering the City," "Ripening Watermelons," "Mutton-fat Jade"); of the corrupt customs of the countryside and the brutal contradictions they bring ("Moonlight," "Snowy Night," "Nectarean Apricot"); of the social changes that define the new era ("Ancestors' Graves," "The Far Journey"); there is also *xiangtu* characters and history ("Lao Huai," "Records of a Dry Pond"). Among these the relatively good works possess the markings of the era, yet can also transcend their era, possessing more general and lasting meanings. For example, "The Far Journey" can be considered a fine work of short fiction: it is both lyrically expressive and thought provoking, with subtle points of linguistic forcefulness. Approaching the 1990s, Benfu's short stories developed steadily from depicting life in the countryside and small rural towns to depicting life in cities, for example "Dreams of Angang," "The Lizard-Bearing Key," "Summer Days," "One Day in the Life of Dispatcher Ma Wanli," "Searching for Moonlight," "The Cobbler and the Mayor," "Woman Luo," "On the Verge," etc. In comparison to his works of *xiangtu* fiction, Benfu's depiction of urban life displays less comprehension; there is some hesitation and the emotion is not as pure. Not only do these writings remind readers of the small towns and the countryside, as

种心灵的矛盾倾向，如《安岗之梦》《收发员马万礼的一天》等。本夫的城市小说可能没有他的乡土小说写得那么精炼、简约、浑然天成，还有些编故事的痕迹。但我前面已提到了本夫的价值观和价值追求，这种矛盾反差的表现可能对于本夫以后的创作（包括长篇），也是必要的和必然的。

这些作品大致上可以说是作家"与时俱进"的创作。不过我认为，本夫短篇中还有一些写"奇人异事"的小说越出了与时俱进的范畴，给人留下了与一般乡土小说不同的深刻印象。这类小说汪曾祺或冯骥才都写过，追求不同，情韵有别，可都需要作家的艺术的敏感发现，和在一般人习以为常后予以再发掘。中国古代的志人、志怪、传奇是这类小说的源头，可在现代意识下能写好更为不易。我觉得除下面将谈到的《绝唱》外，如《铁门》《铁笔》《空穴》《天下无贼》《绝药》《斩首》等一批，也都是比较优秀的短篇。一辈子默默做事、任人差遣的"铁笔"老吕，只因有一点微不足道的个性（"爱尝一口鲜"的嗜好），压倒了领导的尊

in "Searching for Moonlight" and "Woman Luo"; they tend to indicate certain spiritual contradiction as well, as in "Dreams of Angang" and "One Day in the Life of Dispatcher Ma Wanli." Benfu's urban fiction is perhaps not as concise, refined, natural and powerful as his *xiangtu* fiction, as there are still traces of story-yarning. Yet I have already brought up Benfu's values and his pursuit; such contradiction was perhaps necessary and inevitable for Benfu's future writing, including long-form novels.

These works can generally be considered Zhao Benfu's efforts to "keep up with the times." However I believe that within his short stories there are some works that transcend the category of "keeping up with the times," works which write of "strange people and odd things", giving readers a deeply felt impression that differs from conventional *xiangtu* fiction. Wang Zengqi and Feng Jicai have also written this kind of fiction, and while their goals and emotional sensibilities might differ, all require an artistic sensitivity to discover and explore beyond what most people have become accustomed to. The origins for this kind of fiction are pre-modern China's anecdotal stories, stories of the supernatural and romance. And it is even more difficult to handle these subject matters under a modern consciousness. Aside from "Last Song," which will be discussed below, other extremely strong short stories include "Iron Gate," "Steel Pen," "Empty Den," "A World without Thieves," "Refusing Medicine" and "Decapitation". Old "Steel Pen" Lü, who has quietly worked his entire life running errands, is forced into early retirement because, owing to a small defect in his personality (his "love of

严,便被告知要提前退休,只能在街角摆个小摊,给人刻印章,继续默默做人(《铁笔》)。同样是人物小品,县革委会的看门人老卜,外号"铁门",一辈子以靠近权力的尊荣和神秘为荣,最后竟跟着一个上访的修女弃职而去,这真是解构的神来之笔(《铁门》)。《空穴》中的铁姑娘菊在领导鼓励下天天忍饥挨饿还要上工地兴修水利,而领导乔吉则每晚下工后在河湾宰一头羊吃喝并诱奸妇女,小说对于饥饿下的欲望的描写让人难忘,让人想起九十年代的另一种欲望写作。而铁姑娘菊受奸污后生下的男孩则是在"三年严重困难"期间黄坝村唯一受孕生下的孩子。《天下无贼》因冯小刚的电影而更加有名。初看到篇名时我以为它具有反讽的意味。它有着显而易见的矛盾性。可事实上"天下无贼"主要还是一种幽默,而不是反讽,基本上是一个发掘人性和肯定人性美的故事。本夫是以自己的方式应对和处理种种内在的矛盾。傻根从大漠油田带着五年劳动积攒下的六万块钱回乡,火车上遇到了多年作案的窃贼王薄和王丽,王丽忽觉得这乡下人"傻"得就像

trying delicacies"), he impinges upon the dignity of his leader. He is reduced to running a small stand on the street carving wood-block seals for people, which becomes his only means of eking out a dignified life ("Steel Pen"). A similarly modest character is Old Pu, the guardsman at the gate of the county revolutionary committee, whose nickname is "Iron Gate." His entire life he has taken it as an honor to have access to the powerful and their secrets. Yet in the end he leaves his job, eloping with a nun who comes to appeal to the county government to redress her wrong. What a deconstructing work! ("Iron Gate") In "Empty Den," Iron Lady Ju endures hunger every day as she participates in constructing irrigation works with the encouragement of the village leader, Qiao Ji, who slaughters a lamb every night after work by the river, eating, drinking, and seducing women. The depiction of desire under the conditions of starvation is difficult to forget, which reminds readers of other works of the 1990s that deal with another kind of desire. After Iron Lady Ju is defiled, she gives birth to a boy; he is the only child in Huangba village born during the "three year period of severe suffering" (1959—1961). "A World without Thieves" is famous because of Feng Xiaogang's film adaptation. When I first saw the title, I thought that it would be brimming with irony. While obviously paradoxical, "A World without Thieves" is primarily about humor rather than irony. It is, in essence, a story about discovering humanity and affirming its beauty. Benfu uses his own methods to respond to and deal with internal contradictions. Silly Boy sets out to return to his home village from the oil fields in the desert, carrying five years of saved wages, and on the train home he

自己的弟弟，遂决定一路上要保护他免遭偷窃。王薄和王丽是小偷中的"专家"，而另一位隐性人物刀疤脸民警，又是抓小偷的"专家"。有意思的是作家还要把王薄和王丽设计成喜好旅游，分别是学美术和学建筑设计的，对美有着天然的敏感，这才造就了"天下无贼"的悲喜剧效果。社会现实解构和民族心理构成，偶然性和必然性，荒唐的故事和深植人心的自然力量，构成了这些奇人异事小说的底座。实际上我认为，要证明"奇特"，总是要强调它源于"自然"（自然中也包括人性），因为社会是按照现有逻辑，被无数人都依次证明过的，小说要寻求突破，只有探讨"自然"，才能发现和建立起我们所需要的新的价值关系。

本夫创作中还有些写到动物的小说，获得了普遍的高度的评价。除处女作《卖驴》外，譬如短篇《绝唱》、中篇《那——原始的音符》等。《卖驴》中的驴感应着人世间的荒诞和反复及其价值关系，《绝唱》中的百灵又象征着人类的追求及其价值关系，《那——原始的音符》中的義犬表现人类面临生存困境时，人类背

encounters Wang Bo and Wang Li, a pair of thieves who have been in this line for many years. Wang Li feels that this rustic "idiot" is like his younger brother and decides to protect him from being robbed on his road home. Wang Bo and Wang Li are "experts" among thieves, and the other cryptic character, the police officer Scarface, is also an "expert" at catching thieves. What is interesting is that the author designs Wang Bo and Wang Li to be a couple that enjoys travelling; they used to study fine art and architectural design respectively, and therefore are naturally drawn to beauty, and this creates the tragicomic results of "A World without Thieves." The deconstruction of social reality and the national psychology, randomness and necessity, absurd stories and a natural power implanted deeply in the human heart, these are the elements that form the basis of these tales of "strange people and odd things." In reality I believe that if one wants to exemplify the "unusual," one must emphasize that it originates from the "natural" (the natural includes human nature). Social development follows certain well-established logic; its validity has been proved over and over by lots of people. Therefore if novels must search for a breakthrough, it is only by exploring the "natural" can we discover and construct the new values that we require.

Within Benfu's works there are also some fictional pieces about animals, which have gained widespread praise. Aside from his first work "Selling Donkeys," there is also the short story "Last Song," the novella *That Primitive Musical Note*, etc. The donkey in "Selling Donkeys" represents the absurdity and capriciousness of the human world, as well as its values. The lark in "Last Song" symbolizes humanity's search and its values. Xi the dog in *That*

叛自然后所形成的价值关系。其中,《绝唱》中的百灵鸟与关山、尚爷的相互感应,以及百灵鸣叫由十三口到十四口到十五口,还有它一度"叫落"到完成最后"绝唱"的一幕,写得最让人回肠荡气。本夫的这些小说中写到动物,但他仍是在动物与人的关系中写一种价值追求。记得八十年代高尔泰提出美的定义:"美是自由的象征。"这一概括在学理上可能还需要梳理论析,在艺术上却能给人足够多的启发。它表明了,第一,美是一种追求;第二,美是一种象征;第三,自由当然并不意味着摆脱一切规范的约束,可艺术中又必然要蕴有一种在已有规范之上的超越性。于是,美便不在规范,不在表象,它和人,和人的不息的追求(高尔泰说"自由"的追求)建立起不可分割的关系。本夫的创作或也可以从这方面予以解读。他写到动物(以后小说中还出现蚂蚁、蛇等),但并不是动物小说。写农村敝败、衰落,又不是生态小说。写家族历史,却不同于流行的家族小说。譬如家族小说应突出其文化属性,而他则从原始荒野写起,分明是大文化的概念。他还喜欢

Primitive Musical Note epitomizes the values that are created when humanity, faced with the struggle for its own survival, betrays nature. Among these, the description of the emotional responsiveness between the lark and Guan Shan and Lord Shang in "Last Song" is most heart-rending, as is the lark's thirteen, fourteen, fifteen calls, and as it moves towards its "call down" in the final act of its "last song". These novels write of animals, yet they still handle the theme of searching for values through depiction of the human-animal relations. I remember the definition of beauty that Gao Ertai proposed in the 1980s: "Beauty is the symbol of freedom." This definition perhaps, on a theoretic level, still requires more analysis, but in artistic terms, it is insightful. It expresses that first, beauty is a kind of pursuit; second, beauty is a symbol; third, freedom of course does not mean freeing oneself of the strictures of all norms, but art must transcend established norms. As such, beauty is not found in norms, nor is it in symbols; it establishes an unbreakable link with people and people's unending search—the search for "freedom" defined by Gao Ertai. We can perhaps decode Benfu's work from this perspective. He writes about animals (in his later fictions there are ants, snakes, etc.), yet he doesn't produce animal fiction. He writes of the destruction and decline of the countryside, and yet he doesn't write ecological fiction. He writes family history and yet his work is different from popular family sagas. For example, family sagas must highlight their sense of cultural belonging, and yet Benfu writes from a primal wilderness, demarcating a more encompassing concept of culture. He also likes to write of beggars and wanderers, the unique

写乞丐、流浪儿,如《黑蚂蚁蓝眼睛》和《天地月亮地》中的小迷娘,那是本夫作品独特的创造。小迷娘的天性和柴姑的天性对立统一,恰如一个硬币的两面。本夫小说的贡献,在于他一开始便关注人自身的活动,而不仅仅是社会的制约,他以后的故事也就越来越多地表达和开始更自觉地探讨人和世界所建立起来的,以及在我们的文明之旅中所形成的这种价值关系。

二

如果说,本夫在他的短篇创作中已经部分地表现出了自己的价值追求和创作的某种独特性,那么到了中篇的领域,这种独特性的追求就表现得更为鲜明和集中。依然是写乡土,而中篇几乎全部写的都是自己的生命的发源地——乡土生活。赵本夫由此确立了自己的新型乡土作家的身份。短篇是"闪光"的艺术,中篇小说由于一定的叙事长度,便有了某种系统性和方向性。本夫创作的不可取代的特征也就更为突出。在探讨自然和人性方面,在人的本质对象化的活动中,本夫的优秀短篇小说看中开掘的是人

brainchild in Benfu's works, such as Little Miniang in *Black Ants, Blue Eyes* and *Heaven Earth Moonlight Earth*. Little Miniang and Auntie Chai have dispositions that are unified in their opposition, like two sides of a coin. Benfu's contribution lies in that from the start he pays attention to human being's own actions, as opposed to simply focusing on social constraints. In his later stories, he becomes more self-conscious in his pursuit, and gives more expression to the values forged between humanity and the world on our path to civilization.

2

If we say that Benfu, in his short-form works, partially exemplified his search for values as well as the uniqueness of his creativity, then it was in his novella that this unique search found clearer and more focused expression. Of course he was still writing about *xiangtu*, almost all of his novellas are about the fountainhead of his own country life. In doing so, Zhao Benfu solidified his identity as an author of new *xiangtu* writing. The short story is a "flashing" art, while the novella has some narrative length, possessing a certain sense of structure and direction, which highlights the irreplaceability of Benfu's literary achievements. In the exploration of nature and humanity, and in the objectification of human nature, Benfu's best short works examined human nature's social and psychological dimensions; when it comes to his medium and long-form works, he was not content to remain at this level any more, and thus strived to explore the meaning of human nature and

性及其社会的、心理学的涵义；到了中篇和长篇，他便已不满足于此，而是着力开掘人性及其发展和表现出的历史和文化的涵义。我觉得从中篇到长篇，本夫的价值追求与超越性都表现在这种自然和文化的交融上。而他创作的思想成就和艺术魅力，也要从对于这种自然哲学和历史哲学的表现及其艺术感染力上去寻找。

《涸辙》是作家较为看重的一部中篇，发表于1987年。"黄河在这里打个滚，走了。"留下了一片黄泛区。黄河故道也就是"涸辙"，打上了历史的印记。《涸辙》写洪水改道，留下荒原与重建家园；写故道边上最初原始的村庄，和随后种树的村庄、要饭的村庄。它写鱼王庄、鱼王庙等等。斧头的儿子螃蟹8岁便要饭，至17岁喜欢上了开茶馆与照应他的杨八姐，那是一种亦姐亦母亦女人的关系，当然这一切不正常的开始都源于天灾人祸，这也隐喻了历史。小说主要写的还是一个近代的村庄史，经历了抗战、土改、五八年"大跃进"与随后的一次次运动，由此灾难接踵而来，天灾人祸成为常态，历史和各种运动倒弱化了，成为一种形

its development and the history and culture it expresses. I feel that from his medium to long-form work, Benfu's pursuit of values and his sense of transcendence were expressed in this kind of blending of nature and culture. When it comes to his creative thought and aesthetic charm, we must look for them in his expression of natural and historical philosophy and the power of his artistic inspiration.

Dry Track, a novella published in 1987, is regarded highly by the author himself. "Here the Yellow River rolls, leaves." What remains is an area formerly flooded by the Yellow River. The old course of the Yellow River is the "Dry Track," leaving behind its historical traces. *Dry Track* writes of how the flood changes the track of the river, leaving behind barren plains, on which homes would be rebuilt; it writes of the most primitive of villages by the old course of the river, and later villages where trees are planted, villages in which all people are beggars. It writes of Fish King Village, Fish King Temple, etc. Axe's son Crab starts begging at 8 years old, and when he is 17, he falls in love with Eight Sister Yang who runs a teahouse and always looks after him, forming a relationship with her that is part sister, part mother, part woman. Of course all these unconventionalities are due to natural disaster and human suffering; this is a metaphor for history. What the novella mainly writes about is the history of a modern village, which experiences the Anti-Japanese war, Land Reform, the Great Leap Forward in 1958 and the successive movements that followed. Misfortunes come one after the other, natural and man-made disasters becoming a common state of being. History and various movements become less significant and are reduced to a mere

式,灾难自身作为本体凸现了出来。与此相应的便是村民们为生存,挣扎、奋斗与牺牲的过程,一代又一代人与灾难的抗争。有一个细节给我留下了深刻的印象,党支部每年都要开出一批"借饭"(乞讨)的证明,让村民们出外谋生,而开具"成分"则一律写成贫农。有两件事也颇具象征意味,老扁为了支应日本人和不让其砍伐林木,甚至不惜让自己的妻子遭受日本人的奸污凌辱,为了生存,那是何等的忍受!与此不同,老扁动员村民们植树造林,则极为强横、凶狠;而鱼王庄的人无论要饭到了哪里,每年冬至,都一定自觉地赶回来栽树!种树与毁林几乎构成了鱼王庄全部的历史。本夫的这部小说从局部看也是碎片状的,充满着让人惊奇的风俗民情、奇人异事,如独臂汉子、老扁等,还有混乱的血缘关系,然而它在总体上却又自成系统,具备了充分的历史的真实性。重要的是,本夫还把自然和人的关系引入自己的历史创作之中,这是他最早的贡献。

再按时间先后,谈一下本夫的中篇创作。《那——原始的音

formality, as suffering itself emerges as the main subject. In response to this is the struggle for survival, the fight and the sacrifice of the villagers, one generation after another struggling against disasters. One detail left a particularly deep impression on me: every year Party cadres have to write out a bunch of certificates for "borrowing food" (begging), letting the people of the village leave to make a living for themselves, and as to their "class status," it is, without exception, "poor peasant." Two events are replete with symbolism: in order to prevent the Japanese from cutting down the forest, Lao Bian swallows shame and even tolerates his wife being raped by the Japanese—to think what one is willing to bear for survival! Conversely, when Lao Bian mobilizes villagers to plant trees and build up the forest, he is extremely fierce and malicious; and the people of King Fish Village, regardless of where they have gone to make their livelihoods, on every winter solstice must return of their own accord to the village to plant trees! The planting of trees and the destruction of the forest essentially form the entire history of King Fish Village. Seen from its component parts, Benfu's novella is made out of fragments, replete with local customs, strange people and odd events that surprise readers (for example, the One-Armed Man, Lao Bian, intermixed blood relations, etc.). Yet seen in its entirety the work possesses its own system, replete with a vivid sense of historical realism. What is important is that Benfu has introduced the relationship between humans and nature into his historical fiction, one of his earliest contributions in this regard.

In a chronological order, let us discuss Benfu's medium-length

符》发表于1985年，不像一部小说的题目，却发出了作者自己的声音。引子《还生命于自然》中便写到混沌初开和生命成长的自然法则。大自然开始交给人类去管理，但是人类却并没有把这个世界管理得更美好，许多物种濒临绝灭，各种冲突相继出现。故事开始于一个神秘的怪物出现，它在夜间频频袭击人类，伤害人畜。《那——原始的音符》似乎是一部寓言小说，表达天道循环的法则和人类主宰下生命对抗的图景。怪物原来是白驹，传说原是我们的人文始祖伏羲饲养的人类的忠实朋友，又名羲狗，但自私的人类在遇到饥荒的时候，主人却出卖了它，把它卖给了狗屠。经过反抗、逃脱后，羲狗与人类决裂并起而报复人类，最后又退回到了原始荒野。这是一个关于世界的自然生态进而延伸到精神生态的故事。而起点则是人类的背叛，对于自然的背叛和对于伏羲氏（我们的传统人文始祖）的背叛。

《蝙蝠》发表于1988年。又是一些历史的碎片，一些奇奇怪怪的人和事的组合。《挑水夫·老妓女》副标题是"一个失落的童

fictions. *That Primitive Musical Note* was published in 1985, and though it doesn't seem like the title of a work of fiction, it is an expression of the author's voice. Its introduction, "Bring Life back to Nature" writes of the natural law that begins in chaos and governs the growth of life. In the beginning nature is given over to humanity to manage, yet humanity does not manage this world so as to improve it; many species are close to extinction as various conflicts emerge. At the beginning of the story a mysterious and strange creature appears, who in the middle of the night repeatedly attacks humanity, inflicting damage on humans and animals. *That Primitive Musical Note* is seemingly a parable, expressing the law of cyclical life and the prospect of life's resistance under humanity's domination. The strange creature is originally a white colt by the name of Xigou. According to legend he was humanity's most faithful friend, having been raised by Fuxi, our legendary ancestor of human culture. However, in times of famine, its selfish master betrays Xigou, giving him over to a butcher. Xigou resists and, after escaping, splits away from humanity, rising up to avenge itself. In the end all returns to a primitive wilderness. This is a story that not only concerns with the world's natural ecology, but extends itself to the field of spiritual ecology. All starts with humanity's betrayal of nature and its betrayal of Fuxi—the ancestor of our traditional human culture.

Bats was published in 1989. It is also full of historical fragments, a collection of a number of strange people and things. The sub-heading of the work "The Water Carrier and the Old Prostitute" is "A Lost Childhood." The lives of Shiyin and Granny

年"。石印和冉老太的人生都要上溯五十年或四十年，而现实生活只隐隐约约地露出了冰山一角而大部分沉没。《老狼》写县城公安局长宋源的传奇经历。《市井琐记》则表现市井生活、社会世相和时代变迁。都是历史的尘埃。这些片断故事似乎并不相干，小说的社会性意义却在逐渐增强，能感受到的还有作家发出的一种信息，他有些踌躇，似乎一切都在未定之间，历史并未清晰。蝙蝠者，乃是在黎明与白昼、黄昏与黑夜交替时出现的一种生物。小说中写道，它是在"白天和黑夜交合的瞬间飞出的"。

《陆地的围困》发表于1990年，又一次写到了自然生态、社会生态和精神生态的一种交织的图像。"水越来越浅，鱼越来越少"，跨两省十三县的四个湖泊都干枯了，于是渔民们走上了陆地。本夫写鲶鱼湾的船户生活和摊贩们，从老一辈的佘龙子、阿黄到中年的康老大、六妹，再到年轻一代的菱菱、疙瘩、四妮、秀秀等。本夫在这部中篇中写的是一种历史进行时。随着湖水的干枯，鲶鱼湾的"一条街"也发展起来了，矿务局及湖底优质煤的出现，引出了人们生活的转折和精神的迷茫。每一种形象都表

Ran trace backwards forty or fifty years, and real life only tremulously reveals the tip of an iceberg, with most of it sunken down. "The Old Wolf" writes of the legendary history of Song Yuan, the chief of the Public Security Bureau of a county town. "Miscellaneous Notes on a Market Town" represents the way of life and changes across different eras of a market town. Each of these works is the dust of history. These fragmented stories are seemingly disconnected, and yet their social significance become steadily stronger. One can also feel a kind of message that the author is expressing, though he is reluctant, as if everything is in the throes of instability, as if history is unclear. The bat is an animal that only appears in the period when it transits from dawn to bright day and from dusk to night. In the story, it "flies away in the blinking moment when day and night meet."

The Besiegement of Land was published in 1990 and once again presents a picture of natural ecology being interwoven with social ecology and spiritual ecology. "As the water becomes shallower, fish become fewer," the four lakes that cross two provinces and thirteen counties have all dried up, and as a result fishermen have to move to live on land. Benfu writes of the lives of the fishermen and small-stand merchants on Catfish Bay, from the elderly She Longzi and A-Huang to the middle-aged Kang Laoda, Liumei, to Lingling, Geda, Sini, and Xiuxiu of the younger generation. In this novella Benfu writes about what has always been going on in history. As the lakes dry up, the one-street along Catfish Bay develops, the discovery by the department of mining of high-quality coal at the bottom of the lake brings about a turn in people's life and their

现了对于生活和世界的认识、期盼，反映了他们在生活中的欲望和地位。我认为，有些强求的"典型"创作（往往是代表已有精神意象和艺术标准的），有时并不比那些光影俱全、气息充足的形象更有价值。

在八十年代中期文化"寻根"的年代，本夫的中篇便已引入了"自然"和人与自然关系的思考；在八九十年代之交，先锋小说流行，否定"典型"也就是贬抑现实主义时期，本夫的小说仍还是充满着历史感和现实感。他自然也要受"潮流"的影响，但本夫的创作却又始终不在潮流中。事实上，江苏还有许多作家都是不在潮流中的。马克思说，不仅是人的劳动创造价值，大自然（土地和海洋）也是产生价值的源泉。仅仅注意到这一点，便已使本夫的小说和其他人区分开来。

那些断片和碎片状的作品，已为本夫随后的长篇创作做好了准备。除了上面评论的那些中篇外，还有一些中篇或有某种独立价值，或为长篇积累素材，直接或间接地，在故事层面上或精神上可以和他随后的长篇宏大构思联系起来。

spiritual bewilderment. Every single figure represents the understanding and expectation towards life and the world, reflecting the hope and the position they have in their lives. I believe certain "archetypes"— always representing a certain spiritual image or artistic standard out of forced creation—are sometimes not more valuable than those vividly drawn figures brimming with vitality.

In the mid-1980s era of "Roots-seeking" Literature, Benfu's novellas were already engaging in reflection regarding "nature" and the relationship between "nature" and human beings. During the transition from the 1980s to the 1990s when "avant-garde" novels were popular, to reject "archetypes" meant to disparage realism, yet Benfu's novels were still replete with a sense of both history and realism. Of course he was also subject to the influences of "trends," and yet his works never remained stuck within "trends." In fact, Jiangsu has many authors who are not following "trends". Marx said that it is not just human labor that creates value, nature land and oceans are also sources of value. If we pay attention to this point we can distinguish Benfu's works from those of others.

Those fragmented and disjointed novellas have prepared Benfu well for his later long-form novels. Aside from the works already discussed above, there are other novellas that can be linked, directly or indirectly, in terms of story or spirit, to the grand compositions that would come later, either because they have some independent value or because they have accumulated raw materials for his longer novels.

《仇恨的魅力》（1990年）极有艺术创意。它是写土改和阶级斗争的，却并不是写地主"好户"（郝胖）与贫雇农之间的冲突斗争，而是写他们的后代——被郝家收养又不愿意做他闺女而宁可做"下人"的三月，与郝老财的儿子、从广州学医归来的"狼"之间的"仇恨"，不落俗套，充满野性的激情。小说采用了抒情的方式，那是把过去与当下、历史与现实交叉叠加、共时并置的一种叙事和抒情，抒情的主体则是三月。它揭示了一种隐蔽而又复杂，互相需要与对立矛盾中的联系，因而爱恨交替。仇恨的魅力便又包含了一种"爱的魅力"。

《营生》（1991年）中让人喜欢和格外关注的是其人物语言生动有力，充满着来自乡土的生活气息。它同样是有两代乡土人物，上一代的葫芦、丝瓜兄弟和下一代的大木、二木兄弟。同样也有爱恨交织——大木对于张木匠和一村人的恨，以及大木、二木对于芋头的爱。丝瓜说"树要皮养树，人要脸误人"。大木接受了这个观点，他的"营生"就是努力掌握别人的隐私，以达到自己的目的。这使我联想到了《无土时代》的钱美姿与匿名信举报族。

The Charm of Hatred (1990) has a tremendous amount of artistic creativity. It writes of land reform and class conflict, and yet it doesn't write of the struggles between the "good landlord" (Hao Pang) and the poor peasants, but instead writes of their descendants: March, who was raised by the Hao family but was not willing to serve as Hao Pang's daughter and thus resolved to be a "servant"; and Wolf, Old Landlord Hao's son. The depiction of the "enmity" between March and Wolf, brimming with unbridled fervor, can hardly be pigeonholed into any conventional patterns. The novella uses a narrative lyricism that intertwines and juxtaposes the past and the present, history and reality. The lyricism in the novel develops and centers around March. It reveals a concealed and complex relationship defined by mutual needs and antagonistic contradictions, with love and hate interwoven with one another. The magic of hatred also includes the magic of love.

What made people take note of and commend *Livelihood* (1991) was the vivid portrayal of characters and their powerful language which was full of the flavor of *xiangtu* life. It also presents two generations of *xiangtu* characters. The brothers Gourd and Loofah are from the first generation, while brothers Damu and Ermu belong to the next generation. This is also a novel in which love and hate intertwine—Damu's hatred toward Carpenter Zhang and the people of the village, as well as Damu and Ermu's love for Taro. Loofah says, "Trees need bark to nurture themselves, but men are done in if they want to save their face." Damu accepts this outlook, his "business" being rifling other people's dirty laundry so as to control them and achieve his own goals. This makes me think of

这两部中篇可说都是"点"的深入，有其独有的魅力。

《走出蓝水河》（1989年）、《碎瓦》（1992年）和一开始谈到的《涸辙》，在故事层面上便与本夫的长篇三部曲有了更紧密的关系。蓝水河畔的野孩在村里总是挨打，他是一个讨饭姑娘抱回村的，而姑娘所指认的大黑驴此人是否是他大，还未可确认，于是小说一开始就有"寻根"意味，却不是文化寻根，"根"是自然生命。自然的东西在社会中演变成长，才渐渐地融入了文化的因素。小说中的罗爷所讲述的参加法兰西一战的故事，和他与法国小镇上的一位姑娘阿琳娜的浪漫交往，在本夫以后的长篇小说中也完整地呈现过。但"我"回到蓝水河边寻找中学同学徐一海似真疑幻，则又是作者的独特构思。

三

在写《地母》三部曲之前，早期本夫还曾写过两部长篇小说，分别是《刀客和女人》（1984年）和《混沌世界》（1986年）。可我想那时候本夫还没有对世界形成整体的或成体系性的认识，没

Qian Meizi and the anonymous informant group from *An Age without Earth*. These two works, in a similar way, explore a profound theme from a seemingly trivial starting point—there lies the special charm of his writing.

Leaving the Blue Water River (1989), *Broken Tiles* (1992), and *Dry Track*, are all closely related to Benfu's long-form trilogy in terms of narrative. The Wild Child living by the Blue River is always bullied in his village. He is brought to the village in the arms of a returned beggar woman, and whether or not the man pointed out by the beggar woman, Big Black Donkey, is his father is uncertain. As such, the novel from the very beginning has a "searching for roots" flavor to it. Yet it is not a search for cultural roots; the "roots" here are natural life. Natural elements develop and adapt in society, and only then will they be endowed with something cultural. We will see in Benfu's later novels the full development of another story: Luoye tells his experience of fighting in France during the Great War, as well as his romantic entanglement with a young girl named Alina in a small town in France. The "I" that returns to the banks of the Blue River to search for his middle-school classmate Xu Yihai seems terribly illusory; this is also one of the author's unique creations.

3

Before he wrote the *Mother Earth* trilogy, Benfu had written two other long-form novels: *The Knight and the Woman* (1984) and *The Chaotic World* (1986). But I believe that at that point Benfu had not formed a comprehensive or systematic understanding of the

有建立起主体和世界的有效的价值联系,大体上是故事大于历史。他写恩怨情仇,苦难人生,传奇经历,最后都只能从失败而重归静寂,如同长笛在曲终画上了一个呜咽的句号(《刀客和女人》)。他也写少年成长小说,还有一种怅惘之情,一种得到即失去的思情和情怀。主人公得到了猫猫的身体、贞操,又感到自己失去童贞、单纯;得到与黄毛兽斗争的胜利,又失去了质朴的土地和乡亲。感到"冲锋"亦即"陷阵",黄金般的少年时代已经离他而去,自己正走向一个未知的人生里程(《混沌世界》)。一种不确定性在漫延,首尾衔接,无始无终,那是刚开始写作长篇的本夫的真实情状。但那时的本夫已坚持写他的家乡("柳镇"),写到了土匪,也写到和父亲精神上的联系。

在写《地母》三部曲之前,本夫还曾两次到黄河流域和西北地区考察。一次是1985年,他和同伴骑自行车沿黄河故道走了苏鲁豫皖交界的十几个县,行程两千多里。那是一次自力更生的生命的体验。第二次是在相隔二十年后,2005和2006年,他三次到西北漫游,是感受,也是探向。那可能是一次对美和自由的追问,

world, nor had he established a valid value system that related the world to its subject, and generally in these works plot was more important than history. He wrote of resentment and anger, lives of hardships, fantastical experiences, all ending in failure and returning to silence, like a flute completing the song with a whimpering note (*The Knight and the Woman*). He has also written *Bildungsromans*; these have a wistful feeling, a longing for what has been gained and lost. The main character gains Kitty's body, virginity, and yet he feels his own loss of virginity and purity; as he gains victory in his struggle against Yellow-Haired Beast, he also loses his land and family relations. He feels that "struggle/fight" is nothing other than "loss," and his adolescent years, as precious as gold, have already left him, as he moves towards an unknown life course (*The Chaotic World*). A sense of uncertainty extends itself, like an uroboros linking the head and the tail, to have no beginning and no end. That was the real emotional condition of Benfu as he began to write novels. However the Benfu of that era was already writing of his village hometown Willow Town, writing of bandits, as well as his spiritual connection with his father.

Before writing the *Mother Earth* trilogy, Benfu went twice to the Yellow River Basin and the Northwest to investigate. The first time was in 1985, when he and a companion rode bicycles along the old course of the Yellow River, visiting ten counties across Jiangsu, Anhui, Shandong, and Henan. Their itinerary was all-together over two thousand *li*, amounting to some kind of self-reliant and once-in-a-life-time experience. The second time occurred 20 years later, in 2005—2006. He travelled to the Northwest three times, to explore

也是对于历史的沉重的凝视。他出行都不找地方作协，宁可住小店坐驴车，"鸡声茅店月，人迹板桥霜"。而这正是他写作《无土时代》的时候。

本夫对于他所写的三部曲是有自觉的认识的，《黑蚂蚁蓝眼睛》反映的是文明的断裂，《天地月亮地》写的是文明的重建，《无土时代》则是文明的反思。我认为这必然包含着对这个世界及其价值关系的总体认识。

《黑蚂蚁蓝眼睛》是一个荒原故事，写家族的起源，但我宁可把它譬作一个种族的起源。它的神话色彩以及从混沌蒙昧到文明分流的过程，都印证了这一点。家族祖先老石匠所拥有的也并不是有区别性的家族文化，而是黄河边上的一座石屋，与自然对峙，使后人能在一次次的洪水泛滥后存活下来。在文明断裂后曼延的必然是自然人性，于是洪水过后，狼群在荒原上出没，老鸹在天空飞翔，无数"野人"在千里荒野中游荡，生活似乎倒退，又回到了一种"创世纪"的原始和古老的图景。本夫的这部小说是一部奇书，它以自己的充分的想象力，设定了一种人类重新起步的规定情境，写得狂野而又炫丽。它的意义还要联系他随后的两部

and gain a feel for the region. This was a moment to explore both beauty and freedom, as well as to critically examine the burdens of history. On his journeys he did not seek help from the local Writers' Associations, but would rather live in small inns and ride donkey carts. This was precisely the period in which he wrote *An Age without Earth*.

Benfu had his own understanding of the trilogy that he wrote: *Black Ants, Blue Eyes* reflects civilizational rupture, *Heaven Earth Moonlight Earth* writes of civilizational reconstruction, and *An Age without Earth* is a kind of rumination on civilization. I believe that these works must contain a comprehensive understanding of the world and its value system.

Black Ants, Blue Eyes is a wasteland story, writing of a clan's origin, though I see it as a metaphor of the origin of a people. This is testified by the course it charts from chaotic darkness to civilizational progress, as well as its mythical coloring. The ancestor of the clan, the Old Mason, does not possess a distinctive clan culture, but only a stone house alongside the Yellow River, battling against nature, ensuring that his descendants can survive after each and every flood. After civilization ruptures, human nature manifests itself in its natural state. After the flood, life seems to have retrogressed to a primitive and ancient "Genesis" condition: groups of wolves appear on the wasteland, crows circle around in the sky, and countless "savages" roam about across vast barren land. Benfu's novel is remarkable in that he uses his rich imagination to create a scenario in which humanity must start all over again, and the style is both splendid and wild. The book's meaning can only be explained

长篇才能完整释放，但并不等于它就没有自己独立的价值。因为小说所要表现的，它的起点便是自然与人性。

一位神秘女子柴姑由关外经数千里跋涉后来到了石洼村，她是老石匠的后人。老鳏夫父亲感到担忧，她与三个儿子都发生了关系。柴姑所带来的蚁群也蛀蚀着大堤，引起黄河最后一次决口，自此改道带来一片荒原，而柴姑也成了这个家族的女主人。这使人联想到了一个母系社会的开始。遍地的荒凉、沼泽、无人区，伴随着一种初民状态的沉沦，一切道德禁忌和意识形态都可以被忽略，人们只是按照生存要求和欲望法则在生活、行事；但在这种人性与原始本能中实际上也已经有了人类的精神因素的区分。譬如腊、瓦和小迷娘在捕获与贩卖野人，腊与小迷娘不同于瓦的是不杀人和不吃人肉。老大、老二、老三在洪水洗劫后，老大到河滩边搭起窝棚独居并对抗狼群，老二在荒原边境与难民一起流浪，三兄弟都选择了离开和柴姑的群居状态，一定程度上也意味着新的人伦关系的重建。因此最好不要把人性与道德一开始就完全对立起来。老二有着"人害人"的理论和原始状态下人可以随

by linking it to the following two works in the trilogy, though this does not mean that the book does not have a value of its own, for its starting point is humanity and nature.

A mysterious woman Auntie Chai trudges a long distance from outside the Pass to Shiwa village. She is the Old Mason's descendent. Her old widowed father becomes tremendously anxious, as Auntie Chai has slept with all three of her sons. The group of ants that Auntie Chai brings with her corrode the embankment, causing the last break in the dykes of the Yellow River. Since then the course of the River has diverted, creating a vast wasteland, and soon Auntie Chai becomes the female head of the clan. This makes one think of the beginning of a maternal society. Vast wilderness, bogs, no man's land, all of this follows the degradation into the conditions of an early people; all moral restrictions and ideology can be ignored, as people live and act only according to the demands of survival and the law of desire. Yet within this basic human instinct there are already spiritual differentiations. For example, as La, Wa, and Little Miniang capture and sell savages, but unlike Wa, La and Little Minaing are not cannibals. After Senior, Junior and Junior Junior survive the havoc of the flood, Senior constructs a shack by the river bank, where he lives alone and fights off hoards of wolves; Junior roves with the refugees on the border areas of the wasteland; these three brothers all choose to leave the state of collective habitation with Auntie Chai, and to a certain degree this suggests the construction of a new form of ethical relations. As such, it is best not to place humanity and morality in opposition from the beginning. Junior has a theory that "People Hurt People,"

意而行干坏事的主张，但在桃花渡世外桃源他却受到了善的"压力"，救桃花后又仓皇离去；腊离开瓦后，开始思念和要营救女儿梦柳；还有小喜子和梦柳、鬼子和哑女小秋等的关系，都反映了天地初开，善恶萌芽。小说便是在这样的"人性"的基础上，描写柴姑在荒原上收服了江伯、茶、小喜子、老佛等，又把他们引领到老石屋开荒种地，开始重建农业文明，在混沌中分流，步入了历史轨道。

《黑蚂蚁蓝眼睛》最迷人之处和最突出的文学创造，是它塑造了两个互相映衬、又相辅相成的带有标志性的艺术形象：柴姑和小迷娘。尤其是小迷娘，可说是以往小说中罕见的、独特的形象。小迷娘是聪明的，又是凭本能生存的；疏离了物质财富，又满足自身"需要"的。她从七八岁后边开始成为流浪儿，自由不羁，放肆大胆，渐渐地征服了所有的人。在性事上她也是一头"疯狂的雌兽"。她与柴姑似乎构成了对立的两面。柴姑也来自自然，是农业文明的代表；而她则保持自然状态，率性而行。小迷娘在收服了老三（后来成为"三爷"）后也想到荒原去见柴姑。她们并没有产生对立的恶感，似乎只是好奇，就像一个"自我"在注视着

believing that in a primitive state people can do any terrible thing they want. When he goes to the utopian Peach Blossom Ford, however, he feels the pressure of goodness; after saving Taohua, he leaves in a flurried panic. After La leaves Wa, she starts to miss her daughter Mengliu and wants to save her. Also the relationships between Little Xizi and Mengliu, Guizi and the mute girl Xiaoqiu are a reflection of the germination of good and evil in the genesis of the world. On the basis of this "humanity," the novel depicts how on the wasteland Auntie Chai subdues Jiangbo, Tea, Little Xizi, Old Buddha, etc. She leads them to the stone house in order to cultivate the virgin land, and restart an agricultural civilization, which marks a divergence from chaos, and a first step into the track of human history.

The most enchanting and compelling images created in *Black Ants, Blue Eyes* are Auntie Chai and Little Miniang, two symbolic figures that offset and complement each other. Little Miniang is a particularly rare literary creation. She is smart, living on her instinct; distancing herself from wealth, she can still satisfy her "needs." From seven or eight years old she becomes a wanderer—untamed and audacious—who has come to conquer all people around. In terms of sex she is a "crazed female beast." She and Auntie Chai are seemingly two sides of the same coin. Auntie Chai also comes from nature; she represents agricultural civilization, while Little Miniang maintains her natural stat. After Little Miniang subdues Junior Junior who later becomes Lord Junior Junior, she wants to go to the wasteland to see Auntie Chai. There is no enmity between them, but mere curiosity, as if one "self" was looking at

另一个"自我",意味深长。苏珊·朗格认为,艺术在根本上都是一种象征。《地母》可说一开始便为自己确定了一种宏大的象征结构。

我同意本夫在一次采访中所谈的意见,"决定一个作家能走多远的,是他的思想和精神"。其实长篇结构也就最集中地反映了作家思想的深度和边界。《地母》到了第二部《天地月亮地》,神话叙事便更多地转向了历史叙事,文明更替,有了无比的丰富性,也就有了新的矛盾维度和价值追求。本夫所采取的叙事策略是,他在小说十二章中都采取了过去和当下的交叉叙事,这就保持了"创世纪"后的延续性和作家想象中的精神历史的完整的涵义。他写历史进程,从土改、镇压反革命到解放初期的合作化结束,也写柴姑以下一个家族的繁衍生息的历史,在各种生存状态、各种社会力量中,都预留了一种自然的、人性的动力,这就又为创作留下了广阔的空间。

《天地月亮地》中的贫农团长杨耳朵、村长方家远、王胡子区长,还有七子、八音、八音娘、女裁缝等这些人物已经不再是那种"剪影"般的形象,写得都生动无比。这些都是作者熟悉的乡

another "self," profound and significant. Susanne K. Langer believes that all art is essentially symbolic. It can be said that from the beginning the *Mother Earth* trilogy builds for itself a great symbolic structure.

I agree with what Benfu said once in an interview: "What decides on how far a writer can go is his spirit and his thought." In fact, long-form novels perfectly illustrate the depth and limits of a novelist's thought. In the second story in *Mother Earth* trilogy, *Heaven Earth Moonlight Earth*, mythical narration has transformed into historical narration. The alternation of civilizations with its unprecedented magnitude brings new discrepancies as well as new pursuits of values. Benfu's narration intersects the past and the present in all the twelve chapters. This strategy maintains a sense of continuity after "Genesis," and keeps intact the spiritual history unfurled by the author's imagination. He writes of the course of history, from Land Reform, the suppression of counter-revolutionaries, to the end of collectivization in the period immediately after 1949. He also writes of the history of the multiplication of the clan after Auntie Chai. In his depiction of all these ways of living and social forces, there exists the dynamism of nature and humanity, leaving enormous potential for literary creativity.

Heaven Earth Moonlight Earth's characters are written incredibly vividly, none of which are mere "sketched" figures: the head of the poor peasant brigade Ear Yang, the village head Fang Jiayuan, the district chief Beard Wang, as well as Qizi, Bayin, Bayin's mother, the female dress maker, etc. These are all *xiangtu*

土人物，而不是凭想象把握的人物。同样拉近了距离的还有柴姑，她的长孙媳天易娘和天易父亲柴知秋，他们继承了这个家族对于土地的热爱和积攒土地的热情。小说还写到了柴姑和小迷娘的几次交往，它写柴姑去凤城探望小迷娘，有一段精彩的评价。小迷娘似有着一种邪恶的魅力，仿佛一片未开垦的荒原，然而她仍使柴姑产生一种忍不住又爱又恨的欣赏。她们都是能和动物和平相处的，在柴姑的身边总是伴随着无数的黑蚂蚁，而小迷娘则在蛇塔与毒蛇相处，这也是一种暗喻。在接近自然方面，二人有着异曲同工之处。小说中方家远认为，在农村中真正能代表农民思想行为的，不是贫雇农，而是中农甚至包括富农和一些小地主，他们对土地的感情、生活态度和面对苦难时的坚忍不拔，是农民最本质的东西。这可能也代表了本夫的看法。本夫还认为，土地是人类的母亲（"地母"），而当土地转变成了财富以后，一切的争夺、抢掠，和人类的悲剧便开始了。柴姑"迷恋土地"，"只是因为土地的神奇"，她喜欢种地的过程，而对于粮食（财富）却并不在乎。本夫以此表达了他对于土地的一种深刻认识。

characters that the author is familiar with rather than characters that he relies solely on his imagination. Not far from these are Auntie Chai, her eldest granddaughter-in-law Tianyi's mother and Tianyi's father Chai Zhiqiu—they inherit the clan's love of land and the desire to accumulate it. The novel also writes of a number of interactions between Auntie Chai and Little Miniang. In particular, in depiction of Auntie Chai's visit to Little Miniang at Fengcheng, there is a splendid comment on their relationship. Little Miniang has a diabolical charm, like an uncultivated expanse of wasteland, and yet she still generates in Auntie Chai an unbearable admiration that is as much love as it is hate. They both can peacefully co-exist with animals—a kind of metaphor—there are always black ants by Auntie Chai's side, while Little Miniang lives with poisonous snakes in the snake pagoda. In terms of getting close to nature, both of them use different methods to the same effect. Fang Jiayuan, the village head, believes that in the countryside the class that can really represent the peasant ideology is not the poor peasant households, but those medium-income farmers as well as the rich farmers and petty landlords: their feelings for the land, their attitudes towards life, and their perseverance in the face of hardships, these are the true essence of peasants. This perhaps represents Benfu's own perspective. Benfu still believes that land is humanity's mother, and once land has transformed into capital, all struggles, robberies, and human tragedies begin. Auntie Chai's "love of land" "is only because of the magic of the land"—she loves the process of planting, and has no care for wealth. Benfu uses this to express his own deep recognition of the land.

与《黑蚂蚁蓝眼睛》相比，《天地月亮地》的历史叙事加大了密度，也加快了进程。它写了天易父亲的家族，四代人的生活命运；又在有限的篇幅内通过天易娘，追溯到经商的外祖父，写了他母亲家族的衰亡。这中间充满着土匪、绑架、仇杀，惨烈无比。天易的三个爷爷和父亲多次被绑票。而他的大舅、二舅、三舅、六舅又先后在仇杀中死去……但我还是不愿意视它为一般家族小说，因为它并没有突出一种特定的家族文化及其演变，突出的倒是一种文化普遍性，例如对于土地的执著，例如"吃大户"的土匪，它更像是浓缩了一个民族的苦难的历程。在小说的领域，尤其是在长篇创作中，以为我们可以不写社会和历史，光写文化；或是不涉及人类文化、心理，光写生命意识，单纯地取其高端，那都是一种最浅薄的做法。《天地月亮地》是三部曲中内容最丰富的一部作品，它打通了乡土、家族、社会、历史各个领域，也可以说超越了一般的家族小说和一些具体的历史。它还写到建国初期的年轻一代和一些妇女的命运，甚至于写到了同性恋，可能认为"现代"的东西其实在过去也早已存在。

In comparison to *Black Ants, Blue Eyes*, *Heaven Earth Moonlight Earth*'s historical narration is more dense, and it also develops more quickly. It writes of the clan of Tianyi's father, the fate of four generations; it also, in limited length, delineates the decline of his mother's clan, from Tianyi's mother tracing backward to her maternal grandfather, a merchant. The family history is brimming with bandits, kidnapping, murderous vengeance, and incomparable tragedy. Tianyi's three grandfathers and father are kidnapped many times. His second, third, sixth, and eldest uncles are killed in feuds... and yet I am still not willing to look upon the work as a conventional clan novel, for it does not highlight certain clan culture and its development. What is highlighted is, instead, a kind of cultural universalism. The novel is more like a condensation of the historical course of a people and its suffering, as is seen, for example, in its obsession with the land, or in the bandits that "rob rich households." Within the realm of fiction, and particularly in long-form works, it is simplistic to think that one can just write of the sublime—only writing of culture without dealing with society and history, or writing of consciousness of life without touching culture and psychology. Of the entire trilogy, *Heaven Earth Moonlight Earth* is the work with the richest content; it traverses *xiangtu*, clan, social and historical fields, transcending most conventional clan novels as well as historical writing on a specific period. It also writes of the young generation immediately after the establishment of the People's Republic, as well as the fate of some women. It even depicts homosexuality, indicating that such "modern" things have actually existed for a long time in the past.

本夫是按照人性的标准、文化的标准、大文化亦即文明的标准来结构自己的三部曲的，这就形成了关于历史的一种新的概括，同时又衍伸出对于人和世界关系的新的思考。《天地月亮地》最后另一个主人公天易开始出现。他性格怪僻，"固执"、沉默，迷恋黑暗与喜欢"倾听大地呼吸的声音"。那么，它将把我们带向何方呢？

四

去年的七月份，在一次全国文学批评会议上，我见到了多年相识的老朋友鲁枢元先生。我和枢元见面次数不多，但相互信任。他赠我一本研究古代诗人陶渊明的专著，并谈到了自己正在从事的生态文学研究和生态批评。这是一个世界性的话题，涉及文明的走向。随着工业化、城市化的进程，高科技、高物质、高能量的消耗，亦即当前普遍存在着的空气污染、土地沙化、资源枯竭、物种灭绝的现实，我们生活的世界与往昔相比已经变得面目全非。这使我们要重新思考"进步""现代性""现代文明"这些我们多

Benfu constructs his trilogy based on his rationale of humanity, culture as well as civilization, thus forming a new historical framework in which to evolve a new way of thinking regarding humans and the world. In the final part of *Heaven Earth Moonlight Earth*, the novel's other protagonist, Tianyi, appears. He is eccentric, "stubborn," silent, wildly in love with darkness, enjoying "listening to the breath of the great earth." Now, to which direction will he take us?

4

Last July, at a national conference on literary criticism, I saw a friend who I've been acquainted with for many years, Mr. Lu Shuyuan. Although we didn't see each other a lot, we trust each other. He gave me a book that examined the pre-modern poet Tao Yuanming, and we discussed his current research on ecological literature and ecological criticism. This is a global talk, touching on civilization's future direction. Following the processes of industrialization and urbanization as well as the over-consumption of high tech, material and energy, we are faced with air pollution, desertification, resource exhaustion, and the extinction of species as a universal reality. In comparison with the past, our world has changed completely. This has forced us to re-think the consequences associated with the conventional concepts that we have become used to for many years, such as "progress," "modernity," "modern civilization." Literature, of course, cannot solve the ecological crisis or change the course of our current history; however, sensitive

年来已习惯的概念所带来的后果。文学当然不可能解决生态危机或改变当前历史的进程,但敏感的作家却不可能不对现实及人与自然、人与世界的关系发出自己的声音。枢元说,生态批评并不限于自然生态、环境保护一类,它也可以联系、扩大到精神生态。当然,由此还可以分切出更多的层面,社会生态、政治生态等等。他提出的回归自然、"自然哲学"并非是一种消极的主张,自然哲学也决定了其人生哲学,通向历史。枢元从文艺心理学的批评,"向内转"发展到研究陶渊明和生态的批评,似乎有着某种内在的必然性。这使我很敬佩。我也想借助枢元的观点,进一步阐述本夫的《地母》三部曲和《无土时代》。

自然和人性是同一等级层次的概念。在人和自然的价值关系中,包含着我们久已不提的世界观和人生观。前者反映我们对于客体的认识和态度,后者又表明我们关于主体的追求和期许。这种价值观还可能具体地影响到我们的生活态度、情趣、个性追求乃至一些"怪癖"。在《无土时代》中,我看到本夫写了许多"怪人"。如出版社老总石陀是"有巢氏",习惯于坐在木梯上办公,

writers cannot but give voice to the relations between humans and nature as well as humans and the world. Lu Shuyuan said, "Ecological criticism does not limit itself to ecology, environmental protection, etc.; it can also be extended to spiritual ecology. Of course, from this you can branch out a number of different dimensions, including social ecology, political ecology, etc." The "natural philosophy" that he advocated, the notion of returning to nature, is not just a passive position. His natural philosophy also decides his life philosophy, leading towards history. Lu Shuyuan took "the inner turn," moving from psychological literary criticism towards researching Tao Yuanming and ecological criticism, and this development has a kind of inherent inevitability. This makes me admire him greatly. I want to borrow Shuyuan's perspective to further analyze Benfu's *Mother Earth* trilogy and particularly *An Age without Earth*.

Nature and humanity are concepts of the same order. Within the value relations between humans and nature, what is included is our long unaddressed outlook on the world and on life. The former reflects our understanding and attitude toward the object, while the latter addresses the pursuit and hope of the subject. These values can also have specific influence on our attitudes towards life, our interests, our individual aspirations or even a number of our "eccentricities." In *An Age without Earth*, we can see that Benfu writes of many "odd people." For example, Shi Tuo, director of a publishing house is nicknamed Youchao (a legendary king in Chinese history who taught people to build houses in trees to protect themselves against wild animals). He is accustomed to sitting on

晚上则潜行于街上敲开水泥马路，让人和土地接触；作家柴门认为文明伴随着异化，城市在人类发展史上，是培育欲望和欲望过剩的地方，使人扭曲变形，疏离了大地母亲；还有，从乡村进入城市后便失踪了的天易，和木城的各有所思所行的那些奇奇怪怪的政协委员们。怪诞是本夫创造小说故事和人物的一个特征。实际上，《地母》的前两部，乃至于在以往的中、短篇小说中，他也曾写了不少"怪人"。"怪诞"不同于哲学上的"荒诞"那种不可解的内在的悖谬，怪诞作为一种修辞格是可解的，要达到其艺术效果，仍然需要有力的生活与摇曳多姿的故事来支撑。于是我们看到本夫写"怪人"的小说都有鲜明的故事色彩，《无土时代》也不是荒诞小说。同样的，"典型"在认识论上被我们推崇，可那些被我们肯定、赞扬的"典型"又很快被遗忘或淹没，而真正的"典型"却常常是在无意识中形成的，例如贾宝玉、阿Q，他们在当时可能被认为是一些不正常的，当然也是不典型的怪人。本夫也并没有有意识地要创造"典型"，他只是要写"地母"，而从柴姑、小迷娘到《无土时代》中的天易的前生、今世，则已构成了

wooden steps while working in office, and at night he moves stealthily on the street knocking against the cement avenue, so that people can have a chance to touch the soil. The writer Chai Men believes that alienation comes with civilization, and that city is a hotbed of desire, where desire overflows, distorting humans and distancing them from mother earth; there is also Tianyi, who leaves the countryside and disappears in the city, as well as the odd members of the political consultative conference in the Woodtown, each eccentric in their own way. The bizarre is one of the characteristics of Benfu's creation. In reality, there are no lack of "odd people" in the first two stories of the trilogy, as well as Benfu's short and medium-length fiction of the past. "Bizarre" is not the same as the philosophical "absurd," which is a kind of inexplicable inherent preposterousness. "Bizarre" as a figure of speech can be explained, and yet to accomplish its artistic effect it must be sustained by a powerful life and a colorful story. As such, the novels in which Benfu writes of "strange people" all have vivid narrative color. *An Age without Earth* is not an "absurd" novel. Similarly, while epistemically we praise "archetypes", the ones that we affirm are often quickly forgotten or drowned out; the true "archetypes" are often formed unconsciously, for example Jia Baoyu or Ah-Q, who, in their times, were perhaps thought of as unconventional "odd people," certainly not archetypal. Benfu did not consciously set out to create certain archetype; he only wanted to write of "mother earth," and yet from Auntie Chai, Little Miniang down to Tianyi's previous lives and current lives in *An Age without Earth*, he has already created a collective figure that is interconnected and difficult

一种连续的、难忘的集体的形象，又有了一种新的典型意义。

《无土时代》的主要内容就是"寻找"。寻找天易，寻找柴门，最后寻找石陀。由寻找天易所引发，那是一种身世的寻找、身份的寻找，也是在疑窦重重中对于生命本源的寻找。天易是大瓦屋家族中被寄予厚望的、最有出息的孩子，在"文革"大串联后与一个姓梅的俄语教师一起失踪了。他同时也带走了大瓦屋家的魂魄。柴门是一位有才华的作者，石陀要在全国各地寻找他，不仅为他出文集，也暗示寻找一种思想的轨迹。谜一样的石陀又让梁朝东、许一桃等担心、忧虑，"石陀是谁？"寻找石陀也就是寻找怪人的根源和秘密。在这个过程中，出差的大学生编辑谷子也在寻找着她的生身父母。悬疑、神秘、象征、杂糅、变形、夸张、怪诞和"灵魂出窍"的寻找笼罩着这部小说。

我们从哪里来，要到哪里去？

天易乃天意，是柴姑起的名。雅克·德里达在其晚年的力作《马克思的幽灵》中提出，"幽灵"作为一种"遗产"，那是一种不死的灵魂，"从来不是一种给予，它向来是一项使命"，那是"一

to forget, signifying a new archetype.

An Age without Earth's main theme is "searching"—searching for Tianyi, searching for Chai Men, finally searching for Shi Tuo. The search for Tianyi is the search for family history, the search for identity, the search for the source of life amidst great confusion. Tianyi is the most brilliant child in the Great Tile House clan, upon whom the greatest hopes are entrusted. After the Revolutionary Networking Movement during the "Cultural Revolution", he and a Russian language teacher disappear at the same time. He also takes with him the soul of the Great Tile House clan. Chai Men is a talented author, and Shi Tuo searches for him across all corners of the country to get his works published, which also suggests a search of thought. Meanwhile, Liang Chaodong and Xu Yitao fret over the question "Who is Shi Tuo?" who himself is like a riddle. To search for Shi Tuo is to search for the source and secret of the odd people. Within this process the editor Grain, a university student on a business trip, is also searching for her biological mother and father. This search, charged with suspense, mystery, symbolism, hybridization, metamorphosis, exaggeration, bizarreness, like a "ghost hovering over its body", enshrouds this novel.

Where are we from and where are we going?

Tianyi, if understood in its homophone, also means "Heaven's Idea"; it is a name given by Auntie Chai. Jacques Derrida in his late-period work *Specters of Marx* claimed that a "specter" is a kind of "inheritance," a kind of ghost that will not die. "It is never a given, it is always a mission." It is "the waiting of an anxious spirit to come back." In this way, searching for Tianyi (Heaven's Idea) is

种精神焦急的还乡式的等待"。这样，寻找天易（天意）便是人类的使命。

《无土时代》同时给我们呈现了城市和农村的两种画面。一种是繁华的城市，它无度地发展着，不断扩大；一种是日益凋敝的乡村，那一个个即将消失的村庄。一边是贪婪攫取，城里人弥漫着一种焦躁的、无定性的情绪；一边是努力打工，乡下人要改变自己"天然的"或被强迫的身份。一面是一种向上的物质欲求；另一面则表现为一种向下的精神曲线。在草儿洼，村长方全林总要在风雨夜帮人修房，过去农村人进城打工是为了挣钱回家盖房，现在则已舍弃老房，携家到城里寻找居所。农村人宁可到城里捡垃圾，也要生活在城市，例如王长贵。而城里人则要到农村去度假，"久在樊笼里，复得返自然"，享受那份自由、放松乃至原始的性爱，例如木城的女老板麦子。正如《无土时代》的卷首语："花盆是城里人对祖先和种植的残存记忆。"在小说的奇思妙想中，既然农村人口流向城市的过程不可阻挡，那么如天柱带领的草儿

humanity's mission.

An Age without Earth also provides for us two different kinds of tableaus. One is of the prosperous city, its boundless development, its relentless expansion. The other is of the countryside, which becomes increasingly destitute, village after village on the verge of disappearance. On the one hand you have greed and robbery, with cities being suffused with an anxious mood of instability; on the other hand you have hardworking migrant labor, with country people wanting to change the identity that is forced upon them as "ordained from heaven." You have a kind of material desire that pushes ever higher, as well as an enervated spiritual distortion that pushes ever downward. In Cao'r Wa, the village chief Fang Quanlin always helps people on stormy evenings repair their homes. In the past rural people went to the city to work in order to make money so they could return to their villages to build homes. Today they have already given up their old homes, taking their families with them to live in the city. Rural people would rather pick up garbage in cities than live in the countryside, for example, Wang Changgui. City people, on the other hand, want to go to the countryside for holidays—"For a long time I have been in a cage, now again I return to the natural way of life," as Tao Yuanming from the Jin Dynasty said in his poem "Come away Home." And they want to enjoy sexuality that is free, relaxed, and primitive, for example, the lady boss Wheat from Woodtown. Just as it says in the foreword of *An Age without Earth*: "For city dwellers, flowerpots are the last vestige of the memories of the earth and the planting life of our ancestors." Although it seems inevitable

洼的农民工所组建的城市绿化队，决定在改造木城的361块草坪中全部移栽上麦苗，便是把城市又变回了农村。这真是《无土时代》的一个大胆的构想。

石洼村已变成了草儿洼，老石屋家族演变成了大瓦屋家族。在小说故事层面上，天易失踪与天易、石陀、柴门是否是同一个人又疑点不断，模糊不清。譬如石陀不抽烟，柴门则抽烟很凶；另外柴门那些出门的票据与纸条又从何而来，似只能解释为一种幽灵的神秘现象或灵魂出窍。但这些都不用过于追根究底，小说人物"三位一体"是《无土时代》的构思之一，至少在文化性格与价值追求上是统一的。记得在去年的一次作品讨论会上，本夫说，作家的创作归根到底总是要写他自己的，都是一种生活的自叙传或是一种精神的自叙传。当然随着创作发展，其意义又在不断扩大。本夫的小说也总是写他的家乡，"凤城""柳镇"，苏鲁豫皖四省交界处的黄河故道。在《无土时代》的最后，失去了记忆的石陀决定要回一趟自己的故乡，与此同时，木城的天空中又见

to stop rural people from flowing into cities, it is still possible to transform cities back into the countryside. We see this in the urban greening team that Tianzhu leads, made of laborers from Cao'r Wa village, who decide to plant wheat seedlings as they repair Woodtown's 361 lawns. This really is a courageous notion presented by *An Age without Earth*.

Shiwa Village has already become Cao'r Wa village, and Old Stone House clan has already become Great Tile House clan. On the level of the novel's narrative, the disappearance of Tianyi, as well as the question of whether Tianyi, Shi Tuo, and Chai Men are the same person are surrounded in uncertainty. For example, Shi Tuo does not smoke, yet Chai Men smokes like a chimney. Besides, where do Chai Men's travel bills and those slips come from? It can seemingly only be explained as the play of a mysterious specter, or as an out-of-body experience. But these questions do not have to be pursued down to their roots, for "trinity" is the main notion behind the characterization in *An Age without Earth*, an attempt to achieve unison in terms of cultural signification and the pursuit of values. I remember that on a forum last year Benfu said that the roots of an author's creativity are found, on the most basic level, in writing himself; all works are a self-narration of his life or his spirit. Of course, following the development in his creation, the meanings of his work never cease to expand. Benfu always writes of his village hometown, "Fengcheng," "Willow Town," the old course of the yellow river that runs along the borderline around Jiangsu, Anhui, Henan, and Shandong. At the end of *An Age without Earth*, Shi Tuo, who has already lost his memory, decides that he would like to return to his rural hometown, and at that moment people spot stars

到了多年未见的星星和月亮，黄鼠狼也出现了。那是在寻找一种被历史抛弃了的自然和价值的关系，又是一种精神焦急的"还乡"式的期待。马克思早年在谈到人类的理想和追求时说，"共产主义是对私有财产即人的自我异化的积极的扬弃……它是人向自身，也就是向社会的即合乎人性的人的复归……这种共产主义，作为完成了的自然主义，等于人道主义，而作为完成了的人道主义，等于自然主义，它是人和自然界之间、人和人之间的矛盾的真正解决，是存在和本质、对象化和自我确认、自由和必然、个体和类之间的斗争的真正解决。它是历史之谜的解答，而且知道自己就是这种解答"。我想，本夫的全部创作便是呼应了这种自然主义和人道主义的追求。

本夫的长篇可以说是中国生态文学最高水平的成果。它同时也是历史叙事新的创造，提供了新的人物形象画廊和新的故事。《地母》三部曲是他最重要的文学贡献。

2013 年

and the moon in the sky above Woodtown, a rare sight within many years, and the yellow weasel also appears. This symbolizes the pursuit of a relationship between values and nature that history has already abandoned. It is also the anxious longing for "the return of the native". Karl Marx in his early years discussed the ideals and aspirations of human beings. He said, "Communism as the positive transcendence of private property, as human self-estrangement, and therefore as the real appropriation of the human essence by and for man; communism therefore as the complete return of man to himself as a social (i.e., human) being... This communism, as fully developed naturalism, equals humanism, and as fully developed humanism equals naturalism; it is the genuine resolution of the conflict between man and nature and between man and man—the true resolution of the strife between existence and essence, between objectification and self-confirmation, between freedom and necessity, between the individual and the species. Communism is the riddle of history solved, and it knows itself to be this solution." I think that Benfu's entire corpus is an echo of the pursuit of this kind of naturalism and humanism.

We can say that Benfu's novels represent the highest level of accomplishment of ecological literature in China. At the same time they are new works of historical narration, offering a new spectrum of human figures and stories. The *Mother Earth* trilogy is his most important literary contribution.

2013

访谈

文学如何呈现记忆？——赵本夫访谈录

沙家强

沙家强：说实话，我并不是从电影《天下无贼》了解您的，而是因《无土时代》扉页中"花盆是城里人对土地和祖先种植的残存记忆"这样一句话的吸引，让我走进了您的小说世界——《地母》系列三部曲，也进一步了解了您。在研读过程中，我摘抄了近3万字的读书笔记，并按相关内容进行了分类，从中我发现

Interview

How Does Literature Present Memory?
—An Interview with Zhao Benfu

By Sha Jiaqiang
Translated by Jesse Field

Sha Jiaqiang: To tell you the truth, I did not learn about you from the movie *A World without Thieves*. Rather, I was drawn to the sentence on the title page of *An Age without Earth*: "For urban dwellers, flowerpots are the last vestige of the memories of the earth and the planting life of our ancestors." With that, I entered your world, the *Mother Earth* trilogy. And I began to understand you. In the course of my reading, I had taken down nearly thirty thousand characters in notes. I also had classified these notes that yielded

许多很有价值的话题。我的导师何永康先生说，您的小说是个"富矿"，值得细细研究，读后感觉的确如此。可以说，在进行了长时间的心灵对话后，我对文学本质的认识也更深刻了。在此，我秉持的是法国现象学家杜夫海纳这样的文学批评观点："作者并不在那些关于他们的资料里，而就在他们的作品中。"今天，我主要立足于文本，从作家的精神现象的深处来谈谈我的粗见。首先，通读这部系列小说后，我发现您具有浓厚的乡土意识、故乡恋情和书写故乡的愿望。黄河、草儿洼、蓝水河、小城、老祖母等等都是您小说中经常出现的意象，可以想见，故乡是您的精神母体。我的第一个问题是，故乡书写经常出现，故乡山山水水的记忆情怀对您创作有何影响？您感觉这些在您小说的价值意义何在？

赵本夫：作家书写故乡是自然的事。对我来说——其实对任何一个人来说，不仅是作家，当然作家更敏感，故乡记忆是永远的。也许你在故乡仅仅生活了童年或青年时代，之后就离开故乡了。开始的时候，你觉得你可以走遍天下、浪迹天涯，你可以离开故乡，离开母亲了，但实际上你走了很远以后，你会发现你还没有离开。故乡永远是你的背影，是你生存的背影，你的文化、你的修养、你的生命都源于那块地方，实际上你有很多事情脱不

many valuable topics for discussion. My advisor, Mister He Yongkang once said that your stories were a "rich mine" worthy of detailed study, and after reading, I certainly feel the same. I think my understanding of literature has deepened after a long soul dialogue. I affirm the critical view of the French phenomenologist Mikel Dufrenne: "The author is in the work, not in materials about the author." Today I'll base my humble opinions on your texts, exploring the deep center of a writer's spiritual land. First, reading the trilogy, I find in you a deep consciousness of the rural, a rural complex and a wish to writing about the rural hometown (*guxiang* 故乡). The Yellow River, Cao'r Wa, the Blue Water River, small towns, and even grandmothers are all frequent images in your fiction. One gets the feeling that the old rural home is your spiritual matrix. So my first question is: Given the fact that you frequently write about *guxiang* and its natural scenery in your memories, how do these influence your creative writing? How would you define the value and meaning of these in your fiction?

Zhao Benfu: It's natural to write about home, *guxiang*. For me—and for anyone, really, though writers might be more sensitive to it—memories of home last forever. Maybe you only lived at home during your childhood and adolescence, then left it. You began your journey, thinking you could explore all over, travel to the ends of the earth. You believe you can leave your home, your mother. But you can never really leave your home behind, because it's your background, it goes along with you. Your home shadows you, for

开故乡。对于我来说，故乡的意义更大，因为我在故乡生活很久，故乡对我的影响更明显，故乡的影子应该刻骨铭心。我前期生活在丰县，真正调离丰县已经近四十岁了。

沙家强："三部曲"中"草儿洼"由荒凉、繁荣到渐趋消失的变迁过程，很令人启发。这其中与"土地"关系密切，这里蕴藏着赵老师您深厚的"土地哲学"观，所以谈论《地母》系列三部曲就不能回避"土地"这个重要意象。

赵本夫："土地"是个核心问题。

沙家强：其中有四个人对"土地"的虔诚态度让我印象深刻。天易年少时常常俯下身子倾听大地的呼吸，柴姑就是土地的化身、简直以宗教般的情怀崇拜着土地，石陀常常以"神经质"式的方式在混凝土下寻找土地的影子，天柱则始终以一个乡下人的身份极力唤起城市人对土地的记忆，他们的行为也唤起了我们对土地的特别记忆。谈到"记忆"，我就想到了那句话，"花盆是城里人对土地和祖先种植的残存记忆"，"残存"一词让我印象深刻，"残存"让我在震撼中反思：当今繁华的都市给我们留下了什么？又让我们失去

your culture, breeding, your very life all come from that place. In many ways, you can never leave home. To me, home has an especially important meaning, because I lived there so long. The influence of home on me is more obvious; home's shadow is deeply etched in my bones. You know, I lived in Fengxian County until I was nearly forty.

Sha Jiaqiang: Cao'r Wa in the trilogy undergoes a process from barren to flourishing and gradually towards disappearing altogether, a process that is thought-provoking. All this bears a deep relation to earth, and contains your own "philosophy of earth." So to talk about the *Mother Earth* trilogy is to talk about this important image, earth.

Zhao Benfu: Yes, earth is the core issue.

Sha Jiaqiang: There are four characters in the trilogy whose passion for earth leaves particularly deep impressions. Tianyi from a young age often bends down and listens to the breath of the earth. Auntie Chai is an incarnation of the earth, worshipping earth with a religious fervor. Shi Tuo, like a neurotic, is chasing after the memory of earth beneath the cement and concrete. Tianzhu always remains a peasant, reminding urban dwellers of their own memories of earth. The actions of these characters call up our special memories of the earth. On the subject of "memory," I think of the sentence, "For urban dwellers, flowerpots are the last vestige of memories of the earth and the planting life of our ancestors." That phrase "last vestige" really got to me, kept ringing in the mind.

和遗忘了什么？我想，天柱他们要唤醒城里人对土地的记忆这个壮举，是生命本能的坚守。我的问题是，如今城里人对土地失忆了，您在小说中唤醒人们记住土地的深层次旨向是什么呢？

赵本夫：记住土地，实际上就是记住自然。我们住在城市的高楼上，但是不能忘了高楼的地基仍是土地。这是根本。人对自然、对土地的亲近是应有的情结。"大地是人类的母亲"，这不是我发明的，其实大家都知道，这是个常识。但人类恰恰是最容易在常识上犯错误，而在常识上犯错误对人造成的危害最大。就像战争一样，谁都知道战争杀人很残酷、很残忍，但恰恰是战争对人类造成巨大的灾难。

沙家强：这是不是一种悖论？

赵本夫：对，是一种悖论。人在尖端高科技上犯不了错误，没人想造原子弹来贩卖，但恰恰是在常识上犯一些错误，会造成普遍性的危害。人类对自然、对大地的崇拜其实是人类最早的崇拜，是一种原始崇拜。

原始人对日、月、星、辰等自然现象不了解，对此很恐惧，对这些诸如土地为什么会长出各种东西等现象，人类不懂。所以，人崇拜源于无知，源于恐惧，这才有对土地最早的崇拜。然后人

"Last vestige"—What are these cities leaving us with? And what are we forgetting and missing?

The way I see it, characters like Tianzhu are issuing a call to action and to revive urban dwellers' memories of earth. It's an act of self-preservation, the instinct of preserving life. My question is about the purpose of your fiction to call urban dwellers to remember. Anything deep that underlies this call?

Zhao Benfu: To remember earth is to remember nature. We may live in enormous apartment buildings, but don't forget that even those are built on the earth. This is basic. Humans have to feel this intimacy with the Nature and the earth. "Mother Earth is the mother of all." I didn't make this up—this is common sense that everyone should know. But it's common sense that so often trips us up. Ignoring common sense could end up costing humanity everything. It's just like war. Everyone knows war kills, cruelly and ruthlessly, and yet war is just what plagues humanity most.

Sha Jiaqiang: Is that a paradox?

Zhao Benfu: Yes, it's paradox. Humanity thinks it can hardly get tripped up by its cutting-edge technologies—no one wants to fashion and sell nuclear weapons, for example—but it's common sense that so often trips us up and ends up hurting us all. The worship of Nature, of Mother Earth, is the oldest human worship.

Early humans were mystified by the sun, the moon, the stars, and time, which made them afraid. They couldn't understand why things grew from the earth. Worship, then, originates in ignorance,

类有很多宗教，西方有基督教，东方有佛教，阿拉伯世界有伊斯兰教。真正的宗教从本质上是向善的，都是在寻找一种精神归宿。但说老实话，这些宗教对人本身只是寻找一种精神解脱，而真正能给人类以生命托付的还是大地，还是大自然。我们一刻也不能离开。比如阳光、空气、水、植物，大自然为人类提供了一切。人类文明发展到今天，人却离土地越来越远，离大自然越来越远了，对土地概念也越来越淡漠。实际上城市最缺失的就是人对土地的亲近。为什么现在人们那么顽强地开始回归自然，要到户外去、要到城外去寻找大地、寻找山川、河流、森林，所住的自然环境要好一点？这是因为人骨子里这些东西没有消失，但现实中就是缺失了，于是越是缺失就越是要寻找。这就涉及一些哲学命题。比如，我们通常说人类文明是世界上最高级的文明，我就质疑这种说法。事实上，最高级的文明应当是自然文明，大自然的奇妙有多少密码，我们知道吗？所以有仿生学，人类在向大自然学习，在不断探索、研究，但无法穷尽它。人类文明只能算自然文明的一小部分。再比如，人本质上是理性力量大、还是本能力量更大？我一直在思考这种问题。我觉得，人的本能力量更

in fear. The worship of earth was the earliest form. Afterward came other religions, Christianity in the West, Buddhism in the East, Islam in the Arab world. True religion leans toward the good, seeks a haven for the spirit. But the truth is, the major religions all seek the liberation of spirit, whereas Nature and Mother Earth provide the necessities of Life itself. We can never do, not even for a moment, without what are provided by Nature—sunlight, air, water and plants. But following civilization, humans become more distant from the earth, more distant from Nature. Their idea of earth turns thin and insubstantial. What cities lack most is intimacy with the earth. Why is it today we have so many turning back to Nature, demanding to go outdoors, seeking Mother Earth outside the city, among mountains, rivers and forests and living in better natural environment? It's because Nature, which remains in our bones, is lost in our real life; so the more it's lost the more we seek it.

This touches on certain philosophical propositions. For example, we often say human civilization is the highest in the world. But I'm skeptical of this claim. In fact, the highest civilization ought to be that of Nature. Do we even know how many marvelous secrets Nature holds? That is how bionics comes into being. Humans look to Nature for lessons, exploring, studying, yet never reaching the end. Human civilization can never count as more than a small portion of natural civilization. Another example is, which is a stronger force in the basic quality of humanity: reason, or instinct? I

强大。

沙家强：人有一种无意识的本能行为。

赵本夫：我们知道，人与动物的区别是人是理性的，人可以约束自己，人与社会是要规范的，但人本能的东西你根本压抑不住。比如我们生活中的吃、喝、拉、撒这些最俗的本能，但你用再好的理性也不能抑制住这些。文明在某种意义上是一种秩序，文明社会需要秩序，但任何秩序对生命个体都是一种束缚，甚至是一种扼杀、一种灾难。因为任何一个生命个体都是生而自由的，不希望被束缚，一草一木都是如此，何况人呢。所以，文学有时候不是判断文明好与不好、人的本能好与不好，而是常常要表现这种无奈、痛苦和挣扎。

沙家强：在《无土时代》，我发现有一处很长的几句话，说城市人"为权为名为得为生存而拼搏而挣扎而相煎而倾轧而痛苦或精疲力竭或得意忘形或幸灾乐祸或绞尽脑汁或蝇营狗苟或不择手段或扭曲变态或逢迎拍马或悲观绝望或整夜失眠或拉帮结派或形单影只或故作清高或酒后失态或窃笑或沮丧或痛不欲生等等所有这些，都属于城市特有的表情。城市把人害惨了，城市是个培育

have long wondered. I think instinct is the stronger.

Sha Jiaqiang: People exhibit unconscious, instinctive behavior.

Zhao Benfu: We know that reason is what makes humans different from animals. Humans can constrain themselves, and human society has rules, but instinct cannot be repressed. Eating and drinking, shitting and peeing, for example, are the most common of instincts, yet you will be hard-pressed to stifle them, no matter how good your reason is. Civilization means order, and civilized society requires order. But any form of order is also a constraint on Life, and at worst may stifle and lead to disaster. Any individual organism is born free and hopes not to be constrained, and that includes grass and tree as much as human. That's why literature does not always judge the good or evil of civilizations or human instinct, but rather expresses helplessness, pain, and struggle.

Sha Jiaqiang: In *An Age without Earth*, I found some long descriptions about urban dwellers.

"They fight and struggle and suffer and jostle for power for fame for gain for existence and in pain in fatigue to rise to dizzying success or fall down in disaster racking their brains and searching for gain some perverting the right and the true and some flattering and fawning some losing hope and others losing sleep, some working in packs and others all on their own, some proud and pretentious and others drunk and despairing or sly or dazed or too hurt to keep on living and all these are faces found first in the city. The city

欲望和欲望过剩的地方，城里人没有满足感没有安定感没有安全感没有幸福感没有闲适没有从容没有真正的友谊"。这里由于没用标点，所以整个句势显得很有压迫感。在这里，您似乎在强调城市的现代文明发展给人带来诸多问题？

赵本夫：我不用标点完全不是玩形式，借用这种形式是为了人物内心表现的需要，他很急迫地很汹涌地表达一种观点，就像我们平时说话很快、很急、很冲动时，语不加点，甚至口吃，他就是要急迫表达一种观点，那是人物性格人物内心表现的需要。所以，我始终认为形式是为内容服务的。

沙家强：从中我们可以看出那种无奈、困惑和愤怒的情绪。城市的发展和现代文明的进步是两面的，是充满悖论的。

赵本夫：城市、人类的发展面临很多话题，作家、政治家你都可以从不同角度来探索，我选择的是从土地这个角度来探索。今年 10 月份我要到法兰克福参加一个国际书市，其间有几场演讲，我演讲的主题就是"城市和无土时代"。我还是讲大地这个话题。

沙家强：对，我第一次见到您时，就特别感觉到您时常关注

traumatizes people the city incubates desires a place of excess desire. People of the city get no satisfaction no peace no safety no happiness no leisure and no true friendship."

The lack of punctuation here turns the sentence's power into something repressive. It seems that you really wish to emphasize the many problems that come from cities as developments of modern civilization. Is that right?

Zhao Benfu: I don't eschew punctuation just to play with form, but rather adopt this form out of the needs of the character's internal state. He is expressing a view in a very hurried and distressed manner, and it comes out somewhat like how we often speak: fast, urgent, impulsive, without the right pauses, stammering, even. He expresses his view out of distress and such are the needs of his internal state. Form must serve content, I always say.

Sha Jiaqiang: We can see here feelings of helplessness, confusion, and indignation. There are two sides to the development of the city and the development of modern civilization. It's paradoxical.

Zhao Benfu: The development of cities and humanity touches on many topics, and writers and politicians can approach from many different perspectives. My own perspective starts from the earth, the land and soil themselves. At the Frankfurt Book Fair in October this year, I will give a lecture called "The City and an Age without Earth." Once again, my topic will be Mother Earth.

Sha Jiaqiang: Right, the first time I saw you, I felt that you

人类话题，是不是您内心深处对土地也有着宗教般的情怀？

赵本夫：是，我一直觉得以前那些宗教信仰都是好的，我都很虔诚地尊敬它们，但我认为人类最早的宗教、真正的宗教是对大自然的崇拜，这是人类最原始的宗教。我一直相信这不仅仅是最原始的崇拜，而且应当是一种终极的崇拜，这样人类才有希望。

沙家强：在漫长的几千年文明史中，人与自然、人与土地的关系相当密切，文学本身往往有一种诗性特色，但这种特色现在似乎正在遭受某种挑战？

赵本夫：人和大地这种关系，中西方是相通的，中国神话里面女娲用黄土造人，泥土是造人用的最原本的东西。西方《圣经》里也是用土造亚当，亚当又用肋骨造了夏娃。所以，中西方造人都是用土这种原料。人本质上都是源于土，人最初从土里生，最终死亡又回归大地。自有人类以来，死了多少人？死去的人哪里去了？和土地融为一体了。所以今天的土地成分中，是有人类、动物、植物分子的。土既是生命的源头，又是生命的归宿。

沙家强：我发现，三部曲在叙事时间上很有特点。整个系列

paid particular attention to broader topics of humanity. Would it be correct to say that deep down, you approach the concept of earth with a religious feeling?

Zhao Benfu: Yes, I've always felt there was something good about religion and faith, and I respect it, but I feel humanity's earliest religion, and really truest religion, is the worship of Nature. This is the primal religion of humanity. And I've always believed that it's not only the primal form of worship, but also deserves to be the ultimate form of worship. It's humanity's only hope.

Sha Jiaqiang: Over thousands of years of civilization, people have had a very intimate relationship with Nature, with the earth. And literature itself has frequently a special poetic quality, but is this special quality undergoing a major challenge now?

Zhao Benfu: China and the West are in perfect accord regarding the relation of people to mother earth. In Chinese mythology, Nüwa (女娲) created humans from the yellow earth. Mud was the original substance used to make humans. In the Bible, earth was used to make Adam, and a rib of Adam was fashioned into Eve. So in both China and the West, earth was the original material. Human originates in earth, humans are born from earth, and in the end they return in death to Mother Earth. How many humans have died since humanity began? Where did all the dead go? They are one with the earth. Thus the earth today contains portions of humans, animals, and plants. They are its ingredients. Earth is both the originator and the resting-place of life.

小说不像《刀客与女人》那样时常出现"民国五年""一九三六年"等等这样明确的时间界限，在文本中，我们几乎看不到具体的时间指向，而是以具有显著时代特征的事件来进行叙事的。如柴姑大概活了100岁以上，我没猜错的话，故事大致从19世纪60年代开始的；还有一些重要事件的隐露，如八音"支持七子去抗美"、贫农、地主阶层的划分、天易是在"文化大革命"期间在北京失踪的、草儿洼"常年外出打工的不下一千人"，从这里"文化大革命""打工"术语的运用可以看出，小说时间的流动已经绵延至当下甚至就近在咫尺。我的问题是，以这些具有时代特征的事件来推动故事进展，您是有意的吗？这是不是一种特殊的记忆方式，作家对某个特定时间段往事的记忆更会获得生命存在的确切感受。不知您是否赞同？还是有着什么样的思考？

赵本夫：我这样写，不确定哪一年、哪一月的具体时间，这与整个系列三部曲的基调是一致的，整个系列基调是混沌的，它基于我对整个人类、大地、宇宙的认识。

沙家强：赵老师，我插一下，这种"混沌"是不是指其本身就不是清晰的、没有明确界线？

Sha Jiaqiang: I noticed the trilogy has an unusual way of dealing with time. In *The Swordsman and the Woman*, there were specific years mentioned, like "the fifth year of the Republic," or "1936," but not in this trilogy, where we see almost no specific dates, but instead descriptions of events that mark the era. That Auntie Chai lives to be one hundred, for example, indicates that the narrative begins around 1860, if my guess is correct. There are also indirect references to important historical events, as when Bayin supports "all seven of her sons going off to fight against the Americans in Korea," or when the class line between poor peasant and landlord was drawn, or how Tianyi was missing in Beijing during the "Cultural Revolution," or how in Cao'r Wa, no fewer than a thousand spent years working as migrant labor elsewhere. Terms like "Cultural Revolution" and "migrant labor" reveal a flow of time all the way up to the present. Do you have some particular purpose in narrating time using such historical events? Perhaps it is a special form of memory, one in which the author retains precise feelings of life during certain periods of the past. Do you agree? What else might we say on that?

Zhao Benfu: Writing like this, leaving out the specific dates, is of a piece with the basic tenor of the work: undifferentiation, *hundun*. It's based more on my holistic view of humanity, earth, and the universe.

Sha Jiaqiang: Excuse me, but does this "*hundun*" mean that there is no clarity? No distinct boundaries?

赵本夫：对，它本身就不应是清晰的，很多观念是贯穿始终的，它是一团混沌，你根本就搞不清楚。这是东方哲学。东方哲学和西方哲学有很大的不同。西方哲学是要把什么都搞清楚，什么都要分出是非。我是对的，你就是错的。但东方哲学不会这么说，你是对的，可能我也是对的。所以中国会有很多相反的话可以并行，所以中国人讲和而不同。西医和中医，西画和中国画，包括一些政治理念，都可以看出东西方的不同。文学的背后，其实是哲学。文学作品也必会有所不同。但好的文学作品一定是混沌的。你今天让我自己来谈《无土时代》，说真的，我自己就不清楚，因为我把自己整个生命中的很多东西、生命的所有积累和感悟都砸进去了。这其中就可能包括很多东西，以至于连我自己都说不清，这很正常，中外很多作家都有这种体会。不同的读者会读出不同的东西，这才叫好作品。我经历过很多苦难的生活，经验过很多特别的生活，不仅有家族和周围人的困难，而且曾差点病死、饿死，还因为写小说受过半年多的批斗，差一点进了监狱。我上世纪七十年代，参加过六次农村工作队，看到太多的人间苦难。我也参观过很多监狱，和犯人有过很多次的接触和通信。我

Zhao Benfu: Yes. It's not clear to begin with. Many concepts are completely interconnected. It's all one undifferentiated mass that you can't analyze. This is Eastern philosophy, which is very different from Western philosophy. Western philosophy wants clarity, wants to distinguish truth from falsehood. I am right and you are wrong. But Eastern philosophy isn't like that. You are right, but maybe I am, too. That's why in China, many contradictory statements can be upheld at the same time. In China, people can disagree yet still find accord. We can see this distinction at work in Chinese medicine versus Western medicine, in Chinese painting versus Western painting, and even in certain political concepts. *Hundun* is Chinese philosophy. Behind literature we always find philosophy. Literary works have their differences, but good literature always exhibits this *hundun*. Here you are now, asking me about *An Age Without Earth*, but to tell you the truth, it's not clear to me either, because I stuffed it full of so much from life, so many accumulated feelings. This can include more things than I even know, which is only normal. Many authors, Chinese or not, have this experience. Different readers can discover different things in any good work of literature. I've been through very tough times, very strange times. I've seen suffering in my family and among those around me. I've also almost died of illness. And of hunger, too. Once, I was struggled against the better part of a year, just because I was a writer. I was nearly put in prison. Back in the 1970s, I served six times in rural work teams, where I saw

曾经独自一人去西部采风五个多月，回来像个鬼，其间看到太多太多，我当然读过很多书，但我不是从书斋里走出来的作家，我是从人间走出来的亲历者。

沙家强：是的，我看您的作品更多是从故乡、民间苦难写起的。

赵本夫：有一年我母校丰县中学校庆时，我代表校友发言，就特别回忆起上世纪六十年代求学时是怎样熬过来的一些亲身经历，那时很多同学都是浑身浮肿着坐在教室里听课，老师也是浮肿着站在讲台上，好像又回到那个岁月，很多同学、老师都哭了。

沙家强：这些苦难记忆应该是您写作的重要资源。

赵本夫：这种记忆我是永远不能忘记的。

沙家强：赵老师，刚才您说过您作品的基调是"混沌"，其实作为读者，我在拜读您的作品时，往往会发现您可能没有特别注意的内蕴，这其中我就发现作品的"孤独"意识，即《地母》系列里的孤独是隐含在文本里的，这也让小说具有更大的阐释空间。这里有黄河决口后荒原的荒凉与孤寂，有蓝水河的静寂和凄凉，

too much suffering. I've also paid visits to jails, where I established frequent contact with convicts there. Once I spent five months in China's far west, collecting materials, studying culture, and I saw so much, so very, very much. When I returned, I looked like a ghost. And of course I read many books, too. But I'm not a writer out of the bookstore, I'm a witness, someone who has learned from the experience of life.

Sha Jiaqiang: Right, I can tell most of your work is about rural towns and the struggles of ordinary people.

Zhao Benfu: I remember at an anniversary celebration of my alma mater, Fengxian Middle School, I gave a speech on behalf of the alumni, reminiscing how much we had to go through to get some schooling in the 1960s. The students, even the teachers, were starving, their swollen bodies fatigued as they stood at the lecterns or sat listening at the desks. It was like we really had gone back to those old times, and we all started to cry, classmates and teachers alike.

Sha Jiaqiang: The memories of suffering must be an important source for your writing.

Zhao Benfu: Those are memories you never forget.

Sha Jiaqiang: So, you've said that the basic tenor of your work is *hundun*. As a reader who approaches your work very seriously, I often encounter a theme you might not have noticed: a state of loneliness. The loneliness in *Mother Earth* is implied in the writing, which leaves the work with more room for interpretation. We see

有柴姑最终孤独老去、老大孤身一人生活在黄河大堤上、石陀偏执地寻找土地。要说最大的孤独群体应该是木城人，他们对土地失去了记忆，彼此之间也很陌生，几乎各自是个孤岛。不知我的理解是不是显得有点偏了，这只能是我的一种感受。在此请问赵老师，您是以作家的"孤独"方式在思考着以上孤独的人和物，对于这种"孤独"您寄寓着什么深思吗？

赵本夫：事实上，每个人都是孤独的，只是程度不同。作家艺术家可能会更敏感一点，因为他要追求唯一性，因此一个好的作家艺术家，一定不会和人携手同行。他只用他自己的视角观察世界，解读生活。

沙家强："蚂蚁"意象在系列中出现很少，但第一部《黑蚂蚁蓝眼睛》就以"蚂蚁"来命名。我的理解是，蚂蚁是智慧的象征，而柴姑就是蚂蚁式的智者。"蚂蚁"在文本中有无确切的隐喻内涵？

赵本夫：含义肯定是有的，但我并不想去确认，我依然坚持混沌的状态。比如《无土时代》里有361块麦田，为什么不是362块呢？这与中国古代围棋361个点相似，象征一年360天，是有

the loneliness and austerity of the (flooded) wastes following the breach of the Yellow River, the solitude and desolation of the Blue Water River, the loneliness of the aging Auntie Chai, her son living alone on the Yellow River dyke, and Shi Tuo's stubborn search for land. Perhaps the loneliest group we see are the people of Woodtown, for they have lost their memories of earth and become strangers to each other. It's like each one's an isolated island. Maybe my understanding is biased, but that's the feeling I get. So here's my question, do you handle these examples from the perspective of a "solitary" writer? Does loneliness hold deeper meaning for you?

Zhao Benfu: Everyone is lonely, actually. It's just a matter of degree. Authors and artists are more sensitive, maybe, because they're in pursuit of uniqueness, and so they must always walk alone. They have their own eyes to observe and interpret the world and life.

Sha Jiaqiang: The image of ants seldom occurs in the series, but one appears in the title of the first volume, *Black Ants, Blue Eyes*. My understanding is that ant symbolizes wisdom, and Auntie Chai is one such ant-like person with wisdom. Is there deeper significance to ants?

Zhao Benfu: I'm sure there is, but I wouldn't want to specify it. I prefer to keep things vague. In *An Age without Earth*, for example, there are 361 wheat fields. Why not 362? It has to do with the 361 dots on the ancient Chinese board game, Go, which

周期的。围棋棋盘是方的,棋子是圆的,天圆地方,这里有中国古代哲学思想。这里有什么道理?有没有什么明确的隐喻呢?没有,但它与天地易相有密切联系。蚂蚁也是这样。蚂蚁是智者,蚂蚁是最常见的、也是人最容易忽略的小动物,但实际上它又是最强大的动物。过去古人讲过,"千里之堤,溃于蚁穴",这里是讲千里黄河大堤的崩溃实际上是源于蚁穴,可见蚂蚁是非常有组织的,其力量是非常强大的。蚂蚁看上去很渺小,但我们根本一点也不了解它。而且蚂蚁对世界的索取非常少,然而人很贪婪、索取得太多,所以我说将来地球上可能所有生命都消失的时候,只有蚂蚁可能才会存在下去,因为它需要的太少,所以它才强大,生命才能延续,这与"土地"有一种暗合的隐意。我用天易的那个"易"字,定名时始终在犹豫,后来查了字典,最后用"易"字。为什么用这个"易"字呢?这是因为第一,"易"是《周易》的"易",《周易》本身是不可知的、很深奥的,是中国古代哲学的概念;第二,"易"字的形象又特别像蚂蚁的形象。所以,这中间看似无心实际上又都是有意的,但它是不是一定暗含着某种意义?也没必要把它说清楚,它仍然是朦胧的、混沌的东西。可以

represent the 360 days in a year that is periodic. In Go, the board is square but the pieces are round, just as Heaven is round and Earth, square. Chinese philosophical thought is present here. But is there any reason? Is there a clear implication to it? No. But the figurative symmetry of Heaven and Earth is certainly relevant here. It's the same with ants. Ants are wise, for ants are the most common and easily overlooked of creatures, yet in fact they are also the strongest. There's an ancient saying, "The greatest dam crumbles because of an ant-hole in it." This refers to the real cause behind the collapse of the Yellow River dyke. So we can see that ants are extremely organized, and extremely strong. They look so small, but we don't understand the first thing about them. Another thing: ants take little from the world, while humans are greedy and take too much. That's why I think when all other forms of life are perished from the earth, ants will survive. Spare needs yield strength and long life, which is in accord with the implication of Earth.

I created the name Tianyi, with that character *yi* (易), only after much hesitation and dictionary checking. Why this character? First, it's the character in the *Yi jing*, or *Book of Changes*, a book that itself remains forever obscure and unknowable, a concept from ancient Chinese philosophy. And second, the character is shaped like an ant. So here is something in the work that is very much intentional even if it does not appear so, but is there a specific message inherent to it? Not one that necessarily needs elaboration, but better left as something misty and vague. It can stir associations

让读者去参与联想。

沙家强：说到蚂蚁，我想起您很多作品都写到动物，如《天下无贼》《无土时代》中的狼、狗等，给读者奉献了一种特别的生态世界。我感觉这些动物身上充满人性，从这些动物身上我们可以发现人类残缺的东西，而描写动物恰恰是从另一个角度上唤醒这些"残缺"的回归或呼吁人类要自觉补充这些"残缺"。不知赵老师书写动物是不是蕴含着这种意义？

赵本夫：当然有这种东西在里面，但更主要的是，我很多作品是歌颂生命的。这种生命不仅是人类，任何一种生命包括一花一草一木都有，这些生命都应得到我们的尊重。人应该尊重生命，也应该尊重死亡，两者都同样值得尊重。我在《地母》第一卷《黑蚂蚁蓝眼睛》中写道，生命的汪洋和恣肆，大地不再属于任何人，人类也不再受到文明社会的各种束缚，赤身裸体地生活、播种、行走、做爱，为所欲为，这时才会有汪洋恣肆，那种灿烂、那种奔放、那种原始、那种野性！这时人才是自由的。当然，在现实生活中，又不可能这么无所顾忌。因此文学作品在某种意义上只是对社会生活的一种精神补充。文明社会让人类的生命萎缩得太厉害了，所以我要歌颂生命，歌颂狂野。

in the reader.

Sha Jiaqiang: Speaking of ants, I think of how lots of your work touches on animals, like the wolves and dogs in "A World without Thieves" and *An Age without Earth*. These present readers with a particular ecological world. I feel that the animals possess elements of human nature. We can find in them the basic deficiencies of humanity, which makes writing animals an alternative of calling these deficiencies to awareness, and recognizing the need to address them. Is that what you were thinking when you wrote about these animals?

Zhao Benfu: Of course, but more important is that much of my work is an ode to life. And by life, I mean not only humanity, but all other forms of life, including flowers, grass, trees, all of which deserve our respect. Humans should respect life, and death as well. Both deserve equal respect. In the first chapter of *Black Ants, Blue Eyes*, I wrote that given the teeming boundlessness of life, the earth will no longer be possessed by any human; humanity will not be constrained by any rules in civilized society. Living bare-naked, seeding, moving, making love, acting in accordance with desire: that's what teeming boundlessness means. The resplendent, the untrammeled, the primal, the wild: these are what make humans free. Of course, such lack of scruples isn't permitted in real life. Literature, then, acts as spiritual supplement to social life. Civilized society blights human life horribly, which is why I must make odes to life, in all its mad wildness.

沙家强：那样才是人的本真存在。

赵本夫：《地母》第二卷《天地月亮地》写的是文明的重建，但一旦重建以后，土地又成了财富，人类又开始争夺土地，所以一部人类的文明史就是从对土地的获取、占有开始的。最早的原始部落、原始人类没有这种概念，只从有了部落战争以后，人类开始进入文明社会，就是说这片土地属于专人的，土地一旦变成了财富之后，"文明"就开始出现了。

沙家强：这让我想起《天地月亮地》中有一处写道，柴姑暮年时自己曾经占有的土地越来越少了，最后她只留下满院子一次次卖地时扒出的"地界石"，显现出她要以这种方式来"留住"她曾经的旧梦。当有一天，天易娘还想恢复她们家族曾经的辉煌时，柴姑感觉特别欣慰。

赵本夫：你注意到了这个细节，很好。柴姑很喜欢天易娘这个孙媳妇主要就是这个原因，我在写到这处时心情很激动。少年天易看到柴姑晚年时孤独地打盹、骂人，实际上此时少年天易与柴姑真正有了心灵的沟通，天易成了柴姑的精神传人，他虽然没有承传她的土地，但承传了她的精神。所以，后来天易（也是石陀、柴门）无论走遍天涯海角，土地这个东西已经在他心里种下

Sha Jiaqiang: And only that is true human existence.

Zhao Benfu: The second volume of the *Mother Earth* series, *Heaven Earth Moonlight Earth*, is about rebuilding civilization. Once civilization is rebuilt, however, earth becomes once again wealth to be fought over. The history of civilization begins with invasion, with taking land. The earliest tribes and peoples lacked this concept. With tribal war came the entry into civilized society, with its claims of ownership over land. What we call civilization comes about when land became a form of wealth.

Sha Jiaqiang: I think of the part in *Heaven Earth Moonlight Earth* where old Auntie Chai loses more and more of land she's fought to gain. Eventually she has just the one last courtyard with a heap of border stones which she keeps every time she sold off a piece of her land—clearly her way of keeping alive her dream of holding on to her land. So later, when Tianyi's mother has the idea to restore the past glory of the clan, Auntie Chai is of course pleased.

Zhao Benfu: It's good of you to notice this detail. This part excited me. That's just why Auntie Chai is so fond of her young granddaughter-in-law, and I was really excited writing this part. Young Tianyi sees that Auntie Chai has, in her old age, taken to sleeping a lot and cursing others out of loneliness. They actually have a real emotional connection, and Tianyi inherits Auntie Chai's spirit. Maybe he can't inherit the land, but he does inherit the spirit. So later, no matter where Tianyi goes in the world, the idea of the land has been planted in his heart—this applies to Shi Tuo and

了。天柱开始听说失踪了的天易把家族"魂"带走了时,感到不理解,很疑惑什么样的人能把家族"魂"带走了呢?就决心一定要把天易找到。后来天柱慢慢理解了,这种"魂"就是土地,具体来讲就是对土地的钟爱,对土地的"地母"情结。

沙家强:您这样说,我更理解了"地母"的深厚内涵。刚才您也说过人生存在的"汪洋恣肆"等理想状态,同时您诸多作品常常遥想故乡、反思现代性,我感觉这里有一种潜意识的指向:浪漫情怀的诉求。前一段我也对文学本身做了一番思考,我认为文学的本质应该是理想主义的,文学本身不能不强调"浪漫",但当今人们的生活节奏太快了,生存美学意义上的"浪漫"似乎正在慢慢消失,有很多文学显得很干瘪而缺乏想象力。我想请赵老师您谈谈对文学中"浪漫"特质的看法。

赵本夫:现在的世界是个现实的、世俗的世界,很功利的时代,其实越是这种情况,越是需要浪漫。文学中的浪漫,作家的浪漫理想,事实上是实现不了的,他只是在尽力呼唤。浪漫主义存在的基础是,越是缺失的东西,越是要呼唤。也许我们永远实现不了,但我们仍然要呼唤它。

沙家强:不能让浪漫丢失干净。

Chai Men as well. When Tianzhu hears that the missing Tianyi has taken the soul of the clan with him, he doesn't understand. Who could take away the soul of a clan? He decides then and there to find Tianyi. Later, he comes to understand that "soul" means land, or more specifically, the love of land, the emotional attachment to Mother Earth.

Sha Jiaqiang: Now that you put it that way, I understand better the deeper meaning of Mother Earth. You said just now that people existed in a golden age of "teeming boundlessness". Much of your work also reminisces of old rural homes and reflects on modernity. I detect here a subconscious appeal to the romantic mindset. Previously, I've been reconsidering the basic nature of literature itself, and I think literature has to be idealistic. Literature must emphasize "romance." But the pace of life today is too fast, and romance in the aesthetic sense is being lost. So much of literature seems dull, unimaginative. Please talk a little about the quality of romance in literature.

Zhao Benfu: The world today is a practical one, a vulgar one. We live in an age of utility. But the more things go in this direction, the more we need romance. The romance of literature, the romantic ideals of an author, can never actually come to pass. He can only make an urgent appeal through literature. The basis of romance is to call for it the more we lack it. Maybe we'll never realize our ideals, but we mustn't stop calling on each other to try.

Sha Jiaqiang: It would be a shame to lose all the romance.

赵本夫：人类不能没有梦想，当今时代可能是我们所处最繁荣的时代，但这个时代仍然是不完美的，它有很多问题存在。可能一个人一生已经过得很不错、很幸福了，但实际上他回想起来常会感觉到还缺少很多东西，有很多遗憾，这就是文学存在的理由。他不是能实现而不去努力，而是他本身就无法实现。生活中有很多无奈，最大的无奈还是无奈。就只好做梦。

沙家强：赵老师，事实上当我从记忆角度开始关注您小说中的"孤独""焦虑""怀想"等这些精神现象时，我发现"孤独""焦虑""怀想"是在记忆精神现象的统摄下才更具深度，这里就涉及我很长时间以来关注的"文学记忆"这个话题。有很多学者担忧地说，现在的文学缺少记忆，甚至就没有记忆。甚至"新生代"作家"什么记忆也没有，只有写当下生活了"。我的理解是，当下文学不是没有记忆，而是在消费时代语境下，记忆发生了异变，"消费性"记忆或者说城市生活记忆在当下更为突出，而"严肃性"记忆、乡村记忆则似乎退居次要位置了。在此我想请赵老师对当前作家"记忆"状况谈谈自己的看法。

赵本夫：有这种情况存在，但要视情况而定。现在的年轻作

Zhao Benfu: Humanity can't go without dreams, and while we are likely living in the most prosperous times ever, it's still far from perfect. Many problems remain. One might be fortunate and his life might have been going well, yet thinking back, he might still feel he is missing something. He might have regrets. This is why literature exists in the first place. It isn't that he doesn't try hard to achieve his goals, but that he simply can't. Life is full of dismay, the worst of which is dismay itself. And so we dream.

Sha Jiaqiang: Actually, when I contemplate the mindset described in your novels, like loneliness, anxiety and nostalgia, in light of memory, I've come to notice that such mental states take on more profound significance from the perspective of memory. And this harks back to the problem of memory in literature, which has been a focus of mine for a long time. Many scholars worry that literature today lacks memory. It might even be that writers of the new generation disregard memory completely and just write about life today. The way I understand it, it's not that literature today has no memory, but that in the discourse of a consumerist age, memory mutates. Consumerist memory, in other words, memory of urban life, is more prominent, and while "grave" memory, memory of the rural, seems to fall back to a secondary position. I wonder if you might tell us some of your own thoughts on the state of memory among contemporary writers.

Zhao Benfu: What you have pointed out might be true, but it really depends. Certainly younger writers lack breadth, haven't

家的确缺少一些生活的厚度，他们没真正体会过生活的滋味、生活的况味。缺少的东西对于作家来说肯定意味着不健全，像我这种年龄已经经历不少了，但仍然感觉很多不足，我还要去补充或者寻找某种记忆。前几年我到西部采风，从某种意义上我就去寻找童年的记忆，寻找人类的记忆，寻找人类的集体记忆，我极力探寻人是如何发展的、看看人类社会又留下了哪些痕迹。事实上，我正式开始文学创作之前，曾读过中国通史、世界通史，读过一些重要国家的历史，当然也包括政治、哲学、文学、战争、兴亡等，这些都是人类的记忆。我喜欢历史书，阅读历史，你会感觉自己活了几千年，看问题会有纵深感。作家写东西，当然可以只写当下，但有历史的底色，也许会写得更好一些。

沙家强：我发现，的确存在一些年轻作家只写当下消费状况，而不涉及集体记忆的底色。

赵本夫：我相信他们到了一定年龄之后，会改变的。作家需要积累，积累才有分量。

沙家强：一个人的成熟要经历一个复杂的过程。

赵本夫：而且也不能要求所有作家都写一类作品。年轻人有年轻人的生活，他们的一些作品可能我也写不了。

experienced the flavor of life, the tenor of it. Lacking these things certainly means the writer is incomplete. Take me for example, I'm older and have experienced more, but it doesn't feel like enough, and I still want to seek or supplement memory.

My trip west of a few years ago was in search of childhood memory, human memory, and the collective memory of humanity. More than anything, I wanted to know where humans came from, to see what traces human society had left behind. In fact, long before I started writing, I read a lot of Chinese history, world history, and histories of major countries. I, of course, also read lots about politics, philosophy, literature, war, about rises and falls of civilizations. These are the memories of humanity. I love history books. Reading history, you feel as if you have lived through millenniums. You face problems with a deeper perspective. Writers write things, including of course the contemporary world, but putting in a historical undergirding can make the writing better.

Sha Jiaqiang: I've found that some young writers describe only the current state of consumerism without reference to any undergirding collective memory.

Zhao Benfu: I think they'll change when they reach a certain age. A writer must accumulate experience to have fodder for writing.

Sha Jiaqiang: Becoming a mature person is a complex process.

Zhao Benfu: Yes, and we mustn't ask writers to all do the same kind of work. Young people have their own lives, and I wouldn't be

沙家强：赵老师，当我们谈到当下社会语境时，不能不提到"消费时代"这种说法，您认为中国当下进入到"消费时代"了吗？

赵本夫：不能完全说进入到"消费时代"，但可以说超前消费、提前消费的文化状况正在影响着中国和全世界，或正逐步形成一种观念。事实上，就像社会发展一样，从另一角度看，其实发展也是害人的东西。很多方面不要发展那么快。在 2000 年世纪之交时，我曾写过一篇随笔，叫《盘点人类》，就谈人类两千年的发展，有些是必需的，有些是造罪。用电锯代替斧头砍伐森林不是进步，一种专制代替另一种专制不是进步，用热核武器代替冷兵器不是进步。特别最近二三百年发展太快了，世间已经变得面目全非，这肯定会带来许多危机。

沙家强：赵老师，面对当下人记忆的状况，您认为人记忆的理由应该是什么？

赵本夫：记忆也是人生存的需要。从记忆中我们可以获得很多生活的经验，它会指导我们以后应该怎么做。

沙家强：捷克作家克里玛在《布拉格精神》中谈到"文学与记忆"时说："一部真正的文学作品的问世是作为其创造者的一种喊叫，是对于笼罩于他本人、同样也笼罩于他的前辈和同代人、

able to write some of the work they do.

Sha Jiaqiang: Speaking of the current social discourse, we can't fail to bring up the term "consumerist age." Has China entered a consumerist age, you think?

Zhao Benfu: Not completely yet, but the tendency of over-consumption certainly affects China and the whole world. Little by little, this view will gain currency. Just as with social development, development itself is in some ways a harmful thing. In many instances the development shouldn't be so fast. In my 2000 essay "Taking Stock of Humanity," I argue that in the last 2000 years, while some development was necessary, other parts of it proved a curse. Cutting down forests with electric chainsaws instead of axes is not progress. Trading out one form of despotism for another is not progress. Replacing cold weapons with thermonuclear weapons is not progress. Development has been too fast, especially in the last two or three hundred years, leaving the world utterly changed. This is sure to bring about many crises.

Sha Jiaqiang: Under such circumstances, what reason do you think people have for remembering?

Zhao Benfu: Memory is necessary for human life. From memory we obtain much life experience, to guide our actions.

Sha Jiaqiang: Czech writer Ivan Klíma talks about literature and memory in his essay "The Spirit of Prague." He says, "The arrival of an authentic literary work is a cry from the creator, in resistance to being subsumed among his fellows of the same generation,

他的时代、他所说的语言身上的遗忘的抗议。"我也认为，抵抗"遗忘"应该是作家潜意识的行为，您如何看？

赵本夫：这是一种说法，一种表述，也是他的理解。我的作品从来不诠释别人的理论，我坚持说我自己的话，写我自己发现了什么。创作不要证明任何现成的观点，如果从一部作品里能看出作者读过很多书，这部作品一定是失败的。

2009 年

subsumed in his age, subsumed in what is forgotten of the language he speaks." I also think that the author works subconsciously to oppose forgetting, but what do you think?

Zhao Benfu: That's a manner of speaking, of expression, and further, it's his understanding. My works never explicate the propositions of others. I believe my own words and write what I discover for myself. Creative writing mustn't prove pre-packaged views. If you can tell from the work the author has read a lot, then the work is certainly a failure.

2009